The Many Worlds of
L·E·O R·O·S·T·E·N

stories, humor, social commentary,
travelogues, satire, memoirs, profiles,
and sundry entertainments never before published;
with a special introduction,
background notes, revelations and confessions,
all hand-written and themselves worth
the price of admission

HARPER & ROW, PUBLISHERS
NEW YORK, EVANSTON, AND LONDON

ACKNOWLEDGMENTS

"A Book Was a Book." Copyright © 1962 by Madeline Rosten Lee. Originally published in the Chicago *Sunday Tribune*.

Excerpts from *Captain Newman, M.D.*, reprinted with the permission of Harper & Row, Publishers, Incorporated:

"The Happiest Man in the World." Copyright © 1956 by the Curtis Publishing Company. Originally appeared in the *Saturday Evening Post* under the title "Happy Was the Soldier."

"Little Jim." Copyright © 1958 by Leo Rosten. Originally appeared in *Harper's Magazine* under the title "The Guy in Ward Four."

"Mr. Future." Copyright © 1961 by Leo Rosten. Originally appeared in *Harper's Magazine*.

"Hope and Honor and High Resolve." Copyright © 1961 by Leo Rosten. Originally appeared, in longer form, in *Captain Newman, M.D.* as the Epilogue.

"The Creative Idea," reprinted from the *Teachers College Record*, May, 1963 (Vol. 64, No. 8), copyright © 1963 by Teachers College, Columbia University.

Excerpts from *The Education of H*Y*M*A*N K*A*P*L*A*N* by Leonard Q. Ross: "Mr. Kaplan's White Banner," "Mr. Kaplan and Shakespeare," "Mr. Kaplan the Magnificent," copyright 1937 by Harcourt, Brace & World, Inc., and reprinted with their permission.

Excerpts from *Hollywood: The Movie Colony, The Movie Makers* by Leo C. Rosten, copyright 1941 by Harcourt, Brace & World, Inc., and reprinted with their permission.

"The Intellectual and the Mass Media." Copyright © 1961 by Leo Rosten, reprinted with the permission of D. Van Nostrand Company, Inc.

Excerpts from *The Return of H*Y*M*A*N K*A*P*L*A*N*, reprinted with the permission of Harper & Row, Publishers, Incorporated:

"Christopher Kaplan." Copyright 1938 by Leo Rosten. Originally appeared in the *New Yorker*.

"Mr. Kaplan and the Unforgivable 'Feh!' " Copyright © 1959 by Leo Rosten.

"The Confessions of Mr. Parkhill." Copyright © 1959 by Leo Rosten.

"The Case for Mr. Parkhill." Copyright © 1959 by Leo Rosten. Originally appeared in *Harper's Magazine*.

Excerpts from *The Story Behind the Painting*, Doubleday & Company, Inc. / Cowles Magazines and Broadcasting, Inc., 1962:

Profiles on Degas and Rembrandt © 1956 by Cowles Magazines and Broadcasting Inc.

Profile on Leonardo © 1957 by Cowles Magazines and Broadcasting, Inc.

Profiles on Cézanne and Botticelli © 1959 by Cowles Magazines and Broadcasting, Inc.

Profile on El Greco and Introduction to *The Story Behind the Painting* © 1962 by Cowles Magazines and Broadcasting, Inc.

"You Have a Right to Be Unhappy." Copyright © 1961 by Madeline Rosten Lee. Originally published in *Redbook* under the title "Your Right to Be Unhappy."

FIRST EDITION

LIBRARY OF CONGRESS CATALOG CARD NUMBER: 64-18065

An Open Letter
to the Mayor of New York

★

CAN ANY TRUTHFUL OBSERVER *avoid coming to the conclusion that, wherever and whenever possible, his fellow men flee from thinking as they would from a tidal wave? The extremes to which a man will leap in order to buttress a bias, his gymnastics to circumvent a fact that might conceivably alter his opinion, his rage when a sacred cow is pinked or a lofty shibboleth questioned—surely Aristotle was hoping, not reporting, when he called man the rational animal.*

Thinking is hard; it is work; and our conclusions become invested with emotion. To differ with a man is, in most cases, to threaten his self-respect, for he takes disagreement as a rebuff to his reputation, hence to his ego. To revise one's beliefs requires a seasoned, chastened sense of worth that is strong enough to resist the childish and recurrent delusion of infallibility. It takes the kind of joy in process that Edison beautifully demonstrated when, after eight thousand successive failures vis-à-vis a storage battery, he exclaimed in delight, "Well, now we know eight thousand things that won't work!"

These imperishable lucubrations are occasioned by the letters I received after publishing "An Open Letter to the Mayor," a simple enough piece of protest directed against the troubles, inconveniences and stupidities that characterize life on the island of Manhattan these days. I tried to write this appeal to reason in various ways, but they all suffered from one inexcusable defect: they reeked of virtue, which is boring. The device I finally hit on, inventing an obvious idiot who defends the Mayor, seemed to me both amusing and effective.

My feuilleton in Look was hardly on the newsstands before my telephone began to ring. The happy gurgles from friends (and Republicans) lifted my soul, which promptly began to descend under the barrage of indignant calls and poison-pen notes from supralapsarian friends of the Mayor. One lady, who bears a name that is like a star in Manhattan, wrote a torrid, unladylike letter branding me an ingrate, citing the countless wonders of our fair city, telling me that if the floors of our taxis fill up with rain water I should put on rubbers, and ended in this girlish giggle: "I'm off to my favorite little restaurant, of which there are thousands in New York. What other city do you know can make this claim?"

I racked my brain for hours but could not think of another city where she would have thousands of favorite little restaurants to be off to, and I could hardly sleep nights trying to figure out what in the world her favorite restaurants had to do with the disgraceful state of things in Gotham anyway.

I replied to the lady that no city is closer to my affections than New York, "but wouldn't a beautiful woman be more beautiful if the warts were removed from her face?" Her response, a stony silence, was all I could ask for. I think she is still eating her way through those thousands of favorite little restaurants.

*

DEAR MR. MAYOR:

There's a fellow I want to report—so's you can arrest him or deport him or what. He's a real troublemaker who goes around saying awful things about you. I think he's a Communist, or even a Republican.

Last night, whilst shooting the breeze, How do you like living in little old NY? he asks.

I like NY fine, I said.

He looks at me like I'm some kind of Astronut. I mean NY the capital of Noise, Dirt, Muggings and Holes in every street, he says. (Right there I should of realize this guy is carrying around some grudge to grind.) How long, he asks, does it take you to commute to and fro your place of work?

I do not commute, I say, as I work only 30 blocks from here, in the Umpire State Bilding, which takes me 45 minutes to 1 hour.

If that ain't commuting I'd like to know what is, he says. How do you like our Mayor?

OK, I said. His heart's in the right place.

If his heart wasn't in the right place it couldn't pump enough blood to his head to keep him awake, he said, which there's no proof he is.

Ha, ha, ha, I argued.

Want a bargain in a gasmask? he said.

What do I want a gasmask for? I ask.

                    2 pipe cleaners
                    1 sample slipcover material
                    Cellofane (from cigar)
                    Cellofane (from cigarets)
                    Cellofane (from chewing gum)

Plus several objects, he said, whose former identity I prefer not to even think about!

I suppose Mayor Wagner personaly goes around chewing all that gum and opening all that cellofane, I said.

I do not think Big Brain is smart enough to get the cellofane *off* a package, he hollers. The least of our worries is who puts the sheep-dip there. The question is, How can you get it *out*? You can't sweep it out, on account of the dishpans being lower than the doors. You can't vacuum it out, it being mostly water. The only defense is this—(and now he hawls out a Carpenters Drill!) Make holes in the floor.

Water will certainly run right out of a hole, I decided.

Your mother would be proud of you at this moment, he said. And how about the Bus and Subway torture?

How's the Mayor suppose to even know what goes on in Buses or Subways? I said. He rides in a offshul limozine, with a driver to take him to and fro.

Then let's pass a law, he said, making the Mayor and all the politicians *ride in public transportation* for 1 week each year. Just 1 *week* of them dumbells waiting for Buses, getting hijacked into Subways, getting nauzeated from the stink of hotdogs and piazzas frying underground—just 1 week and Brother, you'd get some action! . . . Take Busses. Rush hour, they pass you in wolf packs, they're so full—while right across the street, going in the opp. direction, a fleet of empty Buses is racing like hell to the Bronx, 10 miles away, *so's they can turn around!* Why can't every 2nd or 3rd empty turn around *right there*, instead of racing all the way up to the Bronx?

That would foul up their skedules, I said.

They are suppose to serve people, not skedules, he hollers. What about the holes in the streets?

With all this new bilding, they have to tear up the ground, I said.

They could put a limit on the number of holes, he said, like Mayor La Gardia used to. But not this Mayor, xcuse the xpression. He has raised the Art of making holes to new hights. He has xperts who do nothing but dig holes inside the holes already there. He has inspectors who, if there's a stretch of 3 blocks without a hole, the mistake is corrected before morning.

With so many holes, I am amazed you do not have to crawl to and fro, I said (but he don't even see I have throwed him a spitball).

I carry a board, he said. (You won't believe this, Mr. Mayor, but this kook is now showing me a Ironing Board!) This is part of the NYorker's Survival Kit, to get you across Bewildred Bob's trenches, foxholes, soors and open graves. He is changing NY from a Summer Festival to a All-Year Obstacle Race.

If you don't dig holes you don't get bildings, I defended.

Do you know what type monsterosities they now call bildings? he said.

Sure, I said. There's a new one right outside these windows.

That's why it's so nice and dark in your apt. all day, he said.

I'm not there much during the day, I said.

From the look of things you're not all there most of the time, he said. I will give you a refresher course on Wagner's Bilding Code, or How to Drive Americans Crazy in their Own Home. First, they make the ceilings so low you get an xtra floor every 4 floors—and that overloads all the elevators right there. Second, they make all the walls so thin no one will ever get lonesome. Everyone hears his neighbors gargling, taking a bath, or worse. In 1 new bilding, a tenant went to Florida leaving his TV on and it took the endgineers 2 days to figure out from which apt. the *Sunrise Semester* was coming to educate everyone at 6:30 a.m.

You don't like Mayor Wagner, I hinted.

Neither does my friend Chuck, said he.

Who's Chuck? I said.

Chuck lives in a bran-new rabbit-warn, Neurotic Towers. One night, Chuck hears a man and wife hollering and xchanging blows. When the woman screams No, no, Joe dear, Put down that ax! my friend Chuck dives for the phone. Police, police, Chuck yells, this is Apt. 5-B, Neurotic Towers, and a woman is getting killed here! Which apt. is she getting killed in? ask the cops. Chuck says, Either 5-A or 5-C, which are left and right of me, or 5-H, which is across the hall, or 5-I or 5-J, on each side of 5-H. Or it *could* be the floor below—4-A, 4-B or 4-C, or 4-H, 4-I or 4-J. Or maybe it's the apt. *above* me, Officer, which is 6-B. Or 6-A or 6-C, or 6-H, 6-I, 6-J. . . . Well, by the time the cops nock on the door of these 18 apts., the man has transformed the wife's head into eggplant.

Which apt. did they finally find the victim in? I said.

17-Q, he said.

You're crazy, I reasoned. How could a sound from Apt. 17-Q get down to 5-B?

You don't know these new bildings, he said. The Q apts. in Neurotic Towers are tied in to air-ducks which run next to the kitchen intake fans of all B apts. So naturally 5-B hears a man killing his mate in 17-Q, 12 stories above and to one side.

movie, which was finally called It's Only Money *and starred Frank Sinatra and Jane Russell, was no great shakes either at the box office or in my estimation—but Mr. Marx did play the part of Emil to my everlasting satisfaction.*

The following piece first appeared, more or less, in Look. *I say "more or less" because I have riffled into it many paragraphs from a later article, "The Lunar World of Groucho Marx," I wrote for* Harper's. *I don't think anyone will really care which stuff originated where: I just hate to omit certain passages from this gathering.*

★

ONE DAY IN CALIFORNIA, MY TELEPHONE RANG AND A NASTY VOICE RASPED, "This is Professor Waldemar Strumbelknauff."

"Who?" I asked.

"Let's not quibble," the voice said coldly. "Aren't you ashamed of yourself, beating your children up that way? You Cossack! If you were a man you'd come over here and knock my teeth out. If you were half a man, you'd knock half my teeth out. I'm sick and tired of your calling at all hours of the night to ask for specimens of my nail-clippings."

"Who *is* this?" I fumed.

"This is the Secretary of the National Committee to Free Georgia. And I suppose you'll tell me you don't even know her! A fine kettle of fish! . . . This is Groucho. How are you? As if I really care."

I should, of course, have known it from the first. No one else could have delivered so brazen and bewildering a monologue, in so indignant a tone, with such a mixture of defiance and contempt.

My life was never the same after Groucho Marx learned my phone number. At one time or another I have been telephoned by a barnacle-scraper named Formosa Greulenheimer, by the president of the Society for Counterfeit Money, and by one Captain Raoul P. Clamhead, of the Iranian FBI. I have been awakened at ungodly hours to be chivvied about why I should have my wife Simonized, my lawn paved, or my children sold. I have been identified to strangers as the brain behind the International Uranium Cartel, the man who invented the spiral notebook, and a tapioca-runner from Acapulco. My friends have been tipped off that originally I had two heads and my son has been accused of being a midget, graduated from Yale in 1908, whom I keep undersized by the injection of anti-growth gland juices. It hasn't been an easy life. . . .

Being a friend of Marx's isn't something you do lightly: You have to be in perfect physical condition. During the worst days of World War II rationing, Oscar Levant flew into Los Angeles on a concert tour. Groucho said, "Oscar, you look tired. Why don't you come to my house for dinner? I've got the most wonderful cook in town, and I've saved enough ration coupons for a steak four inches thick."

Levant cried gratefully, "What's your address?"

"Wouldn't *you* like to know?" said Groucho, and departed.

The war, incidentally, was the occasion for one of his most celebrated ad libs. He was waiting in a general's office, prior to entertaining the troops, when the phone rang. Marx picked up the receiver and crooned: "World War Two–oo."

Earl Wilson's wife was once rash enough to make conversation with Marx by venturing, "I made a stew last night."

"Anyone I know?" asked Groucho.

He once expressed interest in joining a certain beach club in Santa Monica. A friend told him uneasily, "You don't want to apply for membership in that beach club, Groucho."

"Why not?" asked Marx.

"Well, frankly, they're anti-Semitic."

Marx, a Jew whose wife wasn't, said, "Will they let my son go into the water up to his knees?"

He possesses the singular faculty of *hearing* with originality. One night, while he was driving me to a preview, I suddenly remembered that it was my father's birthday. "Would you mind stopping at a Western Union office?" I asked. "I want to wire my father."

"What's the matter?" inquired the master. "Can't he stand by himself?"

Marx once asked a friend, "How did you like my radio show last night?"

"I only caught the first ten minutes," the friend apologized. "I was called away——"

"A fine friend you've turned out to be," Marx exclaimed indignantly. "I listened to the program from start to finish. That's the kind of friend *I* am!"

When a young actress asked his advice on how to succeed in the theater, Marx replied, "My advice to you and to all struggling actresses, is this: Keep struggling. If you keep struggling, you won't get into trouble—and if you don't get into trouble, you'll never be much of an actress."

My favorite anecdote about him involves the time he was driving back from Mexico and, like everyone re-entering the country, was stopped at the border. The immigration satrap asked him, "Are you a citizen?"

"Certainly," replied Marx.

"Birthplace?"

"New York."

"Occupation?"

"Smuggler."

He is a man who simply abhors the obvious. A dowager once violated our privacy, while I was lunching with him at the Brown Derby, to gush: "Oh, *do* pardon me—but aren't you Groucho *Marx?*"

"No," Marx murmured, "are you?"

When a tippler slapped him on the back with the gambit "Groucho, you old son-of-a-gun, you probably don't remember me!" Marx fixed the poltroon with his wall-eyed glare and declaimed: "I never forget a face—but in your case I'll be glad to make an exception."

When a curvaceous blonde tried to flatter him by cooing, "You're a man after my heart," Marx leered, "That's not all I'm after." And he left one dinner party with this farewell to his host: "Don't think this hasn't been a dull evening, because it has."

He is a master of verbal ambush and likes to startle the Philistines with comments such as: "I was always awkward, even as a young girl," or "I want to apologize for not returning your call. I've been so busy not returning calls that I just couldn't get around to not returning yours in time."

Some years ago the natives of Hollywood were extolling the supernatural powers of a spiritualist who was cashing in on séances for the gullible. This sorcerer might still be plying his occult wiles had not some friends challenged Marx, who had listened to their raptures with icy reserve, to appraise the psychic's wizardry for himself. Groucho went to a séance. He sat silent and baleful through a demonstration in which the spiritualist answered the most arcane questions, broke the barrier between those who are here and those who are hereafter, plumbed awesome secrets from beyond the grave, advised, warned, instructed, and uplifted. After an hour of this exhausting omniscience, the seer intoned, "And now my spirit grows weary. . . . Our journey into the unknown draws to a close. There is time for only one more question."

Marx asked it: "What's the capital of South Dakota?"

Performing, Groucho is unlike any other comedian in the republic. He does not tell stories. He does not tell jokes. He does not use contrived "situations." He does not follow a script. He does not present guest stars. He does not employ straight-men, bit players, or stooges. He does not swap banter with the orchestra. He does nothing, in fact, except chat with his contestants, and about the most mundane matters: "Are you married?" "Have you any children?" "How many banks have you broken into lately?" and so on. The reason you hear such strange, loud noises from the audience (sounds known in the trade as boffs, yaks and boffolas) is that his disarming questions lead to complications of an unearthly character. I can only try to reproduce their flavor from a dazed memory:

GROUCHO: Are you married?

MAN: Well . . . yes and no.

GROUCHO: Good for you! That's the way to be. What do you mean, yes and no?

MAN: I mean I'm going to marry the same woman I was once married to.

GROUCHO: Didn't it *take* the first time?

MAN: Well, I guess not.

GROUCHO: No guessing, please. Not on this quiz show. Tell me, Fallen Arches, how did you meet your wife?

MAN: We were kids together.

GROUCHO: Well, that's possible—but how did you meet her?

MAN: You see I drive a truck—

GROUCHO: You ran over her?

MAN: No; she was in the barn—

GROUCHO: You drove the truck into a barn?

MAN: No. You see, she was a farmer's daughter, and they had been missing their chickens—

GROUCHO: They were lonely for chickens?

MAN: No, they had been *missing* them, so they turned a light on in the barn yard, and one night I drove up to get some turkeys, and her father said the turkeys were in the barn—

GROUCHO: You married a *turkey*?

MAN: No, no. As I went to the barn, a skunk started for the chicken house—and she yelled, "Get that skunk!"—

GROUCHO: A fine way for her to talk about her future husband.

MAN: —and I jumped on the skunk, and she fell on the skunk, too, and we started going out together because no one else could go out with either of us.

On one program a schoolteacher confessed she was "approaching forty," and Groucho queried, "From which direction?" To a Chinese contestant who said he was twenty-four, Groucho asked, "In years or yen?" When the boy said you don't count age in yen, our man replied, "Oh, no? I have a yen to be twenty-one again."

Trying to carry on a conversation with Groucho gives you the feeling that you've fallen into an automatic washer with Betty Hutton. You get dead-panned, misunderstood, misquoted and—in the end—routed by whatever wild notion flits into that demoniacal mind. In the middle of a political discussion, he is liable to rise gravely and announce, "Gentlemen, they have fired on Fort Sumter." If you are around him during one of his free-flight moods you feel like the bird that flew too low and got caught in a badminton game.

Mr. Marx has a wall-eyed stare, the lope of an arthritic roué, and a real moustache. His leer, the most distinguished characteristic of an otherwise chologizings. The confidence that a mood will pass, that some things simply take time, that not everything needs to be explained or debated, may be a good deal more desirable than unsolicited missions of salvation. A soul in distress is not necessarily doomed.

We have all been bamboozled into thinking that it is our sacred duty to "understand." This is nonsense. There is a good deal about others, even those we know well, that we will never understand, and there is a good deal about ourselves that we should not try to understand too much. It is enough to know that each of us is often irrational, petulant, childish, and unfair. The why is less imporant than the effort to keep others from suffering because of us.

Whosoever is human must reconcile himself to being imperfect. We must surrender our infantile dream that anyone really lives happily ever after. To even the most successful and "well adjusted" of us, a large part of life involves duties that are dull and routines that are disagreeable.

Happiness is rare, not common. Bliss, save in precious and transient moments, is an invention of poets, clung to by genuine neurotics. If we spent less time trying to have "fun," we might discover the endless rewards and resources of that internal self which is at home with contemplation and solitude, which can accept disappointment or ungratified desire. Only the very young or the hopelessly naive expect life to give them everything they hoped for, or dreamed of, or read about.

Fairy tales, at least, were labelled tales, and involved imaginary people in imaginary peril, saved by luck or virtue or magic. It is one of the unhappy (but not so terrible) facts of life that virtue does not always prevail, that fate is utterly indifferent about how and when it doles out fortune, and that Pollyanna was a pretty silly, to say nothing of tiresome, little girl.

The Power of Words

★

THESE BRIEF PARAGRAPHS were written for National Library Week, to introduce an article in Look *that featured some marvelous photographs by Art Kane, dramatizing passages from the Bible, Shakespeare, Hans Christian Andersen, and others. I cheerfully seize this (or any other) excuse to resurrect "The Power of Words" from the files.*

★

THEY SING. THEY HURT. THEY TEACH. THEY SANCTIFY. THEY WERE MAN'S FIRST, immeasurable feat of magic. They liberated us from ignorance and our barbarous past.

For without these marvelous scribbles which build letters into words, words into sentences, sentences into systems and sciences and creeds, man would be forever confined to the self-isolated prison of the scuttlefish or the chimpanzee.

"A picture is worth ten thousand words," goes the timeworn Chinese maxim. "But," one writer tartly said, "it takes words to say that."

We live by words: LOVE, TRUTH, GOD.

We fight for words: FREEDOM, COUNTRY, FAME.

We die for words: LIBERTY, GLORY, HONOR.

They bestow the priceless gift of articulacy on our minds and hearts—from "Mama" to "infinity."

And the men who truly shape our destiny, the giants who teach us, inspire us, lead us to deeds of immortality, are those who use words with clarity, grandeur and passion: Socrates, Jesus, Luther, Lincoln, Churchill.

During National Library Week, Americans, caught between affluence and anxiety, may again give thanks for the endless riches in the kingdom of print.

The Kaplan Stories

★

IT WAS 1935. I was living in Washington, wallowing in research on the capital's corps of newspapermen, for my Ph.D. thesis. I had been awarded a "field fellowship" from the Social Science Research Council. A field fellowship did not mean I had to work in a meadow; it meant I was supposed to conduct research away from libraries, "in the field."

It is a rare and marvelous thing to be in your twenties, bursting with juices, living in the elegant, if unbearably hot, city of Washington, working with a cachet which, in those distant days, attended any research deemed important enough to be subsidized by a foundation. I would have made a debonair sight had I lounged against the bar of the National Press Club, my eyes narrowed, my ears tuned to every gossamer wisp of gossip. Actually, I got much better information in the club's poolroom, which a coterie of us younger bloods had all to ourselves: Paul Ward of the Baltimore Sun, Clifford Prevost of the Detroit Free Press, Kenneth Crawford, later of Newsweek, and a reporter whose uncle was head of the G.P.U. in Moscow, leaving that unusual post only when his brains were blown out by his comrades in proceedings that were never properly publicized.

I was, I may say, a fairly proficient wielder of a pool cue, having perfected that part of my education at the University of Chicago in private tournaments with the red-headed, very pale son of a bishop. I didn't know that my freckle-faced companion was a Negro until some fraternity brothers soberly informed me that it would be better for the reputation of our lodge if I spent more time with them and less time with him. I chose to spend less time with them, upright though they were, and proud as I was of their lineage.

I slaved away in Washington for a year, when I fell in love with a Model A

Ford. I saw it on a used car lot and it was going for $125. My heart pined for the black beauty, a rakish two-seater with a canvas top and a rumble seat. To readers too young to know what a rumble seat is, or was, I should say that this dashing symbol of the Jazz Generation was the trunk—whose top opened not as present-day trunks do, but from above and its front, thereby unfolding into a crowded back sofa into which gay blades and pliant maidens inserted themselves as if into king-sized sardine cans. It was, because cramped, ideal for necking. This glorious predecessor of the convertible let your face and hair catch the wind—and, unfortunately, the rain. The owner of the car customarily kept an old poncho or slicker in the rumble seat, for his cargo to use as a hand-held canopy if the rains came before Louis Bromfield. Anyway, I thought of my Ford as Annabelle, for some reason, and a part of my heart remains with her, wherever her parts may be, to this day.

To get the $125, I wrote a story one weekend about a character I called Hyman Kaplan. It was vaguely based on a student I had briefly known in a night-school class I had occasionally taught to help pay my way through college. The story was sold to the New Yorker, and Annabelle was sold to me.

I had not the faintest notion of writing more than one Kaplan story, but soon Annabelle needed a tire, so I wrote another. I must make it clear that I was careful to write it, as well as all non–social-science prose, on weekends. I figured that the Social Science Research Council deserved my full, undivided brain and ergs from 9 A.M. every Monday to 12 P.M. every Friday. Saturdays and Sundays were mine, do you hear, mine.

The idea of writing a book of fiction, in addition to The Washington Correspondents, the book I was already writing, did not even dawn on me until Annabelle conned me into replacing her plugs and refurbishing her top. The motive force behind my literary efforts was, accordingly, automotive.

All of my clandestine tales about Mr. Kaplan appeared in the New Yorker —the first of many stories, sketches, and travel pieces I sold that illustrious journal. Years later Harold Ross, the mysterious and laconic editor, told me in a burst of reluctant praise, "Goddamit, you've gone longer without a rejection slip than any damn writer we've ever printed." It was dizzying.

I submitted all my writing under a pen name, Leonard Q. Ross, because I felt indentured to the S.S.R.C. and was fearful of my humorless professors back in Chicago, before whom I would have to appear with an indigestible doctoral dissertation. I used a literary agent, making heartfelt pleas to him to keep my identity secret. This he did so well that the New Yorker staff organized a pool, the jackpot to go to whoever guessed the real name of the

Christopher K★a★p★l★a★n

To mr. parkhill the beginners' grade was more than a congregation of students yearning to master English. He took a larger view of his responsibilities: to Mr. Parkhill the American Night Preparatory School for Adults was an incubator of Citizens. To imbue the men and women of a dozen nations with the meaning of America—its past, its traditions, its aspirations—this, to Mr. Parkhill, was the greater work to which he had dedicated himself.

So it was that on the eve of any national holiday, Mr. Parkhill devoted at least half an hour to a little excursion into our history. In the spring, it was Decoration Day that enlisted his eloquence. In the fall it was Armistice Day and Thanksgiving. (He always regretted the fact that the Fourth, grandest holiday of them all, fell in a month when the school was not in session.) And this Monday night in October, on the eve of Columbus Day, Mr. Parkhill opened the class with these ringing words: "Tonight, let us set aside our routine tasks for a while to consider the man whose—er—historic achievement the world will commemorate tomorrow."

Expectancy murmured its sibilant path across the room.

"To this man," Mr. Parkhill continued, "the United States—America— owes its very beginning. I'm sure you all know whom I mean, for he—"

"Jawdge Vashington!" Miss Fanny Gidwitz promptly guessed.

"No, no. Not *George* Washington— watch that 'w', Miss Gidwitz. I refer to——"

"Paul Rewere!" cried Oscar Trabish impetuously.

Mr. Parkhill adjusted his spectacles. Mr. Trabish had formed some peculiar psychic union with "Paul Rewere": he had already written two rhapsodic compositions and made one fiery speech on his beloved alter ego. (The compositions had been called "Paul Revere's Horse Makes History" and "Paul

31

Revere. One by Land, Two by the Beach." The speech had been announced by Mr. Trabish as "Paul Rewere! Vhy He Vasn't Prazidant?" He had been quite indignant about it.)

Mr. Parkhill shook his head. "Not Paul 'Rewere.' It's a 'v,' Mr. Trabish, not a 'w.' You spell it correctly when you write, but you seem to replace the 'v's with 'w's—and the 'w's with 'v's—when you speak. Class, let's not guess. What *date* is tomorrow?"

"Mine boitday!" an excited voice sang out.

Mr. Parkhill ignored that. "Tomorrow," he said firmly, "is October twelfth. And on October twelfth, 1492—" He got no further.

"Dat's mine *boit*day! October tvalf! I should live so! Honist!" It was (but why, oh why, did it have to be?) the proud, enraptured voice of Hyman Kaplan.

Mr. Parkhill took a deep breath, a slow, deep breath, and said cautiously, "Mr. Kaplan, is October twelfth—er—really your birthday?"

Mr. Kaplan's eyes widened—innocent, hurt. "*Mister* Pockheel!"

Mr. Parkhill felt ashamed of himself.

Stanislaus Wilkomirski growled, "Kaplan too old for have birtday."

"October tvalf I'm born; October tvalf I'm tsalebratink!" Mr. Kaplan retorted. "All mine *life* I'm hevink boitdays October tvalf. No axceptions!"

Mr. Parkhill said, "Well, well, well. That *is* a coincidence. October twelfth. Hmmm." He cleared his throat uneasily. "I'm sure we all wish Mr. Kaplan many happy returns."

Mr. Kaplan beamed, rose, bowed, beamed, and sat down, beaming.

"Phooey," muttered Mr. Plonsky under his breath.

Miss Mitnick, feeling the occasion called for good will and peace among men, stammered "Congratulation."

"Denks," said Mr. Kaplan, all *savoir faire*.

"However," Mr. Parkhill raised his voice, "the particular historical event we are commemorating tomorrow pertains to—Christopher Columbus. For it was on October twelfth, 1492—"

"*Colom*biss!" Mr. Kaplan's rapture passed beyond containment. "Christover *Colom*biss?!"

Excitement seized the beginners' grade.

"Columbus!"

"Columbia Day," breathed Olga Tarnova. "Romahnteek."

"Colombos discovert America!"

"Oy!" That was Mrs. Moskowitz. No one could groan a "What?" or moan a "Why?" with one-tenth the eloquence Sadie Moskowitz put into her "Oy!" She was the Niobe of the beginners' grade.

"Yes, class, on October twelfth, 1492—"

Pole is important as North, maybe more."

"Ha!" parried Mr. Kaplan. "Averybody *knew* vas a Sot Pole, no? All Edmiral Boyd did vas go dere!"

Miss Mitnick turned white. Mr. Plonsky was so infuriated that he turned his back on Mr. Kaplan and, facing the rear wall, appealed to the gods: "Crazy! Cuckoo! How can you argue with a Mr. Opside Don?"

"Admiral Byrd is big *hero*," Miss Mitnick faltered, wetting her lips. "He went through terrible things for humanity—cold, icebergs, alone, freezings."

"Edmiral Boyd *vent mit all modinn conweniences!*" ruled Hyman Kaplan.

Miss Mitnick made a strangling sound and shot an S O S to Mr. Parkhill.

"Er—it's 'Admiral *Byrd*,'" Mr. Parkhill repeated. Nobody paid any attention to him. For Miss Caravello, a never-dormant volcano, had erupted: "Is only da one Columbus! No more lak—before, behinda!" To Miss Caravello, beyond any peradventure of doubt, Columbus would forever be enshrined as a peculiarly Italian phenomenon, unparalleled, incomparable. Admiral Byrd, she said flatly, was a "copying cat." For great Columbus, Miss Caravello concluded hotly, nothing short of a thousand Bravos would do. She proceeded to give three of them: "Bravo! Bravo! Bravo!"

The Messrs. Kaplan and Pinsky broke into applause.

"Class—"

Now Mr. Gus Matsoukas demanded the floor, and took it before Miss Mitnick could recognize him. "Colomb' good man, no doubts about," he began magnanimously. Columbus was, indeed, worth all that Mr. Kaplan and Miss Caravello had claimed for him. But after all, Mr. Matsoukas insinuated, how could any but the uncultivated regard Columbus as more than a dull descendant of the first and *greatest* explorer—Ulysses? (Ulysses, it turned out, was born no more than seventeen kilometers from Mr. Matsoukas' birthplace.)

"Boit*days* are more important den boitplaces!" Mr. Kaplan proclaimed.

Mr. Matsoukas, startled, could think of no rejoinder to this powerful and unexpected postulate. He retired, mumbling.

"Anybody else wants to say few words?" asked Miss Mitnick anxiously.

Mr. Kaplan thrust his hand into the air.

"Floor is ebsolutely *open*," Miss Mitnick announced, keeping her eyes where Mr. Kaplan could not meet them. "*Any*body can talk."

Mr. Kaplan promptly rose, said "Foidinand an' Isabel. Ha!" and sat down.

Uneasy murmurs raced across the room. Miss Mitnick flushed and twisted her handkerchief around her fingers. "Mr. Kaplan," she stammered, "I didn't catch."

Mr. Kaplan got up again, repeated "Foidinand an' Isabel. Ha!" and again sat down.

"Why he is anger?" whispered Mrs. Tomasic.

"He is mod, mod," groaned Olga Tarnova.

"Er—Mr. Kaplan," Mr. Parkhill began, "I do think—"

"Axplain!" Mr. Blattberg sang out. "Describe!" (It was through such clarity and persistence that Aaron Blattberg had become one of the best shoe salesmen on Second Avenue.)

Mr. Kaplan snorted, but said nothing.

"Keplan wants to talk or Keplan *not* wants to talk?" Mr. Plonsky inquired of the rear wall bitterly.

"Y-yes, Mr. Kaplan," Mr. Parkhill frowned, "I do think the class is entitled to some explanation of your—er—comment."

"All of a sodden Mr. Keplen makes fun Foidinand Isabel!" protested Mrs. Moskowitz. "Not even saying 'Axcuse' can he make 'Ha, ha!' on kinks and quinns?!"

This frontal attack stirred the royalists into action.

"Talk, Kaplan?"

"You got the floor, no?"

"Tell awreddy!"

A more formal dialectician cried, "Give your meanink dose remocks!" That was Mrs. Yanoff, an epistemologist dressed, as always, in black.

Mr. Kaplan rose once more and turned to face his challengers. "Ladies an' gantlemen, Mr. Pockheel—an' chairlady." Miss Mitnick lowered her eyes. "Ve all agreeink Colombiss's joiney vas vun de most movellous tings aver heppened in de voild." Cries, calls, grunts of affirmation. "*T'ink* abot det treep, jost *t'ink*. Viks an' viks Colombiss vas sailink—tru storm, lighteninks, tonder. Tru vafes high like Ampire State Buildink. Fodder an' fodder Colombiss vent—alone!" Mr. Kaplan paused to let the awesome data of that ordeal sink home. "Vell, mine frands, in *vat kine boats* Colombiss made det vunderful voyitch?" Mr. Kaplan's eyes narrowed. "In fency sheeps? In fine accommodations? No! In leetle, teentsy chizz boxes! Boats full likks! Boats full doit, joims, vater commink in! *Som* boats for discoverink Amarica! An' det's vy I'm sayink, '*Shame* on you, Foidinand! *Shame* on you, Isabel!' " Mr. Kaplan's eyes flashed. "Couldn't dey give a man like Colombiss batter transportation?"

Outrage exploded in the classroom.

"*Viva* Columbus!" cried Mrs. Rodriguez, upon whom it had just dawned that Columbus owed much to Iberia.

"Crazy talk," muttered Mr. Matsoukas, thinking of the raft of Ulysses.

"Maybe in 1492 they should manufacture already a SS *Qvinn Lizabeth*?" Mr. Plonsky asked the rear wall sarcastically.

A storm of retorts, defenses, taunts, disclaimers filled the air. Miss Mitnick, staggering under the responsibilities of arbitration, kept pleading, "Mr.

Mr. K★a★p★l★a★n and Shakespeare

It was miss higby's idea in the first place. she had suggested to mr. Parkhill that the students came to her grade unaware of the *finer* side of English, of its beauty and, as she put it, "the glorious heritage of our literature." She suggested that perhaps poetry might be worked into the exercises of Mr. Parkhill's class. The beginners' grade had, after all, been subjected to almost a year of English and might be presumed to have achieved some linguistic sophistication. Poetry would make the students conscious of precise enunciation; it would make them read with greater care and an ear for sounds. Miss Higby, who had once begun a master's thesis on Coventry Patmore, *loved* poetry. And, it should be said in all justice, she argued her cause with considerable force. Poetry *would* be excellent for the enunciation of the students, thought Mr. Parkhill.

So it was that when he faced the class the following Tuesday night, Mr. Parkhill had a volume of Shakespeare on his desk and an eager, almost an expectant, look in his eye. The love that Miss Higby bore for poetry in general was as nothing compared to the love that Mr. Parkhill bore for Shakespeare in particular. To Mr. Parkhill, poetry meant Shakespeare. Many years ago he had played Polonius in his senior-class play.

"Tonight, class," said Mr. Parkhill, "I am going to try an experiment."

The class looked up dutifully. They had come to regard Mr. Parkhill's pedagogical innovations as part of the natural order.

"I am going to introduce you to poetry—great poetry. You see—" Mr. Parkhill delivered a modest lecture on the beauty of poetry, its expression of the loftier thoughts of men, its economy of statement. He hoped it would be a relief from spelling and composition exercises to use poetry as the subject matter of the regular Recitation and Speech period. "I shall write a passage on the board and read it for you. Then, for Recitation and Speech, you will give

45

short addresses, using the passage as the general topic, telling us what it has brought to your minds, what—er—thoughts and ideas."

The class seemed quite pleased by the announcement. Miss Mitnick blushed happily. (This blush was different from most of Miss Mitnick's blushes; there was aspiration and idealism in it.) Mr. Norman Bloom sighed with a businesslike air: you could tell that for him poetry was merely another assignment, like a speech on "What I Like to Eat Best" or a composition on "A Day at a Picnic." Mrs. Moskowitz, to whom any public performance was unpleasant, tried to look enthusiastic, without much success. And Mr. Hyman Kaplan, the heroic smile on his face as indelibly as ever, looked at Mr. Parkhill with admiration and whispered to himself: "Poyetry! Now is poyetry! My! Mus' be progriss ve makink awreddy!"

"The passage will be from Shakespeare," Mr. Parkhill announced, opening the volume.

An excited buzz ran through the class as the magic of that name fell upon them.

"Imachine!" murmured Mr. Kaplan. "Jakesbeer!"

"*Shake*speare, Mr. Kaplan!"

Mr. Parkhill took a piece of chalk and, with care and evident love, wrote the following passage on the board in large, clear letters:

> Tomorrow, and tomorrow, and tomorrow
> Creeps in this petty pace from day to day,
> To the last syllable of recorded time;
> And all our yesterdays have lighted fools
> The way to dusty death. Out, out, brief candle!
> Life's but a walking shadow, a poor player
> That struts and frets his hour upon the stage,
> And then is heard no more; it is a tale
> Told by an idiot, full of sound and fury,
> Signifying nothing.

A reverent hush filled the classroom, as eyes gazed with wonder on this passage from the Bard. Mr. Parkhill was pleased.

"I shall read the passage first," he said. "Listen carefully to my enunciation and—er—let Shakespeare's thoughts sink into your minds."

Mr. Parkhill read: "Tomorrow, and tomorrow, and tomorrow . . ." Mr. Parkhill read very well, and this night, as if some special fire burned in him, he read with rare eloquence. "Out, out, brief candle!" In Miss Mitnick's eyes there was inspiration and wonder. "Life's but a walking shadow . . ." Mrs. Moskowitz sat with a heavy frown, indicating cerebration. "It is a tale told by an idiot . . ." Mr. Kaplan's smile had taken on something luminous, but his eyes were closed: it was not clear whether Mr. Kaplan had surrendered to the spell of Shakespeare or to that of Morpheus.

"I shall—er—read the passage again," said Mr. Parkhill, clearing his throat vociferously until he saw Mr. Kaplan's eyes open. "Tomorrow, and tomorrow, and tomorrow. . . ."

When Mr. Parkhill had read the passage for the second time, he said: "That should be quite clear now. Are there any questions?"

There were a few questions. Mr. Scymzak wanted to know whether "frets" was "a little kind excitment." Miss Schneiderman asked about "struts." Mr. Kaplan wasn't sure about "cripps." Mr. Parkhill explained the words carefully, with several illustrative uses of each word. "No more questions? Well, I shall allow a few minutes for you all to—er—think over the meaning of the passage. Then we shall begin Recitation and Speech."

Mr. Kaplan promptly closed his eyes again, his smile beatific. The students sank into that reverie miscalled thought, searching their souls for the symbols evoked by Shakespeare's immortal words. Olga Tarnova was uttering those husky, throaty moans that, in her case, signified either speechlessness or rapture.

"Miss Caravello, will you begin?" asked Mr. Parkhill.

Miss Caravello went to the front of the room. "Da poem isa gooda," she said slowly. "Itsa have—"

"It *has.*"

"It has a beautiful wordsa. Itsa lak Dante, Italian poet—"

"Ha!" cried Mr. Kaplan scornfully. "Shaksbeer you metchink mit Tante? *Shaksbeer?* Mein Gott!"

It was obvious that Mr. Kaplan had identified himself with Shakespeare and would tolerate no disparagement of his *alter ego.*

"Miss Caravello is merely expressing her own ideas," said Mr. Parkhill pacifically. (Actually, he felt completely sympathetic to Mr. Kaplan's point of view.)

"Hau Kay," agreed Mr. Kaplan, with a generous wave of the hand. "But to me is no comparink a high-cless man like Shaksbeer mit a Tante, dat's all."

Miss Caravello, her poise shattered, said a few more words and returned to her seat.

Mrs. Yampolsky's contribution was brief. "This is full deep meanings," she said, her eyes on the floor. "Is hard for a person not so good in English to unnistand. But I like."

"*Like!*" cried Mr. Kaplan. "*Like? Batter love,* Yampolsky. Mit Shaksbeer mus' be *love!*"

Mr. Parkhill had to suggest that Mr. Kaplan control his æsthetic passions. He did understand how Mr. Kaplan felt, however, and sensed a new bond between them. Mrs. Yampolsky staggered through several more nervous ambiguities and retired.

Mr. Bloom was next. He gave a long declamation, ending: "So is passimistic ideas in the poem, and I am optimist. Life should be happy—so we should remember this is only a poem. Maybe is Shakespeare too passimistic."

"You wronk, Bloom!" cried Mr. Kaplan with prompt indignation. "Shaksbeer is passimist because is de *life* passimist also!"

Mr. Parkhill, impressed by this philosophical stroke, realized that Mr. Kaplan, afire with the glory of the Swan of Avon, could not be suppressed. Mr. Kaplan was the kind of man who brooked no criticism of his gods. The only solution was to call on Mr. Kaplan for his recitation at once. Mr. Parkhill was, indeed, curious about what fresh thoughts Mr. Kaplan would utter after his passionate defenses of the Bard. When Mr. Parkhill had corrected certain parts of Mr. Bloom's speech, emphasizing Mr. Bloom's failure to use the indefinite article, he said: "Mr. Kaplan, will *you* speak next?"

Mr. Kaplan's face broke into a glow; his smile was like a rainbow. "Soitinly," he said, walking to the front of the room. Never had he seemed so dignified, so eager, so conscious of a great destiny.

"Er—Mr. Kaplan," added Mr. Parkhill, suddenly aware of the possibilities which the situation (Kaplan on Shakespeare) involved: "Speak *carefully*."

"*Spacially* careful vill I be," Mr. Kaplan reassured him. He cleared his throat, adjusted his tie, and began: "Ladies an' gantleman, you hoid all kinds minninks abot dis piece poyetry, an'—"

"Poetry."

"—abot dis piece *poetry*. But to me is a difference minnink altogadder. Ve mus' tink abot Julius Scissor an' how *he* falt!"

Mr. Parkhill moved nervously, puzzled.

"In dese exact voids is Julius Scissor sayink—"

"Er—Mr. Kaplan," said Mr. Parkhill once he grasped the full import of Mr. Kaplan's error. "The passage is from *Macbeth*."

Mr. Kaplan looked at Mr. Parkhill with injured surprise. "*Not* fromm *Julius Scissor?*"

"No. And it's—er—'Julius *Caesar.*'"

Mr. Kaplan waited until the last echo of the name had permeated his soul. "Podden me, Mr. Pockheel. Isn't '*seezor*' vat you cottink somting op mit?"

"That," said Mr. Parkhill quickly, "is 'scissor.' You have used 'Caesar' for 'scissor' and 'scissor' for 'Caesar.'"

"My!" Mr. Kaplan exclaimed, marvelling at his own virtuosity.

"But go on with your speech, please." Mr. Parkhill, to tell the truth, felt a little guilty that he had not announced at the very beginning that the passage was from *Macbeth*. "Tell us *why* you thought the lines were from *Julius Caesar*."

"Vell," said Mr. Kaplan to the class, his smile assuming its normal serenity,

"I vas positif, becawss I can *see* the whole ting." He paused, debating how to explain this cryptic remark. Then his eyes filled with a certain enchantment. "I see de whole scinn. It's in a tant, on de night bafore dey makink Julius de Kink fromm Rome. So he is axcited an' ken't slip. He is layink in bad, tinking: 'Tomorrow an' tomorrow an' tomorrow. How slow dey movink! Almost cripps! Soch a pity de pace!'"

Before Mr. Parkhill could explain that "petty pace" did not mean "Soch a pity de pace!" Mr. Kaplan had soared on.

"De days go slow, fromm day to day, like leetle tsyllables on phonograph racords fromm time."

"Mr. Kap—"

"'An' vat abot yestidday?' tinks Julius Scissor. Ha! 'All our yestiddays are only makink a good light for fools to die in de dost!'"

"'Dusty death' doesn't mean—"

"An' Julius Scissor is so tired, an' he vants to fallink aslip. So he hollers, mit fillink, 'Go ot! Go ot! Short candle!' So it goes ot."

Mr. Kaplan's voice dropped to a whisper. "But he ken't slip. Now is bodderink him de idea fromm life. 'Vat is de life altogadder?' tinks Julius Scissor. An' he gives enswer, de pot I like de bast. 'Life is like a bum actor, strottink an' hollerink arond de stage for only vun hour bafore he's kicked ot. Life is a tale told by idjots, dat's all, full of fonny sonds an' phooey!'"

"'Full of sound and fury!'" Mr. Parkhill cried desperately. But inspiration, like an irresistible force, swept Mr. Kaplan on.

"'Life is monkey business! It don' minn a ting. It signifies nottink!' An' den Julius Scissor closes his ice fest"—Mr. Kaplan demonstrated the Consul's exact ocular process in closing his "ice"—"an' falls don dad!"

The class was hushed as Mr. Kaplan stopped. In the silence, a tribute to the fertility of Mr. Kaplan's imagination and the power of his oratory, Mr. Kaplan went to his seat. But just before he sat down, as if adding a postscript, he sighed: "Dat was mine idea. But ufcawss is all wronk, becawss Mr. Pockheel said de voids ain't abot Julius Scissor altogadder. It's all abot an Irishman by de name Macbat."

It was some time before Mr. Parkhill could bring himself to criticize Mr. Kaplan's pronunciation, enunciation, diction, grammar, idiom, and sentence structure. For Mr. Parkhill discovered that he could not easily return to the world of reality. He was still trying to tear himself away from that tent outside Rome, where "Julius Scissor," cursed with insomnia, had thought of time and life—and philosophized himself to a strange and sudden death.

Mr. Parkhill was distinctly annoyed with Miss Higby.

Mr. K★a★p★l★a★n's White Banner

IT WAS ONLY LOGICAL THAT, HAVING DRILLED THE CLASS BEFORE THE HOLIDAYS on the writing of personal letters, Mr. Parkhill should now take up the business form with the beginners' grade. Business letters, indeed, might be even more practical from the students' point of view. They might want to apply for a job, or answer an advertisement, or things of that sort.

"The general structure of the business letter follows that of the personal letter," Mr. Parkhill had said. "It, too, requires the address, the date, a salutation, a final greeting or 'complimentary close.'" Then he had gone on to explain that the business letter was more formal in mood and content; that the address of the person or company to whom you were writing had to be included in the form of the letter itself, on the left-hand side, above the salutation; that both the salutation and final greeting were formalized: "Dear Sir," "Dear Sirs," or "Gentlemen," and "Yours truly," "Yours very truly," "Very truly yours." Mr. Parkhill was a conscientious teacher and, aware of the queer things some of the students had done with previous exercises, he was careful to introduce the beginners' grade to business letters with particular care.

All had gone well—very well. So much had Mr. Parkhill been pleased by his success that, for homework, he had assigned a composition entitled "A Short Business Letter."

And now the students were presenting their homework on the blackboard for class analysis. Mrs. Tomasic, anticipating some halcyon day in the future, was applying for a position as private secretary to the President of the Good English Club. Mr. George Weinstein was ordering "a dozen assoted colors by size 12 raon" from a well-known department store. Mr. Norman Bloom, ever the soul of business, was inscribing a polite but firm note reminding "St. Levin—Inc.—Jobbers" that they still owed him $17.75 for merchandise

50

pantomime. That narrowing of the eyes, that lethal stare, that doomsday tone—to any who knew Mr. Kaplan these signified but one thing: Hyman Kaplan had issued that formal *caveat* which precedes a declaration of war. There could be no doubt about it. Whenever Mr. Kaplan bestowed so malevolent a glare on a colleague, it was for only one reason: his honor had been slurred, and demanded satisfaction in battle.

But who was the student at the far end of the front row? He was one Fischel Pfeiffer. He had been admitted, originally, to Miss Higby's class, but after the very first recess Miss Higby had escorted Mr. Pfeiffer into Mr. Parkhill's room, where, with excessive casualness, she had informed Mr. Parkhill that although Fischel Pfeiffer was a most rare and conscientious pupil, a scholar of undeniable promise, he was "not *quite* ready" for the heady heights of Composition, Grammar, and Civics. In Miss Higby's considered opinion, Mr. Pfeiffer needed basic "drill, drill, drill" where certain fundamentals of the tongue were involved.

During the whole of Miss Higby's recitation, Mr. Pfeiffer had remained standing, silent, baleful, his lips pressed tight, his face all gloom. None but the blind could have misread his mood: Mr. Pfeiffer was mortified by demotion. He was a thin, dapper man with rimless glasses, a polka-dot bow tie, and a cream-colored suit the sleeves of which were as sharp as knives.

"We're glad to have you with us," Mr. Parkhill remembered remarking in a reassuring manner. (At least it reassured Mr. Parkhill; it made no dent on Mr. Pfeiffer's conspicuous discontent.) "Class, this is Mr. Pfeiffer. Mr.—er—Fischel Pfeiffer. Won't you take a seat, please?"

Mr. Pfeiffer lifted his eyes just high enough to survey the reaches of the Siberia to which he had been exiled.

"There is a place in the front row," said Mr. Parkhill.

Without a word, in his own miasma of humiliation, Mr. Pfeiffer started toward the empty chair at the far end of the front row. It was at that moment that Mr. Parkhill had felt a premonitory twinge. For in order to get to the seat at the end of the front row, Mr. Pfeiffer had to pass directly in front of Mr. Kaplan. And Mr. Kaplan, by leaning forward generously, had managed to follow the entire colloquy between Miss Higby and Mr. Parkhill with the most avid fascination. . . .

As Mr. Pfeiffer crossed in front of Mr. Kaplan, that self-appointed protector of the weak and the homeless had sung out, "Valcome, Fischel Pfeiffer! Valcome to beginnis' grate!"

Mr. Pfeiffer had paused, eyed his unsolicited cicerone, and uttered a monosyllabic sound the mere recollection of which still made Mr. Parkhill's forehead damp: "Feh!" That was all he had said: "Feh!"

Now "Feh!" was an expletive Mr. Parkhill had heard before—but in the *corridors* of the American Night Preparatory School for Adults, never inside a classroom. The expression had, in fact, rather interested him: it was a striking example of onomatopoeia. Just as "moo" or "quack" or "coo" conveyed their meaning with supreme accuracy, so "feh!," however inelegant, was a vivid vehicle for the utterance of disdain.

"Feh!" The class had caught its collective breath; then all eyes turned from Fischel Pfeiffer to Hyman Kaplan, a man of the most delicate sensibilities.

His jaw had dropped; his cheeks had reddened in disbelief. "Feh?" Mr. Kaplan echoed dazedly. "*Feh? For de cless?!*"

"Our exercise tonight is Open Questions," Mr. Parkhill had announced quickly. Long, hard experience in the beginners' grade had taught him how to apprehend the first faint alarums of discord, and how to canalize aggression by diverting attention. "The floor is open, class. Any questions at all, any problems you may have encountered in reading, writing, conversation. Who will begin?"

Up rose the hand of Sam Pinsky.

"Mr. Pinsky," said Mr. Parkhill lightly.

"I ebsolutely agree with Mr. Keplen!" proclaimed Mr. Pinsky stoutly. "A student shouldn't make 'Feh!' for——"

"*That*," said Mr. Parkhill crossly, "is not a question. Mr. Matsoukas."

Gus Matsoukas emitted his immemorial growl, consulted a dog-eared envelope, and asked his question. "Which is for describing furniture: 'baboon' or '*bam*boon'?"

"Mr. Matsoukas," said Mr. Parkhill, knitting his brow, "a ba*boon* is an animal, an ape, whereas bam*boo*, not 'bam*boon*', is a—er—wood." Mr. Parkhill explained the difference between the anthropoid and the ligneous in patient detail. (Mr. Matsoukas, who customarily referred to his dentifrice as "toot ponder," had much to learn.) "Miss Shimmelfarb?"

" 'Mail' in 'mailbox,' where you putting letters. Is this a masculine?" asked Miss Shimmelfarb.

"N-no," said Mr. Parkhill, and described the difference between the postal and the human. "Mrs. Rodriguez."

"Why 'scissors' have 'c' and 's' but no two 'z's?" asked Mrs. Rodriguez. "I *hear* 'z's!" (That dreadful word "scissors," Mr. Parkhill reflected ruefully, must have plagued every teacher of every course in English ever offered in in any land or time.)

"I'm afraid 'scissors' is just spelled that way," said Mr. Parkhill, with genuine regret.

The students entered into Open Questions with zest. They loved Open Questions. It offered them freedom, amplitude, respite from the constricting ruts of instruction.

"What is the League of Women Motors?" Hans Guttman, a man devoted to learning, asked.

"Who is Hannahlulu?" chirped Mrs. Tomasic.

"What kind candy is 'valley fudge'?" Mrs. Yanoff inquired.

Mr. Parkhill had worked his way deftly through all these linguistic snares and swamps. He, too, enjoyed Open Questions—its challenge, its unpredictability; yet that night, he remembered, he had been unable to shake off a sense of foreboding. For in the caverns below consciousness, the flatulent memory of "Feh!" still echoed. It was difficult enough to preserve decorum in a class torn by fierce vendettas, a class that included such antithetical types as Hyman Kaplan and Reuben Plonsky, or Mr. Kaplan and Carmen Caravello, or Mr. Kaplan and Miss Mitnick. To add to this scholastic powder keg so incendiary a type as Fischel Pfeiffer, a man foolhardy enough to give the affront direct to Hyman Kaplan—Mr. Parkhill had felt a surge of outright displeasure with Miss Higby.

But all that was behind him now, Mr. Parkhill reminded himself. This was two nights later. The roll had been called, the decks cleared for action. There was work to be done. Mr. Parkhill put his attendance sheet to one side, cleared his throat, pretended he had not noticed the mordant pantomime Mr. Kaplan had addressed to Mr. Pfeiffer, and announced, "I have corrected the compositions you handed in last Thursday, class, and one thing that stands out in my mind is the number of—er—*dangling participles*." He paused for the briefest moment to let this sink in. "I shall read some compositions—without identifying the authors, of course. Let's see how many of us recognize the errors. . . ."

He launched his apprentices on a brisk quest for dangling participles which did not end until the bell rang for recess. And in all that time, Mr. Parkhill noticed with mounting uneasiness, Mr. Kaplan said nothing, and Fischel Pfeiffer sat wordless, stony and withdrawn.

After the recess, Mr. Parkhill announced, "Now, class, suppose we have a little exercise on—vocabulary."

"Vary useful," declared Mr. Plonsky.

"I like," said Mr. Studniczka.

"Oooh," breathed Olga Tarnova from her reservoir of unutterable griefs.

"Pencils and papers, please. Everyone."

"Hau Kay," sighed Hyman Kaplan.

The room rustled like aspens under a high wind. Thirty-odd scholars opened briefcases, handbags, portfolios, shopping bags.

"I shall write five words on the blackboard," Mr. Parkhill said, picking up a piece of chalk. "Use each word in a sentence, a—er—full sentence, that is. Five words, therefore five sentences." He smiled. There was no harm in leavening the bread of learning with the yeast of levity. "Write your sentences carefully, class. Remember, I shall grade not just your spelling, but entire sentences—diction, syntax, punctuation. . . ."

"Oy," moaned Mrs. Moskowitz, fanning herself with her notebook. It was arduous enough for Mrs. Moskowitz to spell one word right; to spell five words correctly, and put them into five whole sentences in which all the *other* words had to be spelled right, *and* selected properly, *and* fitted into the terrifying architecture of syntax—that, for Mrs. Moskowitz, was piling new Ossas upon already overburdened Pelions.

Mr. Parkhill gave Mrs. Moskowitz a therapeutic smile and turned to the blackboard. In large block letters, he printed:

1. CHISEL
2. LAMP
3. GROAN
4. POTATOES
5. CLIMAX

"Oy!" came from the unnerved depths of Mrs. Moskowitz once more.

"Moskowitz," called Mr. Kaplan, "you doink a lasson or givink a concert?"

"You have five minutes," said Mr. Parkhill quickly, wiping the chalk dust off his fingers. He moved down the aisle, nodding encouragement to a student here, alleviating anxiety in a student there, stiffening the morale of the faint of heart.

How pregnant the moment before commitment always was. The eyes of his neophytes were racing across the five words on the board, appraising them like frontiersmen in a trackless forest, alert to the dangers that might skulk behind the most innocent façade, on guard against linguistic ambushes, reconnoitering "chisel" warily, taking the measure of "lamp" in stride, hurdling the limpid "groan" to reach the obvious "potatoes," resting at last on the word Mr. Parkhill, with his unerring sense of the appropriate, had chosen to close the maze—"climax."

"I'm sure you all know the meaning of these words," said Mr. Parkhill.

"I'm not," wailed Mrs. Moskowitz.

"Come, come now, Mrs. Moskowitz. Try."

Mrs. Moskowitz heaved into the unknown.

Miss Mitnick bent her head over her notebook, the bun of her hair like a doughnut on the nape of her slender neck, and began to write with sedate dispatch. Mr. Plonsky unbuttoned his vest, cleaned his bifocals, uncapped his pen, and inscribed his first sentence on a letterhead of Statue of Liberty Remnants, Inc. And Mr. Kaplan, ever undaunted, cocked his head to one side, repeated each word aloud in a clear, approving whisper, adding an admiring

"My!" or "Tchk!" of homage to Mr. Parkhill's incomparable gifts as a teacher, exclaimed "Fife fine voids!" and shot Fischel Pfeiffer a glower designed to remind him of the riches the beginners' grade had always spread before the worthy.

Mr. Pfeiffer saw it not. After one deprecatory glance at the blackboard, the thin-lipped malcontent had set to work with absolute decision and startling speed. Before most of the students had even cleared the troubling reefs of "chisel," Fischel Pfeiffer slapped his pencil down and announced, with contempt, "Done!"

The appearance of an archangel would have caused no greater astonishment.

"*Done?*"

"Finished?"

"So *fest?*"

Heads were shooting up all around the room in wonderment.

"What we have here, a *ginius?*" asked Miss Goldberg, and consoled herself with a piece of chocolate.

"A ragular spid dimon?" Mr. Kesselman queried.

"Pfeiffer expects to graduate before midnight!" said Mr. Pinsky acidly, glancing towards his captain for approbation. Mr. Kaplan looked as if he had seen Beelzebub.

Before the sensation created by Mr. Pfeiffer's velocity had even spent its force, that fleet paragon stepped to the blackboard, seized a stick of chalk, and began to transcribe his sentences with careless disdain.

"We generally *wait* to go to the board until——" Mr. Parkhill's voice trailed off.

Words were flowing from the end of Mr. Pfeiffer's chalk as if it were a magic wand.

In the congregation of watchers, all work ceased. The class sat transfixed. Then a chorus of "Oh!"'s and "Ah!"'s and "Fentestic!"'s cleaved the air.

For on that plain, black board, in most beautiful script, a script both sumptuous and majestic, Fischel Pfeiffer had written:

1. In Chicago, pride Lake Michigan, many shops sell Mexocan jewelry made by small, sharp *chisels*.

A new hymn of admiration ascended from the seated—not only for the exquisite calligraphy, which would have done credit to a Persian, but for the mettle of a man intrepid enough to tackle as recondite a word as "Michigan," as exotic a name as "Mexocan."

"Dis man writes like an artiss!" cried Oscar Trabish.

"*Like* an arteest? No! He *is* an arteest!" flamed Miss Tarnova. Then she throbbed, "*This mon has soffert! This mon has soul!*" (Olga Tarnova, a Slavophile who considered herself a reincarnation of Anna Karenina, believed that all humanity could be divided into two categories: those with and those without "soul.")

A burst of glee issued from Mr. Blattberg. "Kaplen, you watching?"

"Pfeiffer makes you look like a greenhorn!" jeered Reuben Plonsky, searching for his nemesis through his bifocals.

White, crestfallen, Mr. Kaplan said nothing. He was staring at the board—abject, incredulous—where Mr. Pfeiffer was finishing his second grand sentence:

2. In Arabean Nights, famous story, is Alladin's wonderful *lamp*.

Now the "Oh!"'s and "Ah!"'s fell like a shower, garnished by a lone, reverential "Supoib!"

"*Mamma mia*," gasped Carmen Caravello.

"Pfeiffer, congradulation!" chortled Mr. Plonsky.

"Mr. Kaplan, what you see?" grinned Stanislaus Wilkomirski.

"Pfeiffer, you raddy for college!" cried Shura Gursky, carried away.

Mr. Parkhill tapped the desk with his pointer. "Now, now, class. Order . . ." But he was, in truth, as fascinated as his flock. And why not? The years in the beginners' grade had taught him to expect, for a sentence using "chisel," say, "I have a chisel," or "Give me chisels," or even "I like chisels." For a word like "lamp," Mr. Parkhill had long since become conditioned to sentences such as "Take the lamp," or "Who stole this lamp?" Into such a pedestrian world had come a Hector, a man who dared write "Arabean Nights" when the harmless "old book" would have sufficed; who did not flinch before Aladdin, where the timorous would surely have written "boy"; who even had the audacity to use an appositive ("famous story") he could have sidestepped entirely. It was indeed "supoib."

And while the murmurs of tribute were still rolling down the ranks, Mr. Pfeiffer transferred his three remaining sentences to the board with a celerity that was to become a legend in the American Night Preparatory School for Adults:

3. Life is not only suffring and *groans*.
4. No one finds diamonds in *potatoes*.
5. What is Man? A bird? A beest? No! A *climax*.

To a symphony of praise as excited as any Mr. Parkhill had ever heard in a classroom, Mr. Pfeiffer turned from the board, stifled a yawn, and returned to his seat.

"Oh, Mr. Pfeiffer," sighed Miss Mitnick.

"Wohnderful," crooned Olga Tarnova. "*Khoroscho* for an arteest!"

"Keplan," mocked Mr. Plonsky, "you have nothing to say? Not a single criticize?"

Not only had Mr. Kaplan nothing to say, he seemed to be in a state of shock. And Mr. Parkhill felt vaguely sorry for him. True, a man with so reckless a confidence, so luxuriant an ego, might well be exposed to occasional reverses; still, Hyman Kaplan had a certain flair, a panache not often seen among the earthbound.

"Time is slipping away, class," said Mr. Parkhill. "We are not—er—finishing our assignments."

They sighed and stirred and resumed their labors, and soon Mr. Parkhill sent a contingent of six to the board. They copied their sentences soberly, dutifully, but the heart seemed to have gone out of them. They wrote without that spirited counterpoint of comment or soliloquy which usually enlivened performances at the blackboard. For over all their heads, like an unscalable summit, shone the glittering handiwork of Fischel Pfeiffer.

How feeble, by comparison, seemed Mr. Marschak's "Actors give big *groans*," how lackluster Miss Gidwitz's "By me are old lamps the best," how jejune even Mr. Scymzak's brave foray into aesthetics: "Any piece Hungarian music has glorious *climax*." With apologetic gestures and self-deprecating shrugs, the listless six shuffled back to their places.

"Good!" said Mr. Parkhill brightly. "Discussion . . . Miss Ziev, will you read your sentences first?"

Miss Ziev, who had been quite vivacious since her engagement to a Mr. Andrassy in Mr. Krout's class, read her sentences *sans esprit*—and the discussion thereof died stillborn. Not a spark of life was struck by even Miss Ziev's "The boy has certainly *groan* lately."

Mr. Marschak followed Miss Ziev, and the discussion was as spiritless as the utterances of a stricken child. No outburst of "Mistake!" or "Hoo ha!" greeted Mr. Marschak's "He eats fright *potatoes*."

Mrs. Rodriguez followed Mr. Marschak, and once again Mr. Parkhill, unable to put heart into his charges, had to carry the entire discussion by himself—even unto Mrs. Rodriguez's defiant "Puerto Rico has nice, hot *climax*! ! !"

"Miss Gidwitz, please."

There was but desultory response to Miss Gidwitz's "Mary had a little *lamp*."

An equally pallid reception greeted even Mr. Pinsky's unprecedented use of the word "chisel." (Mr. Pinsky, who seemed to consider "chisel" the diminutive of "cheese," had written: "Before sleep, I like to have a little milk and *chisel*.")

It was Mr. Parkhill alone who pointed out lapses in diction, the stumbling of syntax, the neglect of prepositions. The spirit of discussion had fled the beginners' grade. Gone were the *sine quibus non* of debate: strong convictions, stanchly held; the clash of opinions bravely defended; the friction of one certain he is right rubbing against another positive he is wrong.

Now only Mr. Pfeiffer's sentences remained to be read. Mr. Parkhill teetered back and forth on his heels. "Mr. Pfeiffer."

A hush fell upon the classroom. All waited. All listened. And what all heard, in utter astonishment, was the high, thin voice of Mr. Pfeiffer reciting in shrill sibilance: "In Sicago, pride Lake Missigan, many sops sell Mexican joolery made by small, sarp *tzisels*." There was no getting around it: Mr. Pfeiffer had said "Sicago" for "Chicago," "Missigan" for "Michigan," "sarp" for "sharp". . . .

"A Litvak!" a clarion voice rang out. It was Mr. Kaplan, rejuvenated. "Mein Gott, he's a Litvak!" He wheeled toward Mr. Parkhill. "Must be! Fromm Lit'uania! He prononces 'sh' like stimm commink ot of a pipe!"

The heavens opened above the beginners' grade.

"Shame, Koplan, shame!" howled Miss Tarnova.

"Can Pfeiffer *help* he is a foreigner?" protested Mr. Trabish.

"In class is no place to condemn!" shouted Mr. Plonsky, so agitated that his glasses almost slipped off his nose.

"I *described*," said Mr. Kaplan icily, "I did not condamn."

The riposte only fanned the flames that swept through Fischel Pfeiffer's defenders.

"Not fair!" charged Mr. Blattberg hotly.

"Not fair?" Mr. Kaplan echoed. "If a customer calls vun of your shoes a 'soo' vould you give him a banqvet entitled, 'Hoorah! He's ruinink de langvidge!'?"

"But discussion should be about the *work*," Miss Mitnick pleaded, "not the personal."

"Mine remocks are abot de prononciational, not de poisonal!" rejoined Mr. Kaplan.

"Class, *class*," Mr. Parkhill kept saying, "there is no reason for such—"

"Kaplan, *bad!*" blurted Mr. Wilkomirski. (Mr. Wilkomirski, who was a sexton, often confused error with sin.) "New man writes like king!"

"Ha!" cried Mr. Kaplan. "He writes like a kink but talks like a Litvak!"

"*Gentlemen—*"

"Kaplan, you plaina jalous!" roared Miss Caravello.

"Who's makink poisonal remocks now?" asked Mr. Kaplan piously.

"Mr. Kap—"

"Stop! Caravello put her finger on!" boomed Reuben Plonsky. "Keplan picks on small ditail!"

"A mistake," said Mr. Kaplan, "is a mistake."

"Pfeiffer needs *praise*, not pins!" Miss Mitnick objected tearfully.

"Are ve in cless to praise—or to *loin?*" Mr. Kaplan flashed.

"You dun't give the Litvak a chence!" moaned Mrs. Moskowitz, all bosom.

"I vouldn't give an *Eskimo* a chence to drive 'sh' ot of English, eider!"

"Ladies—"

"You got to make allowance for frands!" stormed Mr. Blattberg.

"If mine own brodder makes a mistake," Mr. Kaplan retorted, "do I pretend he desoives the Nobles Prize? If Pinsky makes a mistake, does Keplen say, 'Skip, skip, he is maybe a cousin Einstein's'?"

"Gentlemen—"

"What's got Einstein to do with Fischel Pfeiffer?" asked Mr. Plonsky in bewilderment. "*Stop!*"

"Koplan, *you got no pity?*" importuned Miss Tarnova.

"Piddy?" Mr. Kaplan drew erect, implacable in his wrath. "You esk piddy for *de man who sad 'Feh!' to de cless?!*"

Now Mr. Parkhill understood. Now the mainspring of Mr. Kaplan's wrath lay revealed. "Class!" said Mr. Parkhill severely. "There is no need whatsoever for such intense dispute. Nothing is to be gained by—er—passion. We are—" The upraised hand of Mr. Pinsky caught his eye. "Yes?"

"How do you spall 'passion'?"

Mr. Parkhill cleared his throat. " 'Passion,' " he said, regretting his impulsiveness. "P-a-s-s-"

Before he could complete "passion," the bell rang. The contesting students rose, assembled their effects, and began streaming to the door, arguing among themselves, calling the familiar salutations. "Good night, all." "A *good* lasson!" "Heppy vik-end."

It had been a difficult evening, Mr. Parkhill reflected, a most difficult evening. The road to learning was long and hard, and strewn with barriers of the unforeseen. He noticed Miss Mitnick approaching the chair of the man who, responsible for all the tumult and the shouting, had been entirely forgotten in the heat of battle.

"Mr. Pfeiffer," Miss Mitnick blushed, "your writing is splendid. Also your sentence structure."

Mr. Blattberg joined them with a hearty "Pay no attention to *Professor* Kaplen!" He twirled the gold chain from which two baby teeth dangled, and favored Mr. Pfeiffer with that half-fraternal, half-subversive smile he reserved for those he tried to recruit to the anti-Kaplan forces.

Then, to Mr. Parkhill's surprise, Mr. Kaplan stepped up to Mr. Pfeiffer, extending his hand in comity. "Pfeiffer, I congradulate. I hope you realize I vas only doink mine *duty*. I didn't minn to hoit fillinks."

"You sabotaged his self-respact!" hissed Mr. Blattberg.

"You made mish-mash from his recitation!" Mr. Plonsky glared.

"You—you acted *hard*," Miss Mitnick stammered, biting her lip.

Mr. Pfeiffer adjusted his bow tie nattily. "If you esk me," he said, "Mr. Kaplan was right."

"Hah?"

"*Who?*"

"Keplan?!" The Blattberg-Mitnick-Plonsky task force could not believe their ears.

"A mistake is a mistake," said Fischel Pfeiffer, quoting Mr. Kaplan *verbatim*, oblivious of the coals he was heaping on the heads of his partisans. "A fect is also a fect. I pronounce bad."

"Pfeiffer, dobble congradulation on you!" Mr. Kaplan cried. "You honist! Batter an honist mistake den a snikky socksass! So you made a mistake! Who dozzn't? Still, you made on me a *fine* imprassion. Soch beauriful hendwritink! Not iven Mitnick writes so fency. So tell me, vhere you loined it?"

"I heppen to be in embroidery," said Mr. Pfeiffer.

"Aha!" Mr. Kaplan beamed. "Good night, Plonsky. Good night, Mitnick." He went to the door, where he turned, narrowing his eyes as of yore, and said in a measured tone, "Ve can vipe ot de 'Feh!', Pfeiffer. But vun ting you should know: You ken write like Judge Vashington, you can spall like Vinston Choichill, but ve got a titcher, Pfeiffer, a movellous titcher, who onlass you prononce 'sh' like a mama to a baby an' *not* like you booink at a ball game, vill kipp you in beginnis' grate if it takes fifty yiss!" He was gone.

As Mr. Parkhill locked his desk, he had the uneasy feeling that Mr. Kaplan was right, and hoped against hope that he was wrong. Fifty years . . .! Unless —yes—*Fata viam invenient*.

The Case for Mr. Parkhill

IT WAS A MISERABLE EVENING. ALL DAY LONG THE RAIN HAD COME DOWN, IN
sudden, driving shafts, the way it used to descend upon Camp Quinnipaquig,
the summer he had spent there as a counselor. Mr. Parkhill put on his rubbers and his Burberry, opened his big black umbrella, and sloshed through
the streets. It was only two blocks to the little restaurant on Ninth Street,
and when he got there he ordered half a grapefruit, the clam chowder, and
the steamed Maine lobster. He desserted on a delectable deep-dish apple pie,
and, because it was a special occasion, drank *two* cups of Sanka. It was his
birthday.

He had received a lacy birthday card from his Aunt Agatha, mailed, as it
was each year, so as to arrive exactly on date, and containing, as it did each
year, a crisp five-dollar bill with the tart instruction: "To be spent on something *foolish*." Aunt Agatha always underlined the "foolish."

The only other letter he had received (and what a surprise that had been)
was from Mr. Linton, headmaster of Tilsbury:

Dear Parkhill:

The other night Mrs. Linton and I were reminiscing about past boys, and as we
browsed through the old school annuals we came upon your photograph (the
year you were awarded the Ernestine Hopp Medal for School Spirit). When Mrs.
Linton reminded me of the time you astonished us all, as a freshman, by parsing
that sentence from Cicero during tea, we laughed merrily.

The only other boy Mrs. Linton remembered so well was Wesley Collender
('33), who placed a copper contrivance in the fuse box at Farwell which inter-
mittently expanded and contracted so that the "lights out" bell rang on and off, on
and off, for a goodly ten minutes before Mr. Thistlewaite could ascertain the
cause, and effect the remedy. Thistlewaite is no longer with us. He is, I believe, at
Claremont or Carmel or some such place in the western states that begins with
"C."

Be that as it may, Mrs. Linton called my attention to the birth date under
your picture. "Why, that is next Tuesday," she exclaimed, and indeed it was.

I extend, accordingly, our felicitations, and express our joint wishes for, in *loquendi usus*, "many happy returns."

Faithfully yours,
Amos Royce Linton

It had been awfully nice of Mr. Linton to write. Mr. Parkhill could not help feeling touched. The last time he had seen "Old Molasses," which was what the boys privately called Mr. Linton, was six years ago, when his class had presented the school with a fine, carved newel post for Modley Hall.

Mr. Parkhill remembered the first time he had gone back to visit Tilsbury. It was the year after he had received his B.A. When Mr. Linton had asked him what he was doing now, Mr. Parkhill told him he had taken a substitute teaching post, just for the experience, at the American Night Preparatory School for Adults.

"Parkhill," Mr. Linton had boomed in his no-nonsense manner, "what on earth is that?"

"It is a night school, sir."

"College entrances? Cram courses? That sort of—"

"Oh, no, sir. This is an elementary school."

"A *what*? Speak up, Parkhill!"

"An *elementary* school, sir," Mr. Parkhill repeated, raising his voice. "For adults."

Mr. Linton must have gotten hard of hearing, for he had gazed at Mr. Parkhill steadily for a moment and mumbled something that sounded like "Good God!" But that could not have been it; that was not at all like Mr. Linton; it was probably "Great Scott."

Mr. Parkhill often found himself thinking back to that little episode. He could understand that a man like Mr. Linton had no way of knowing what a fine institution the American Night Preparatory School for Adults really was. After all, Mr. Linton had led a rather sheltered life: Exeter, Harvard . . . He wondered, for instance, what Mr. Linton would have said when Hyman Kaplan named our leading institutions of higher learning as "Yale, Princeton, Hartford."

Tilsbury . . . What a different world that had been. What a different world it *was*. Mr. Parkhill felt a rush of pleasant, almost poignant, memories: that lovely campus, so tidy, green, serene, composed; the broad river that overflowed its banks in the spring; the school pond on clear winter days, a burnished white mirror; the path across Main Quad, that none but lordly seniors were permitted to use. . . . Those were happy days in a happy world, a world ten thousand miles and years away.

Occasionally, Mr. Parkhill caught himself wondering what it would have been like if he had returned to Tilsbury as a master. (Mr. Linton had never even sounded him out on that, to be frank about it.) Life was so curious. Who would have thought that the teacher whom Mr. Parkhill had temporarily replaced at the American Night Preparatory School for Adults would never return? No one even knew what had happened to him.

Mr. Parkhill recalled how Aunt Agatha used to ask him, whenever he visited her, if he intended to spend the rest of his life "among those people in New York." Aunt Agatha, who had never even set foot in New York, did not understand the special rewards adults provide someone who regards teaching not as a job, but as a mission. He had once had a little fun at Aunt Agatha's expense by saying, "Why, Aunt Agatha, just as your father brought God to the heathen, I bring Grammar to the alien."

Aunt Agatha never brought the subject up again after that.

"Miss," Mr. Parkhill called.

The waitress, who had done everything well except wait, slouched toward him from the kitchen.

"Check, please." (For some reason, Mr. Parkhill remembered the night Mr. Kaplan, chivvied by his critics and cornered by his foes, who demanded that he explain the "R.S.V.P." he had, in a reckless burst of elegance, tacked onto a composition, rejoined, "It minns 'Reply, vill you plizz?' ")

He paid his bill, put on his coat and his rubbers, stepped into the street, and opened his umbrella. The rain was, if anything, worse.

He began to walk quite briskly. He could hardly wait to get to the school. Sometimes, when he entered that old, unprepossessing building, he felt as if, like Alice, he was walking through a looking glass, into an antic and unpredictable world beyond.

"Miss Goldberg . . . Mr. Scymzak . . . Mrs. Rodriguez . . ."

As Mr. Parkhill called the roll he could not help noticing that Mr. Kaplan had not yet arrived. The seat in the exact center of the front row, that seat directly in front of Mr. Parkhill's desk, was empty. When Mr. Kaplan occupied that place, he seemed to loom out like a mountain, blotting out the rest of the class; and when Mr. Kaplan was not in that seat, as now, it seemed a good deal emptier than any other seat could possibly be.

"Miss Pomeranz . . . Mr. Wilkomirski . . ."

It was not simply that the corporeal Mr. Kaplan was missing; a certain point of view was missing, a magnetic pole, a spirit that expressed itself every moment the class was in session—with a gesture or a sigh, a whisper or grunt, a cluck, a snort, a gloat, a sneer, an approving "My!" or an admonishing "Tsk!", a commanding "Aha!" or a triumphant "Hau Kay!" Mr. Kaplan's "Hau Kay!" often sounded like a judgment from on high.

"Miss Mitnick . . . Miss Gidwitz . . . Mr. Kap——"

The voice of Sam Pinsky cut the fateful name in half. "Mr. Keplen asked me I should say he is onawoidably ditained. For maybe hefenarr."

Mr. Parkhill's long years in the beginners' grade had equipped him to translate "hefenarr," without the slightest break in his stride, into "half an hour." "Thank you." He put the attendance sheet to one side. "Well, class, suppose we devote the first part of the evening to—Recitation and Speech."

Smiles, grins, and dulcet affirmations issued from the Messrs. Plonsky and Marcus, and the Mesdames Gursky and Tomasic: they loved Recitation and Speech. Groans, moans and piteous suspirations drifted out of Mrs. Moskowitz and Peter Studniczka: they hated Recitation and Speech.

"May I remind all of you, once more, to speak slowly, carefully, enunciating as clearly as you can. Recitation and Speech can be one of our most valuable——"

"It gives me goose-dimples," wailed Mrs. Moskowitz.

"From prectice you will *learn*," attested Miss Ziev, gazing at the diamond ring with which Mr. Andrassy had re-pledged his troth.

"I should live so long." Sadie Moskowitz fanned her many chins with a notebook.

"Now, now, Mrs. Moskowitz," said Mr. Parkhill with a smile, "nothing ventured, nothing gained." And probably because of that note from Mr. Linton, *Empta dolore docet experientia* leaped into his mind. How appropriate: "Experience wrought with pain teaches." He noticed the hand of Oscar Trabish in the air. "Yes?"

"What it means?"

"I beg your pardon?"

"What it *means?*" Mr. Trabish repeated. (Mr. Trabish was a cleaner-and-dyer.)

Mr. Parkhill cleared his throat. "What does—er—what mean?"

"Those words you just gave. About adwentures and games——"

"Ah!" Mr. Parkhill could not help exclaiming. "I said, 'Nothing ventured,' not '*ad*ventured,' Mr. Trabish, 'nothing *gained*,' not—er—'games.' It is a saying. It means that if we never try, how can we hope to succeed?"

"Pssh!" cried Mr. Pinsky, closing his eyes and slapping his cheek with his palm. "Will Mr. Keplen be mat he wasn't here to hear those words!"

"'*Mad*,' Mr. Pinsky, not 'mat,'" said Mr. Parkhill earnestly. "And it really would be better to say that Mr. Kaplan will be 'disappointed,' or 'sorry,' instead of 'mad.' 'Mad' means insane, or—er—crazy."

"Exactly the woid for Keplen!" grunted Mr. Plonsky.

"Wait till he *comms* before you insult!" said Mr. Pinsky indignantly.

Miss Caravello gave a derisive laugh. "Ifa Kaplan is scratch, Pinsky holler

FLEECE
FLEAS

Not a single scholar broke into the welcome responses to revelation. Not a single "Ah!" or "Oh!" or "Hoo ha!" ascended from the lyceum.

"Mary's little lamb," Mr. Parkhill frowned, "had a *'fleece,'* class, not 'fleas.' " He went on to delineate the disasters which might follow the replacement of the sibilant with the fricative. "Why, the entire meaning of a word, or a sentence, or an idea, can be radically altered if one says *'zzz'* when one means 'sss,' or *'sss'* when one means 'zzz.' "

"You hear?" whispered Cookie Kipnis.

"Imachin," breathed Mr. Guttman.

Mrs. Moskowitz was snoring softly.

"For example . . ." On the board Mr. Parkhill printed:

PEAS
PEACE

"Ah!"s and "Ooh!"s and a reverent "Holy Smoky!" from sexton Wilkomirski greeted "peas" and "peace."

Mr. Parkhill struck again, while the pedagogical iron was still hot. "Or these words . . ."

KNEES
NIECE

Now the class was beside itself with cognition.

"A niece and a pair knizz is som difference!"

"Just on accont one little latter!"

"Sss! Zzz!" went one group of students. "Zzz! Sss!" went another.

The room buzzed as from a swarm of energetic bees.

"And sometimes, class," Mr. Parkhill plowed on, exhilarated by success, "two words are spelled alike, exactly alike, yet are pronounced differently *and have entirely different meanings!*"

This, alas, was too much for the beginners' grade.

"Hanh?" cried Mr. Marschak incredulously.

"No," groaned Rochelle Goldberg, and consoled herself with a bonbon.

"Same word, same spell, no same mean?" was the way Peter Studniczka put it.

Mr. Parkhill's chalk fairly flew across the slate as he printed:

CLOSE
CLOSE

He turned to the class: "Now these, for instance, are two entirely different words!"

At this point Mrs. Moskowitz, returning to sentience, saw CLOSE spelled twice on the board, heard Mr. Parkhill's "two entirely different words" and released a heartrending "Oy!"

" 'Close,' " said Mr. Parkhill anxiously, "is an adjective, which means near. But 'cloze,' pronounced with the 'z,' is a verb, which means to shut, as in 'Close the door——.' "

As if in some perfectly timed dramatization in reverse, the door was flung open. All heads turned. There, his clothes dripping, his face wet but his smile incandescent, his glistening hair wreathed in a sort of halo from the light in the corridor beyond, stood——

"Mr. Keplen!" cried Sam Pinsky.

"Et lest!" grinned Fanny Gidwitz.

Not all his comrades greeted Mr. Kaplan in such joyous accents.

"About time!" scowled Mr. Plonsky, squinting at his watch to see what time it actually was.

"You had to stop maybe on the way at City Hall?" asked Mr. Blattberg scathingly.

"You arriving or leaving?" inquired Miss Gursky.

Mr. Trabish acidly announced, "Mr. Kaplan isn't late; the class is *early*!"

Mr. Kaplan suffered these taunts nobly. "I couldn't find fest vat I vanted," he said mysteriously. "An' texis are scerce like a chicken's toot."

"Good evening, Mr. Kaplan," said Mr. Parkhill dryly.

It was just like Mr. Kaplan to enter a room that way. Any other student arriving this late would have courted invisibility, opening the door like a mouse, entering on tiptoes like a thief, creeping to the nearest vacant seat, speaking only if spoken to—and then only to mumble some agonized incomprehensibility. Not Hyman Kaplan. He could not even arrive late without endowing it with the attributes of a world première. He made his tardiness an occasion that called for public rejoicing.

Mr. Parkhill noticed that Mr. Pinsky was signaling to Mr. Kaplan with surreptitious flippings of his hand, accompanied by clandestine emissions of "Psst! Psst!" But Mr. Kaplan merely nodded with a certain insouciance and made not the slightest move to enter the room.

"Do come in," said Mr. Parkhill, not without a tinge of sarcasm.

"Axcuse me," said Mr. Kaplan; but his expression was not at all like "excuse me." "You blockink de dask."

Mr. Parkhill could hardly have been more astonished. He had indeed moved, without thinking of it, from the blackboard to the side of the desk nearest the door; but why that should impede Mr. Kaplan's passage from the door to his seat, a path entirely unobstructed by Mr. Parkhill *or* the desk, Mr. Parkhill could not for the life of him comprehend. "Mr. Kaplan," he for an instructor in a night school on the West Side of Chicago. I was not an accredited teacher, and have since become a discredited substitute, because my talents, such as they were, had not yet been crippled by Required Courses in Education.

I committed pedagogy for an instructor who had sensibly suffered a nervous breakdown. Wild horses will not drag out of me the name of the school, which I remember with the deepest affection.

"Why did you move the scene from Chicago to New York?"
It seemed natural. It seemed appropriate. It seemed inevitable. Stories about immigrants in a night school just have an irresistible tropism for that marvelous carnival of a city. Besides, New York has an annual mean rainfall.

"Did you actually have a student like Hyman Kaplan?"
No. Life is not that beneficent.

There was put at my mercy, briefly, a student who, had he acted the way he *should* have acted, would have resembled Mr. Kaplan. The student, being only human, never did. (One of my favorite fans is a lady who wrote to me for years, offering treasures withheld by Scheherazade if she could but meet the creator of the man she insisted on calling "Human" Kaplan.)

Mr. Kaplan is, I suppose, the projected image of certain traits of personality, nourished by narcissism and pushed to the outermost boundaries of yearning. A famous psychoanalyst once analyzed Mr. Kaplan and concluded he was my alter ego. I sometimes think it is the other way round.

"Were you Mr. Parkhill?"
I don't know. But I also don't know who else he could have been, or where else he could have come from.

Not all of me, I hasten to add, is Mr. Parkhill, nor all of him me. Part of him, I suspect, is that portion of me which is conventional, slow-witted, virtuous beyond belief. Other facets of him, which are not me, I deeply envy and admire: infinite patience, kindliness, restraint, an incorruptible faith in man and unshatterable faith in his perfectibility.

What puzzles me about Mr. Parkhill is that he seems to think that every man and woman on earth can be taught, can learn, can improve, can stand at last before the Throne. I, who have the greatest difficulty in persuading my children that the evidence is all against this, am often accused of being reactionary when I am only trying to be realistic, and am often charged with being cynical when I am only trying to be detached. It has gotten to the point where I open my prayers each morning with two lines from Bertrand Russell: "It has been said that man is a rational animal. All my life I have been searching for evidence which could support this."

"Was there a real Miss Mitnick?"

Miss Mitnick neither was nor *is* real. I found this sweet, shy maiden, with whom I am madly in love, in a neglected glen of my reveries.

"Do you have a special way of writing?"

Yes. I use a special fountain pen, which I fill with my blood.

"Is it harder to write humor than serious things?"

Yes. God, yes.

"Is dialect harder to write than other forms of humor?"

Much. It is also more risky, more tricky, more perplexing, and more dangerous.

Humor is the affectionate communication of insight. (Satire is focused bitterness, and burlesque the skewing of proportions.) Humor is, I think, the subtlest and chanciest of literary forms. It is surely not accidental that there are a thousand novelists, essayists, poets, journalists for each humorist. It is a long, long time between James Thurbers.

Comic dialect is humor plus anthropology. Dialect must seduce the eye to reach the ear and be orchestrated in the brain. It must tantalize without irritating, and defer without frustrating. It must carry a visual promise to the reader that what he does not instantly recognize can be deciphered with ease and will be rewarded by pleasure. The reader must be cued into making what he thinks is his own special and private discovery—a discovery of delight which, he suspects, neither the character nor the author fully appreciates.

Dialect is not transcription. Nothing is more depressing than a passage of broken English exactly transcribed from the spoken. The "accurate ear" for which a writer is praised is as inventive as it is accurate. It is creative, not literal, for the writer transforms that which he hears into that which you could not.

In the antic freedom of phonetics, some mortals say "ship" when they mean the source of wool, or "sheep" when they mean a vessel. Others throw "bet" around with the abandon of a gambler—to mean either "bat," "bet," "bad," or "bed."

The writer must therefore create exact, if camouflaged, contexts within which the reader's responses are firmly controlled. He must convey without explaining. Mr. Kaplan may say "fond mine fife fit don," which suggests a devoted shaft of flutes fit for an Oxford tutor. But if the clues have been properly structured, and the channels of association properly cut, the reader will have to do no heavy lifting to know that Mr. Kaplan, having lost something, found it five feet down.

Or take Mrs. Moskowitz. Poor, dear Mrs. Moskowitz. She says, if I were to record it with absolute rigor, "I hate the brat." But that is not at all what she made him turn princes away from his door while working, Rembrandt Harmens van Rijn set forth once more to explore the human mystery. The subject he chose was well known to artists: Heraclitus and Democritus, "the Dark Philosopher" and "the Laughing Philosopher." Heraclitus he fixed in a half-profile, losing him in shadows at the left. Democritus, who maintained four hundred years before Christ that reality consists of atoms and void, and (anticipating modern physics) that matter is indestructible—Democritus would be Rembrandt himself. For the Laughing Philosopher had preached what Rembrandt now knew: that the greatest good is tranquility.

He put the pigment on the canvas thickly, with his thumb or palette knife, in juxtaposed gobs of color, building up layer upon layer, scratching through the paint with his nail or brush handle to let the color beneath break through, covering pigment with glaze and scratching through and putting pigment on again, creating images the critics would deride as "wild smears"—until, two hundred years later, some French geniuses would smash the bonds of the literal, just as he dared to do, to bring the breathtaking new visions of Impressionism into the universe of art.

"Don't stand close to the picture," Rembrandt warned visitors to his studio. "The smell of the colors will bother you." This was nonsense, and a ruse: he wanted his painting to be viewed from a distance—so that the eye of the beholder would fuse the separated flashes of color, so that the viewer's mind would participate in the making of the magic illusion, so that light and shadow could move and float and play out their drama. He lured the eye into the canvas, seizing its attention with highlights, teasing it with adumbrations of the half-caught, the half-hidden, the half-revealed. He used color with unparalleled richness and splendor. He used shadows like music, somehow enlisting senses other than the visual. He used light like the blast of a trumpet.

No painter before had so directly confronted emotion, or entered so deeply into it. No artist captures *our* feelings with such immediacy. In his haunting self-portrait, the roughhewn features of this untidy, arrogant, introspective man move out to us in an expression that symbolizes triumph over suffering.

One year later, Rembrandt was dead.

Degas

In 1886, the Impressionists presented their eighth and final exhibition, among which was a startling group of pastels described by the artist as "a series of nude women, bathing, washing, drying, rubbing down, combing their hair.

. . ." The art world of Paris, so proud of its sophistication, was both astonished and scandalized.

Degas had brought the boudoir into the salon. The anonymous woman in "The Tub," for instance: this was no recognizable woman, no familiar nude, carefully posed, reclining in grace and splendor; this was no ethereal goddess in female form, no voluptuous model for the mythology of Greece or Rome. This was not a woman: this was a body—arrested in natural movement, drawn without a face, apprehended in the unexpected grace of the ungraceful. This picture denied the aesthetic assumption of centuries: that the model is most beautiful when *posed*—and, in posing, presupposes an audience. This was art, the artist cynically confessed, "as if seen through a keyhole."

The critics fumed, calling the artist "a cruel observer," a man "morbid and neurotic." Even Emile Zola, the great and uncompromising apostle of realism, voiced displeasure with pictures that made women "vulgar," distorting their movements, trivializing their beauty.

To all of this, Edgar Hilaire Germain Degas responded with icy disdain. Elegant, scornful, a snob, this eldest son of a French banker and a Creole mother from New Orleans held fast to his creed: "Drawing is not what one sees, but what others have to be made to see."

Behind his astonishing draftsmanship, the tilted perspective (so reminiscent of the Japanese), the iridescent play of light on soft flesh, under which strong muscles rippled—behind all this lay one mordant strain of irony: Degas despised women. He portrayed them not because he thought them beautiful, but because he was fascinated by motion. He caught them off guard in moments of exertion—with a fresh and dispassionate vision that anticipated the candid camera. His nudes were oddly unsensual, unlike Rubens' corybants, and most unluscious, unlike Titian's golden nymphs.

When one Parisian *grande-dame* asked indignantly why he showed women as ugly, Degas replied: "Because, madame, in general women *are* ugly." Once, he declared: "I show women deprived of their airs and affectations, reduced to the level of animals cleaning themselves."

His passion for cascading light and color and movement led Degas to haunt the cafés of Paris, the race track, the opera, the ballet he adored. But it was not the exquisite ballerinas he chose to paint; it was "the little rats" of the *corps,* the underfed dancers who worked for a few sous and yearned, with single-minded vulgarity, to catch a "rich gentleman friend." Women came to his attic studio as models—shopgirls, dancers, laundresses, prostitutes—and he endowed them with a kind of accidental loveliness. He captured, with singular understanding, the lonely moments of their moods. Even his "brainless creatures" were suffused with reflectiveness. He painted with a compassion of which he was unaware.

Hollywood

★

I WAS A movie fan, in the hot etymological sense of the word ("fan" comes from "fanatic"), ever since I was five. I did not see a real play until I was fourteen, but I saw movies at least once a week, often much more—and for at least three decades.

My childhood appetite for films was fed by the angelic fact that for several years we lived next door to a movie theater. It stood, proud and corrupting, on Kedzie Avenue, and bore a melodious, if misleading, name: The White Palace. On those hot, blistering nights that any refugee from Chicago knows too well, when all the side doors of The White Palace were open to catch some semblance of respite from the murderous heat, I could hear from my bedroom, or my sigh-laden perch at the window, the tinny arpeggios of the pianist who, in the paleozoic age before talkies, sat to one side of the screen, making music appropriate to the images he saw floating above him. You would be surprised to know how many deathless death-bed scenes were perfectly scored by "Hearts and Flowers," how many storm-tossed moments were underscored by "The Poet and the Peasant." Oh, it was a happy era.

I do not suppose that ever again will a generation know the special magic, the transports of imagination, the hilarious excitement and throat-parched terrors that I and my gaping friends derived from the movies of Douglas Fairbanks or William S. Hart, Buster Keaton or Harold Lloyd. As for loyalty, I defy the future to match the adulation we brought, each Saturday morning, to a serial such as The Midnight Man, *starring no less a god than the heavyweight champion of the world, "Gentleman Jim" Corbett. It was from movies that my generation learned manners, decorum, the nuances of courtship, the quintessences of courage and style and pride. And through the movies we were ushered into the shimmering world of wealth and fame, and times of glory long since gone.*

I always nursed a secret fantasy that one day I would get to Hollywood to become part of the empyrean of films. It was a piece of infantile wish-fulfillment, I suppose, taken not too seriously, yet cherished and nurtured as an adumbration of desire. I did not dream that I would arrive in Hollywood by accident (it was cheaper to buy an excursion-special to Los Angeles, from Washington, than to Phoenix, Arizona, where I was headed on a mission of mercy), or that I would start a short-lived career as a screenwriter soon after passing my exams for a higher degree in political science.

I first worked as a movie writer in 1937 and part of 1938. Nothing I wrote for Major Pictures, hallowed be its name, ever reached the screen. Instead, the studio went bankrupt before my eyes. I was much too inconsequential to have caused this cataclysm all by myself. I was disemployed, but scarcely discouraged; working in a studio, sweating out story lines, hanging around sound stages, talking shop with the odd wizards of the cutting rooms, observing the wiles of producers and resisting the blandishments of starlets—all these were to prove priceless to another purpose. They gave me entrée to the dinner tables and swimming pools of the movie colony—as a professional, not a gawker.

During my first year and a half in Hollywood, an idea kept growing within me. Middletown, by Robert and Helen Lynd, an ethnological foray into the everyday life and mores of Muncie, Indiana, was being hailed as a landmark in social analysis. I could not get out of my mind the notion that a sociological study of Hollywood, a place I thought unequalled as an incubator and mirror of cultural symbols, could illuminate a part of American society that had until then been described only in rollicking anecdotes or merciless parodies. I wanted to analyze the community that makes movies for the world the way an anthropologist might study the Maori.

I applied to the Carnegie Corporation for a grant to set up a two-year study of Hollywood. It was my good fortune to be received by that remarkable man, the late Frederick Keppel, whose enthusiasm paved the way for me. Late in 1938, I hired several sociologists and a statistician, and opened an office at 7046 Hollywood Boulevard. The lettering on the door read, MOTION PICTURE RESEARCH PROJECT. *When the Carnegie stipend was exhausted, eighteen months later, the Rockefeller Foundation stepped into the breach with additional funds and encouragement.*

I used about eleven assistants on the Hollywood study, at one time or another, some paid, some volunteer, the latter producing their own M.A. or Ph.D. theses from research I supervised. The study took me two and a half years; the writing, which I did concurrently, almost three.

My information came from innumerable hours of interviewing, scrutiny of the special trade journals of "show business," and lengthy questionnaires mailed to the 1,753 members of the Screen Actors Guild, the 600-700 members of the Screen Writers Guild, and the 232 movie directors. We also distributed questionnaires, through their unions, to assistant directors, film editors, cartoonists, etc. I have an unpleasant recollection that we analyzed around 12,000 questionnaires in all.

My opus on Hollywood retains one indisputable and historic distinction. It was reviewed, with hosannas of praise, on the front page of the Sunday New York Times book section, in a long and laudatory review in the Sunday New York Herald Tribune, and in Sunday book sections up and down the republic—on December 7, 1941. I had received advance copies of some of these encomiums, and I took my breakfast, that lovely Sunday morning, preening with pride and telling myself that the years of drudgery were really worthwhile: the gruelling gobs of statistical analysis, the inescapable disappointments and frustrations, even the rumors with which my name had been blackened. (The Communists in Hollywood regarded my politics and my project with special venom, and spread canards that I was a secret agent of the producers; that I was really being financed by the Chase National Bank to undermine the guilds—I was a member of the Screen Writers Guild; that my "naïve liberalism," evidenced in government services for the Roosevelt administration, was a snare designed to deceive the proletariat and reduce their militancy.) I thought of all this charitably now, reflecting that all over America people were reading the tributes to my brain-child, and tomorrow they would hasten to bookstores and buy ————. The telephone interrupted my blissful reverie, and a friend's voice, oddly thick, asked: "Have you been listening to the radio? I just caught the goddamnedest news bulletin. This announcer says the Japs have bombed Pearl Harbor."

Yes, it was Sunday morning, December 7, 1941. And when historians in the future reconstruct that terrible day, they may say that what America was reading at Armaggedon was—of all things!—a sociological tome on Hollywood. But they will be wrong. Pearl Harbor, Hitler's declaration of war, our entry into war with Japan—during such days, who cared about the gaudy night life of the stars?

The next morning, December 8, I received a phone call from Lowell Mellett, one of President Roosevelt's six assistants with "a passion for anonymity."

(The phrase was Louis Brownlow's, and it is still a dandy.) I had been serving as consultant to the National Defense Advisory Commission, working on ways to use film for training purposes in the armed forces and for what later became known as the I.E.&O. (Information, Education, Orientation) program. I flew to Washington, was enlisted by Archibald MacLeish for his Office of Facts and Figures, and subsequently became Deputy Director of the Office of War Information.

But all that, as they say, is another story—another time, another universe. Here is a sampling of observations and ideas from Hollywood: The Movie Colony, the Movie Makers. *I have not included any of the statistical materials, on salaries, spending patterns, picture costs, profits, marriage and divorce, and so on.*

★

The Legend

Hollywood is generally dismissed—by the cynical or the bewildered—as "screwy." The movie colony is believed to be dominated by maniacs, operated under the laws of lunacy, and populated by an assortment of illiterates, "geniuses," divorcees, crackpots, and poltroons. The millions who read the gossip columns or have seen those classic delineations of Hollywood's folly, *Once in a Lifetime* and *Boy Meets Girl*, are quite familiar with the producer who tried to hire Chaucer, the director who wears earmuffs to spare himself from hearing the actors, the actresses who carry monkeys on their shoulders and spend their lives shuttling between Yuma and Reno. . . .

In reality, there is nothing particularly screwy about Hollywood; or, better, Hollywood is no more screwy than other and less conspicuous parts of our society. The aberrations of our culture are simply more vivid, more conspicuous, more dramatic in Hollywood than in New Bedford or Palo Alto. Our values are extended to the strident and the unmistakable in Hollywood's way of life. If we look at Hollywood against the larger context of the society in which we live, if we compare the motion picture industry to other businesses at a comparable time in *their* sudden heyday, if we compare the *nouveaux riches* of the movie colony to the *nouveaux riches* of banking, railroads, or real estate, we discover startling parallels between the practices of Hollywood and New York, between the mores of Bel-Air and Oyster Bay.

Hollywood was not created out of a void; its people did not descend from Shangri-La. They brought to Hollywood appetites which have been gratified, aspirations which have been realized, in this rich and indulgent community on the Pacific. The citizens of Kalamazoo who possess the unique and sometimes distressing temperament of actors, writers, directors, producers would

thin? They'll fatten her up. Can Fanny Jones act? Well! Can Hedy Lamarr? They'll teach her. All that Fanny Jones really needs for a stab at glory is that elusive, indefinable quality for which, she has read, movie producers are always searching in palpitating desperation—"Personality." And Luck.

What fatal blemishes can the Fanny Joneses (or the John Joneses, for that matter) actually admit that will preclude them from the new Valhalla? Hollywood's wizards will coach them, dress them, raise their eyebrows, straighten their teeth, lift their bust lines, lower their coiffures. Brilliant writers and directors will dedicate themselves solely to the expoitation of hidden talents. The one thing Fanny Jones really needs for a chance at glory is physiological cohesion, the faculty of remaining intact before a camera. Yes, Fanny Jones can continue to dream of a contract with RKO, a home at Malibu Beach, and a shiny convertible with an automatic top. For Fanny Jones can legitimately feel that all she needs is—luck. The movie scout happening to stop for a malted at her fountain . . . the movie magnate happening to see her face somewhere, sometime, somehow. . . .

The conclusive point is that these things do happen, and the movie pages hammer them home to a world that never tires of the Cinderella story.

The movies are one of the very few fields of enterprise left in America in which youth is promised high rewards, in which youth is, indeed, an advantage rather than a burden. The would-be movie star needs no capital, no training, no skill. (A reviewer once said of a famous movie actress: "She has two expressions—joy and indigestion.") The fortuitous arrangement of facial components may be enough to shoot a name onto the theater marquees. It is no wonder that Hollywood is a perpetual magnet to hope.

The first premise of our system of values is that the rewards of our society go to those who have skill, make sacrifices, and behave soberly. Our culture is saturated with the attributes of what Max Weber called "the Protestant ethic." But society, particularly in an era of crisis, does not fulfill these promises, and to the degree that our economy fails to reward those who try hard and train themselves and shun evil, the role of luck becomes increasingly important, and the individual becomes increasingly aware that luck is a crucial part of success. The very fact that opportunities shrink,* that millions get caught in depressions as in an iron trap, that neither ability, intelligence, nor training guarantees success—these make the role of luck more desperately cherished, more desperately invoked in fantasy or prayer. There is an unconscious point to the dream of Hollywood that millions keep alive in their minds. To Americans raised in the American tradition, faithful to the American concept of unbounded personal achievement, Hollywood is the last frontier. In the movie colony, as in the content of the movies themselves, romantic individual-

* This was written as the United States was struggling out of the depression of 1937.

ism, the most compelling idea in American history, has reached the apogee of its glory.

On Work and Play

Most Americans live in two separate universes, the world of work and the world of play. Our society stresses the idea that play *follows* work, that work is something onerous and sanctions play. But in Hollywood the work is a form of play, and the people love their work, and they are paid handsomely for having fun. The movie makers are paid for doing things other people would like to do without being paid. Is it any wonder that the movie makers are plagued by ambiguous guilts? In a society where work means sacrifice or the performance of distasteful routines, those who are rewarded for having fun may be expected to be ridden by remorse. And where the rewards are as high as they are in Hollywood and, in addition, are coupled with adulation from the populace, the guilts would be all the greater. . . . People in the movie industry jump at the chance to impress the listener with how hard they work. They seem to be defending themselves. They seem to think that no one believes that they do work hard; and when they look at their bank books and their homes, their press clippings and their social calendars, they can't believe that they worked *that* hard.

When Orson Welles (of whom someone said, "There, but for the grace of God, goes God") was first shown through a movie studio, he exclaimed, "This is the biggest electric train any boy ever had!" Movie making is a game and the movie makers play it with great zest. And, as in all games, the players surrender to periodic impatience with the game's illusion and significance.

Hollywood is full of characters in search of a character; they remain a combination of many. It is this that makes them seem "insincere"; it is this, in part, that makes them colorful, unpredictable, and irrational. For here are adults who sustain their juvenility, their creative fantasy, and lend their profession that infantilism which is so typical of the stage and screen.

Hollywood is a one-industry town. Its people "sleep, eat, talk" and think movies. They are engaged in the creation of symbols rather than material goods. Movie making is one prolonged, involuted fantasy. It is often said that the movies are an escape for the masses; it is rarely suggested that they are also an escape for the movie makers. When a movie producer or actor, director or writer, goes to sleep, he may be leaving the world of fantasy and entering the world of reality.

Stories, roles, dramatic artifices monopolize Hollywood's attention, not goods or crops or machines. And this preoccupation with the fanciful must tend to blur perceptions of the real. To personalities lost in fantasy, reality passes through a distorted receiver; either it ceases to seem as threatening as it ought to, as in the case of children, or it becomes excessively ominous, as in the case of psychotics. In either case, the real world—of men and things and events—loses proportion and becomes exaggerated at an extreme. The singular anxiety of some of the movie makers, and the singular indifferentism of others, are end points on Hollywood's psychological horizon. If Hollywood is a community of people who work and live in fantasy, then it is to be expected that their life should take on the attributes of the fantastic. The greater wonder, one visitor exclaimed to this writer, is that Hollywood is sane.

On Youth

The history of movies is crammed with sagas of the "boy genius." Movie production, involving millions upon millions of dollars, is often placed in the hands of very young men. In few other industries is comparable power and freedom delivered into such callow (however gifted) hands. The late Irving Thalberg, for instance, was in his twenties when he began to soar through the movie firmament; he was breaking precedents and box-office records before he was thirty. At twenty-two, Darryl F. Zanuck was writing scenarios for Rin Tin Tin; at twenty-six he became head producer at Warner Brothers; at thirty he was one of the most influential figures in Hollywood, tore up his $5,000-a-week contract, and within a year was put into the top production chair at Twentieth Century-Fox.

Youth is at a premium in Hollywood, which leads to a point not generally given the attention it deserves: the movie people—famous, pampered, rich— are very *young* to be so famous, so pampered, and so rich.

Hollywood's wealth is first-generation wealth, possessed by people who have not inherited it, earned as a reward for talent (or luck). It is not surprising that the movie colony has not achieved stability; it is too young, too new, too uncertain. The people of the movie colony are characterized by showmanship, not breeding; glibness, not wisdom; audacity, not poise. Of Hollywood it might be written, as Parrington wrote of the America of the 1880's, that here is "a society that for the first time found its opportunities equal to its desires, a youthful society that accounted the world its oyster and wanted no restrictions laid on its will."

Anxiety and Optimism

Optimism and insecurity run throughout the movie colony side by side. This is no paradox, for optimism is often used to deaden anxiety, and in Hollywood anxiety serves as a restraint on excessive elation and as a kind of penance for extravagances of income, spending, conduct, or business operations. There seems to be an unconscious need for anxiety in the movie colony, and anxiety is provoked, nursed, and kept alive (note the popularity of gambling) in a manner which can only suggest self-punishment for obscure and disturbing guilts.

Hollywood tries to reduce its anxieties by keeping other people anxious about the same things. It is for this reason that conclaves in the movie colony —whether at the Brown Derby or a Guild meeting—tend to keep attention focused on a threatening future. "Something's going to crack at MGM. . . . Such-and-such is headed for bankruptcy. . . . It can't last. . . ."

Nor are the worries unreal. Actors may become "box-office poison" before they quite understand what has happened. Mae West earned $326,500 in one year, but found it difficult to get a contract the next. Luise Rainer won two Academy Awards and the fame that attends them, then dropped out of movies because her drawing power had vanished.

The volatility of fortune in Hollywood subjects its personalities to a severe and persistent strain. "You're only as good as your last picture" is a byword in the movie colony, and an hour after a picture is previewed the solemn consensus that "Griffiths is slipping" or "Rogers is through" races through the town. This is scarcely a climate conducive to psychological serenity or efficient digestion. The movies require creative—hence temperamental—personalities; the objective conditions of the business are hazardous; and the combination of an erratic milieu and quivering personalities intensifies the insecurity of both.

The movie makers are engaged in an endless search for deference. They seem to be lost in a long, unhappy effort to win respect from symbolic juries. Hunger for praise is marked in Hollywood, and the hunger for orientation amidst the confusions of the world. In an epoch violent with change, the people who play the game of movie making are periodically overcome by the urge to "do something important." For Hollywood is plagued by a vague contempt for the make-believe of its life and work. This perennial dissatisfaction, this relentless comparison of what they are or what they are doing with utterly utopian desires heightens discontent. Such people are driven to surround themselves with an indulgent environment; they demand constant reassurance.

To say that "yes-men" are unnecessary in Hollywood is like saying that gondoliers are unnecessary in Venice. The yes-men are quite necessary to those executives and producers who cannot function without consistent admiration. The yes-man buttresses the ego of his superiors; he shields them from doubt and indecision. The yes-man is not really superfluous; he is simply overpaid. There is a functional niche in Hollywood for those who carry the banner of confidence and forever cry: "That's great! It'll roll them in the aisles!" They pour ebullience into those who cannot create without it.

The movie colony is highly gregarious. The craving for company at almost whose prototype was Phineas T. Barnum, who was described as "a vulgar, greasy genius, pure brass without any gilding, yet in picturesque and capable effrontery the very embodiment of the age."

The first producers were promoters; they combined the talents of craftsmen, impresarios, and circus barkers. They did not cater to small, cultivated circles. They were sensitive to mass desires, for they were of the masses themselves. They had the virtues and the failings of pioneers. They were accused of being vulgar, and with justice; yet it was their very unrefinement which fitted them so perfectly for their function. As Bernard Shaw put it, "Universality of character is impossible without a shade of vulgarity." It was the showmen, not the graduates of proud preparatory schools, who sensed and satisfied the entertainment demands of a nation into which Europe's millions were pouring, millions who could not understand English but were enchanted by the pictures that moved, a nation in which an immense laboring class found no arts within its cultural span and few diversions cheap enough for its pocketbook.

These were the men who forged a medium that entertained more people, at lower prices, than ever before in history. They stamped a vaudeville spirit onto the motion picture industry, and it still bears evidence of their crudity, their imagination, and their vigor. They were masters of "the visceral cliché." They infused a driving, bombastic spirit into the movies, and they breathed that same spirit into the Hollywood that became the world capital of the screen.

Now, many bankers and merchants and magnates also were once peddlers, shopkeepers, barbers—or their sons. They were driven by the same appetites that characterized the ex-salesmen, nickelodeon operators, and furriers who hacked a movie empire out of the entertainment wilderness. They were characterized by the same foibles and given to the same impulsive deportment. For the cellulords, like the pork barons, respond to social values they have not examined, and reach for symbols they had no hand in fashioning. Hollywood, despite its surface singularity, is faithful to social patterns of which it is not aware. Society, not men, sets the molds of prestige and establishes the methods of achieving it. Society canalizes the ways by which power can be won, status achieved, wealth enjoyed.

Hollywood is singularly deferential to others; it is almost craven before politicians, professors, or playwrights. The movie paladins revere, and surely overvalue, the traditional. They have no real sense of their own importance and no great confidence in their right to respect. Their hunger for information, knowledge, "culture" is abysmal. If for no other reason, this would divide Hollywood's elite from the nabobs of other times and places.

Here are men and women dizzied by sudden riches, living boldly, spending recklessly, in an effort to forget that not so long ago they were poor, anonymous, déclassé. They live in great, fine houses. They wear excellent clothes. They ride in sleek automobiles. They have spacious offices and beautiful spouses. As someone said of an earlier generation of *arrivistes*, they try to play the Medici and only capture the spirit of Maecenas. They are caught in the curious trap of unaccustomed wealth, and spend nerves and energy in trying to achieve ease in conforming to expectations, their own and those of their fellow parvenus, to which they have become enslaved. Bright, bold, undisciplined, and crude, they are driven by unconscious urgencies, prodigal of their health, torn by rancor, possessed by rivalry; and beneath all the desperate display they remain lost in their own magnificence, disturbed and uncertain in the false paradise of pecuniary success.

On Wealth and Morals

The rich have always been granted license for behavior denied others. The line between morality and immorality is never as sharply drawn among the Four Hundred as in the middle or lower strata. It is the middle-class that is the moral guardian of society; the elite is worried not by immorality, but by scandal.

To a detached observer, the private life of a movie star would hardly seem more lurid than that of, say, the railroad magnate, Jim Fisk, who poured a ransom "into the laps of wantons." The parties for which Hollywood is notorious are not really wilder than were the yacht parties of William Astor, about which all New York rang. If the business offices of Hollywood provoke smiles, one might recall the offices of the Erie Railroad, which were once situated in a converted opera house and were used for nightly gambling and historic carousing.

The comparison might be carried further, for hallowed American names can offer the satirist material as rich as Hollywood at its weirdest. A movie producer may play host at a dinner party while wearing slacks and a sport jacket, but Oliver Belmont was wont to receive guests while seated on a carved throne with an Egyptian in a Zouave jacket and embroidered fez behind him. The illustrious merchant, Joseph Leiter, once brought a monkey, attired in full evening dress, to a Stuyvesant Fish dinner, and the dinner was carried on with the monkey seated in the place of honor. The wife of a former publisher of the Washington *Post* kept a llama among her pets and once spent $5,000 for a Great Dane. Hollywood cannot surpass these bizarreries. Nor can Hollywood's moguls hope to match the lavishness with which William Randolph Hearst lived, nor the childish greed with which he purchased Spanish castles and Renaissance fireplaces. The movie magnates, like the

If Hollywood were run by a Puritan *Gestapo*, temptation would still thrive. As long as the making of films requires beautiful women and arresting men, especially men and women who can turn emotion on and off at the flick of a camera shutter, Hollywood's amorous sentiments will be characterized by flexibility.

Movies cannot be made by mechanics; movie-making requires creative temperaments, the fructifying interplay of unrestrained personalities, of people with a flair, people who can act or direct or write, people who exploit their fantasies—or their neuroses. Picture makers must be rich in reverie and capable of externalizing their inner fables. Such people are not distinguished for emotional consistency. In the phrase of Gilbert Seldes, movie people have a high "potential for disaster." In Hollywood, mercurial personalities are concentrated in one tight little colony, and they aggravate and maximize one another's inconstancy.

There is a saying that the typical Hollywood triangle consists of an actor, his wife, and himself. The self-centered personality makes a difficult enough spouse; when two supreme egotists take the wedding vows the prognosis can hardly be sanguine. Many Hollywood romances founder on the cold rocks of professional competition, for sometimes the clash between careers is inescapable. The success that one mate enjoys is often an implicit rebuke to the other. Psychological security in Hollywood is inextricably allied to prestige, and few men endure continuous blows to the ego.

With success, moreover, Hollywood's luminaries cease to be individuals and become business institutions. They are guided, protected, surrounded by a corps of agents, lawyers, business managers, press agents, secretaries, maids, hangers-on, friends, relatives, nepots, yes-men, jesters. It becomes increasingly difficult, even for their helpmates, to cut through the court in order to reach the sovereign. "I've got to make an *appointment* to see my wife," one Hollywoodian complained bitterly. Nor does the disordered schedule by which the movie people live encourage domestic serenity. During the hectic periods of production, actors, directors, producers may cease to go home, and forget they are married; night, Sundays, weekends, holidays are burned on the altar of "the picture."

Movie stars, we have suggested, are America's royalty. The aristocratic role not only permits but encourages a certain amount of philandering. The nobility of a society are expected to symbolize its virtues; they are also tacitly charged with the duty of violating the stricter taboos from time to time. This makes the highborn more "human," more endearing to the public, and it provides vicarious gratification to the millions who dare not indulge in the transgressions they may secretly cherish. It is striking that there is at least one black sheep in most of the families of the British aristocracy, and both the families and the truants are the more fondly regarded because of it. In the same fashion, the movie fan may be privately delighted by the romantic acrobatics of his idols. The domestic scandal that involves a starlet does not ruin her career (as producers once feared); on the contrary, it may increase her fame and popularity. A star's fan-mail generally rises after a divorce, according to the heads of fan-mail departments. The divorce creates sympathy for a loved object that has suffered: the divorced star becomes "available" symbolically, and perhaps offers less guilt and more verity to dreams of possession.

The Actors

Actors use their emotions as masons use bricks. "Reactions that occur in more normal employment after five o'clock in the afternoon . . . are discernible on the sets at nine o'clock in the morning. It may be only play-acting, but it cannot but exert some effect on the participants."

Persons skilled in professional make-believe have an extraordinary capacity for private make-believe; how "genuine," indeed, can an actor believe his own emotions to be when he is so expert in fabricating emotion? Acting is a form of deception, and actors can mesmerize themselves almost as easily as an audience. So it is that actors in quest of an undying love are saddened when they discover that, like other roles, the conjugal loses freshness and conviction with the mere passage of time.

The word "hypocrite" is derived from the Greek word for actor, *hypocrites* ("answerer"—the actor who answered the chorus). The enlightened Solon denounced Thespis, the founder of acting, on the grounds that playing roles is a form of public deceit and therefore an act of outright immorality. In Boston, the very word "theater" was invested with iniquity until a generation ago, and the social samurai of that city found a way to patronize playhouses only by calling them "museums."

Skill in mimicry is a revealing characteristic. Children practice mimicry as a means of playing "grown up"; they also use it as a device to master fears by imitating threatening objects. Mimicry, in children, ends when a definite identity is chosen for the self. Adults who prolong, cherish, and refine their talent for playing someone else are, we might say, still exploring the world around them—hoping to discover other characters they might like to be.

Actors are notoriously egoistic. Their careers rest upon either their looks or a talent for simulation; both require consistent attention to the self by the self. An actor's face and physique are his assets and he is compelled to devote as much attention to them as a glassblower to his respiration.

Actors thrive on praise, but praise to an actor for a performance is, in a sense, criticism of the actor as a person. When you compliment an actor for the way in which he played a part you may be underlining a secret sense of insufficiency, for you are congratulating him not for his own character but for his skill in imitating someone else. This writer cannot forget the words of a celebrated Hollywood actor, who mused aloud: "God, what a part I've got in this picture! What a man to play—scientist, scholar, fighter, one of humanity's greatest benefactors. And me"—a shrug— "oh, hell, I'm just a ham."

There are few actors who are not overcome by the thought that their talents, though unique, are not "significant," that their work, though entertaining to millions, is not important, that their personalities—so inflated in publicity, so idolized by fans—are, by their own inner cognizance, vain and shallow. The readiness and frequency with which actors call other persons "phoney" suggests the fear, too close to the surface, that they may be thought to be phoney, too.

A star is a monopoly. A Charles Boyer or a Claudette Colbert has a monopoly on those graces of voice, eyes, manner, attitude which constitute a "personality." There is only one Clark Gable, only one Bette Davis, and although Hollywood is fond of thinking in typologies, and attempts to build up a "Gable type" or a "Davis type," the public is not easily won over to substitutes.*

The uniqueness of a personality, it is easy to see, places that personality in an enviable bargaining position. The competition for stars whose pictures earn profits has always bordered on the frenetic. The movie magnates paid astronomic sums to the movie stars not because they wanted to, but because they had to. The stars who commanded the highest salaries were those who made the highest profits for their employers. The producers who paid exorbitant sums for talent prospered; those who did not, or could not, lost out. As motion pictures made greater and greater profits, stars demanded more and more money; and the producers were able to pay it.

The Writer

To the writer, the most gratifying part of writing, perhaps, is the absolute sovereignty he enjoys over his work, the irrevocable authority over his ideas, story, characters, plot. He is king in the universe of his fantasy. Judgment can be passed only on his finished work; it can be praised or damned or ignored; but no one can change so much as a word or a mark of punctuation. Writers are among the few mortals who can satisfy the yearning for omnipotence, for in their work they are omnipotent.

All this vanishes when a writer enters a studio in Hollywood. He is no longer a creator, working within the self-bounded, one-dimensional world of self-expression; he is an employee, beholden to others.

* It is more than a cliché to say that the name of a star on a marquee guarantees, say, a million dollars in ticket sales.

The very purpose of Hollywood is opposed to the basic motivation of writers. The producer asks, "Will it make money?" The writer asks, "Will it make sense?" The producer wants to gratify popular taste; the writer wants to improve it. The producer wants to make pictures that make a profit; the writer wants to write pictures that make him feel proud. The producer wants to entertain an audience; the writer wants to woo, move, influence, or enlighten the public.

Since the producer is paying the writer to do a job, he expects the writer to do the job to his (the producer's) satisfaction. But since the producer has asked the writer to *write*, the writer expects to be allowed to put his own conceptions and characters on the screen. The paradox lies in the fact that often the writer's version of what will make money is better than the producer's, and often a producer's judgment rescues a writer's work from dullness or pretension.

The writer—no matter how small his talent or how modest his aspirations—tends to identify himself with a calling that has always enjoyed status. Writers are, in a sense, the unofficial oracles of society. They shape the dreams of men; they sing for the mute and dare for the timid. They are, as someone said, the "divine skeptics," enemies of intolerance, rebels against flatulence and platitude. But in Hollywood they say, "We only make movies."

The I AM flock devotes itself to the teachings of the Ninety-Nine Ascended Masters of Saint Germain. These wonderful precepts have been transcribed for humanity by a Mr. and Mrs. G. W. Ballard, the celebrated leaders of the movement. They are referred to lovingly as "Our Messengers of Light," or simply as Papa and Mama Ballard. The head of this immortal household will go down in history as the man who started the I AM single-handed. It seems that he was on a camping trip on Mount Shasta, in sunny California, when suddenly Saint Germain materialized before him and gave him all the dope on the Great I AM Presence, the All-Consuming Flame, the Coming of the Seventh Ray, the Blue Tube of Light, the illusion of "so-called death," and how to stop war, earthquakes, dandruff, and traffic accidents, just by decreeing against them in a loud, firm voice. Saint Germain also told Mr. Ballard about liquor, tobacco, meat, onions, garlic, and sex. Mr. G. W. Ballard promptly rushed down the mountain to Mrs. G. W. Ballard, blurted out the revelation, and mankind passed another milestone on the road to final wisdom. Today the fearless Ballards publish a monthly magazine in violet type (they won't budge an inch on red and black), broadcast Delphic tips several times a week, manufacture I AM books in Braille for those who have lost their so-called sight, and fly all over the land spreading the gospel to thousands of enraptured disciples.

I went to an I AM meeting in the temple in Los Angeles on a Sunday night—a balmy Sunday night. An elderly gentleman—spare and tall and pale, and dressed in white from head to foot—led me down the aisle. There were some five hundred happy converts in the auditorium. Most of them were elderly folk with gray hair and the look of the uplifted. None wore red or black. The whole flock was on its feet singing a hymn. It was a nice, lilting hymn—entitled "Arcturus, We Greet Thee!" They sang it quite loudly. (Arcturus is 29,835,863,103,751 miles from the earth.) When the greeting to Arcturus was completed, everyone sat down and I found a seat.

On a lavishly beflowered stage (yellow, pink and violet flowers only) I saw two people and four panes of glass. The first pane of glass was about four feet high and on it was painted the manly visage of Saint Germain, illuminated from behind. The second pane of glass depicted Our Saviour. The third pane of glass had purple waves painted on it; when lit up, as it was, it looked like blue running water. The last pane of glass I had better describe slowly. Its central motif was a violet flame, within which were two nude male (but sexless) figures, one standing on the head of the other. I mean that the top figure was standing on the head of the bottom figure—only he wasn't really standing, because he had no feet. His legs kind of faded into a path of white light which blended into the head of the man underneath. In other words, the top man seemed to be melting upwards from the bottom man, like ectoplasm. In the background, behind the violet flame and the two andro-gynes, was a snow-capped mountain.

This work of art illustrates the subtle metaphysic of the Mighty I AM. It is called "The Chart." It was explained to us by one of the two mortals on the stage—an exalted young man, dressed all in white, who wore rimless glasses and spoke in a voice that suggested taffy dipped in syrup.

"The I AM Presence is the perfect manifestation of the I AM principle," he began. "The original perfect bodies were of pure light substance, but of course not bodies that you can *see*. Now we have instructions from the Ninety-Nine Ascended Masters so we can rise above life on this octave of light." At this point our Saint Paul went over to the Chart and cleared up a few matters. It was fascinating. I gathered that the under-gentleman represents anyone—you or me or the man who calls for the laundry; by letting the light energy pour into him "until it fills every cell in the body, bursting with pure light radiance," the under-gentleman "rises" into the upper gentleman. Then he is in the Great I AM. Our teacher was a little vague about the mechanics of this elevation. He was, however, ultra-lucid about the mountain in the Chart. "That represents Mount Shasta," he said.

He told us many other things, terribly interesting, which I can only put down just as I heard them: "Mistakes are nothing but a disqualification of energy. . . . The Unfed Flame can burn anywhere, without oil or wood. Why, when you get pure enough you can call on the Flame and hold it right in the palm of your hand—and if you put a bar of steel or iron in the Flame it will be consumed at once but it won't hurt *you*. *Everything* manifests on inner octaves before manifesting here. Like a house on a blueprint."

At this, the other shepherd on the stage took the pulpit. She was a serene, fat little lady—about five decades old—with white hair and a distant look. She was dressed all in pink—a shiny pink evening gown and a flowing pink cape and a tiara of pink flowers in her hair and pink shoes and a pink corsage and her face was all pink too. Her eyes had an ethereal look, even from where I sat. She spoke gently, sweetly, with a beatific smile that didn't leave her face once throughout that whole glorious evening. If anybody was saved, she was. She called us "Dear ones."

I turned to an old woman on my right—she was dressed in pink, too—and whispered: "Who is that?"

The woman sighed ecstatically. "Ratana." A moment later she added, "That is the name the Ascended Masters gave her."

Ratana was saying that she was going to answer questions that had been piling up all through the busy week.

"Is she an Ascended Master?" I whispered.

The woman on my right shook her head, ever so tolerantly. "She is a

Master Unascended. She *could* ascend, of course, if she wanted to, she has been ready for such a long time. But she has decided to stay on this octave of light to do all this wonderful work with us. Like Mr. and Mrs. G. W. Ballard."

"Who was the chap who explained the Chart?"

"Everybody calls him Stanley."

Ratana was waving a letter. "I have here a note from one of the young people in our Ascension Class. You all know about our Ascension Class every Sunday morning at eleven o'clock, studying to make a public ascension? Well, this dear one is a girl in that fine class and wrote me this letter." She smiled and read: " 'To whom it may concern: I have just come down from Venus to usher in the Golden Age.' " Ratana took thought with her I AM, then said: "I think that is going a little too far."

The audience applauded.

"Of course we all know," Ratana continued, "that some spirits *did* come down from Venus to usher in the Golden Age. However"—Ratana gave us a particularly warm smile to soften the blow—"I do not think this particular girl is one of them."

The next letter was from "one of our most earnest and dynamic students" —a mail-carrier. It seemed that this gentleman, putting his heart and soul into things, had donned the I AM veil by renouncing any and all forms of liquor, tobacco, meat, onions, and garlic. (The letter didn't say anything about sex.) What he was writing Ratana about was this: as he was making his rounds for Uncle Sam these days, his mail-sack flung bravely over his shoulders, he was seeing steaks hanging before his eyes. This was accompanied by a strange hollow feeling in the stomach. Alarmed, he had consulted a doctor, and the doctor (a materialist) had told him to start eating meat at once. His letter ended simply: "What shall I do?"

A hush fell over the seekers of salvation. It was plain that a lot hung on Ratana's answer. I have nothing but admiration for the way she handled herself in the crisis. "Of *course* this dear one will feel a little weak for a while," Ratana smiled, taking the bull right by the horns. "But you can eat *poison* when you are in the Great I AM Presence, and take the quality out and change it back to its pristine purity. Why, even the scientists admit that meat-eating people get cancer and fish-eating people get leprosy. *What is the strongest animal in the animal kingdom?* The elephant! And he is a vegetarian."

The next letter was a pip. It was from an acolyte who wrote: "I demand that after so-called death my body be placed on a block of ice for seventy-two hours! No fluid, water, or blood whatsoever is to touch me! Then I am to be cremated at once!!"

This challenge didn't faze Ratana for a moment. "The Ascended Masters do not approve of this sort of thing," she proclaimed firmly. "When our earthbodies reach so-called death, many relatives and so on want funeral services. Do not hurt them. So I do not approve of this dear one asking to have his earth-body laid on a block of ice for seventy-two hours." Ratana finished the whole problem off by remarking: "I want to warn you all that petitions about blocks of ice and cremation after so-called death are being circulated in Los Angeles by certain destructive forces. Watch out for them! Do not do anything fanatical. . . . Let us all stand up and give a decree! And make it loud and strong so the Ascended Ones will get plenty of energy to do their work!"

The audience of 500 rose like one man (or one woman) and Stanley stepped forward and announced: "Let us give the decree for light! Let us give the three times three!" He waved his hands and the audience chanted the decree for light in mighty unison:

"Mighty I AM Presence! Ex-pand thy light in every cell of my body until its ra-di-ance *bla*-zes through my flesh—e-ter-nally sustained!"

Ratana cried, "Keep up the tempo! Do not let it drag!"

The lady at my right was decreeing like mad. Suddenly she shoved several mimeographed sheets at me with a cordial "The decrees!" There were three pronunciamentoes there, in violet ink, and they were wonderful to behold. The first was "The Decree for Annihilation of War in Europe."

There was also a jolly "Decree For Money," which began "Mighty I AM Presence! I must have money!!!"—and a special decree against "Spies, Agitators, Etc." "Spies, Agitators, Etc." was a number to make your hair stand on end. It began blandly enough, calling on Oromasis, the great Archangel Michael, and a Mr. David Lloyd; then it hit its stride and demanded that the Mighty Powers "project the Blue Lightning into every vortex of human discord in America and the world, and EXPLODE! EXPLODE! EXPLODE! everyone this instant!" There was also something about "dissolving all stolen airplanes."

Now Ratana beamed on her children and said, "I hope you will all decree to have the red traffic lights turned to violet."

Then Ratana exclaimed: "We just don't blaze enough light! How much light are *you* pouring forth?" A lot of people in the audience acted pretty sheepish when she put it that way. Whereupon Ratana lit into the evil forces. "I remember when I first got into this wonderful work. I was just an usher in the balcony. Well, a man staggered in and sat down—in the balcony. And, dear ones, how that man smelled! Why, he smelled of liquor and tobacco and meat and all the destructive forces. The smell was so bad I decided to put the Tube of Light around me, but then I closed my eyes"—Ratana closed her eyes—"and suddenly I thought, '*Silly!* Why don't you put the Tube of Light around *him?*' " There was a little explosion of laughter, and admiring nods over Ratana's ingenuity. "So I put the Tube of Light around him, and I put a tiny fragrance of roses around the edges!" We sat there breathless. "And after that beautiful service, dozens of dear ones came up to me and said, 'Ratana, Ratana, did you smell the roses in the temple tonight?'"

A letter challenged Ratana to reconcile the I AM's taboo on spirits (fluid spirits) with Jesus' miracle in turning water into wine. Ratana didn't bat an eye as she replied: "Jesus did turn water into wine—but times were different then! In that region they all ate fish. Well, he could not tell them not to eat *fish*. Why, Saint Germain once said, 'I will give you a ham sandwich but there won't be any pig in it.'" The congregation chuckled merrily at that. "Because it is pure substance. There is just a little *quality* of pig, to give it flavor . . ."

Stanley leered (I don't think he meant to leer; it was just the way he smiled) and relieved Ratana. "The Mighty I AM," he announced in his bold, blurry voice, "is opposed to secret orders and mysticism. There are *no mysteries whatsoever* in the teachings of the Ascended Ones! It is a simple thing which veritably any child can understand." Since no children were present, Stanley went on to explain things. "The ray intensifies and re-intensifies and reduces disqualification, causing pure light to expand in our bodies."

Ratana floated to the fore at this point and interpolated: "I would like to say that our dear Papa Ballard has just gotten a message that during the past few weeks the Ascended Ones have been walking around in Wall Street. They have also been walking around right here in downtown Los Angeles, in the business districts. They are working on the financial crisis!"

There was a roar of appreciation and applause. "Let us sing a hymn! That beautiful number Twenty-three! And make it lively, for the Masters do not like slow rhythms."

I thumbed the numerous pages of the hymn book and read the names of the following liturgies: "Beloved Leto," "O Presence of the Diamond Heart," "Great Sanat Kumara." Even more wondrous were two psalms, the names of which I shall never forget. One was entitled "To Nada, Rex, Bob and Pearl." The other was called "Visualize, Just Visualize."

And now Ratana stepped forward, smiled like an affectionate cherub, and said, "God bless you."

"God bless *you*," the audience echoed fondly.

"God bless you," Ratana called.

"God bless *you!*" chorused the followers of the Ninety-Nine Ascended Masters of Saint Germain.

"God bless you!" Ratana proclaimed for yet a third time.

"God bless *you!!*" the voices of the saved rang out.

The service was over.

We all filed out. The ushers were standing in the foyer in their nice white suits and dresses, beaming at everyone, sending pure light all over the place. The air throbbed with I AM good-nights. Little clusters of the unascended hovered around pedestals inscribed "Love Gift." The more fervent disciples of Mr. and Mrs. G. W. Ballard dropped dimes and quarters as their love gifts. (I didn't drop anything: I wasn't in love.)

Just as I got to the exit a clear-eyed woman with the look of an eagle trapped me. "God bless you," she sang out.

"God bless *you*," I murmured.

"Is this your first time here?"

"Yes."

"Oh, it is wonderful work. It is simply wonderful! You will see how wonderful the work is. Would you like to ask anything about anything?"

I heard some thirty voices chanting furiously from a room upstairs. "Whom are they decreeing against?" I asked.

"Grasshoppers!" she replied at once. "You know this terrible plague in Kern County that's destroying the crops and all? Well, we are working on it. We are working on it with all our powers. We have been decreeing all day just as hard as we can for the Ascended Masters to *drain* the energy out of the insects, to *drain* out their destructive forces. Generally, the Los Angeles chapter decrees against earthquakes and the San Francisco chapter decrees against strikes and revolution."

I started to ask her when Saint Germain had died, or lived, but I caught myself in time and asked instead: "When *was* Saint Germain?"

She blinked: "Oh, many times! You know, of course, that he was Sir Francis Drake. And he wrote all of Shakespeare." Before I could put the Blue Tube around me she had added: "He takes different forms, you see. For the last five years he has just been known as Freedom."

Alone, unloved, I wander far—
On one leg.
Not knowing where or why
For I am blind.

My Mama died when I was four
Oh woe, oh woe,
To join poor Dad who'd gone before
Oh double dreadful woe.

The orphan, I, was shipped in chains
To Madagascar,
A slave to fate, or maybe worse
(Don't ask her.)

But Fortune smiled—oh, life, oh, joy—
Our ship was wrecked!
And all aboard were drowned
Save I,
Who only broke my neck.

Oh friends,
Oh foes,
Such pains,
Such woes.

The good Lord then
Cast on my isle—
She!
Soon two were changed
From two to three,
But fearful pirates, passing by,
Kidnapped the child
And put out my eye.
And my own true love,
Fleeing their vile desire,
Fell into a volcano.

Oh smoke,
Oh flame,
Oh thundering cone,
Why could not fate
Let her alone?

My prayer was answered,
My heart relieved,
My love swam out,
Lava up to her knees,

About to join me—
Oh joy, oh grace—
When, betrayed by a Berber,
She lost more than face.

Oh woe, oh woes,
My heartbreak grows.

She entered a convent,
My one, my own,
With vows of silence,
Herself, alone.

So I wander about
Barely alive,
Waiting for a letter
That never arrives.

Oh woe is me,
Oh woe is you,
Faith in God
Will see you through.

Such is *fado*.

VI

THE WASHINGTON CORRESPONDENTS

conference, the presence of a stenographer, or the vigilant portrait of George
Washington on the wall.

The Washington correspondent must maintain a reputation for discretion.
He must be careful to remain *persona grata* with his news sources. In the
words of the trade, "He must keep his sources open." He may do this by re-
paying his informants in the currency of journalism: he may play up a story
that casts glory on a good news source and play down a story that is embar-
rassing. One veteran newspaperman in the capital has said that "almost every
correspondent has special news sources whose displeasure he consciously or
unconsciously fears." He complained that Washington correspondents are
compelled to operate on a "commercial-friendship basis": "The Washington
correspondent . . . wants to hold friendships and he believes that if he prints
all the news and the truth he cannot do this. Friendships mean news. So the
reporter becomes something of a servitor, a satellite—unknowingly. His truth
is not his own; and, therefore, not the public's. The Washington correspondent today does his work as a business proposition. . . ."

The representative of a large newspaper is interested in national news or
news that, though "local" to him, is charged with national interest. (The
news of New York, Chicago, Pittsburgh, or Detroit has a national market.)
But the correspondent for a small paper, or a string of small papers, is interested primarily in news of interest to his locality alone. (The press associations supply his paper with news of the nation.)

The correspondent for a metropolitan journal can get his information from
a dozen sources. News about a large city, for example, breaks through half a
dozen different Representatives, two Senators, federal agencies with projects
in the city, the Republican and Democratic party organizations, and so on.
But news about Siwash is "bottle-necked" at two points: the Representative
of the district in which Siwash falls, and, to a lesser degree, the Senator from
Siwash state. These men control the political jobs to be distributed in Siwash,
and the pork-barrel appropriations. The reporter for the Siwash *Siren* is pretty
much at their mercy. If they choose to "freeze up" on him he is in a difficult
position because he has no alternative sources of information. The news
involving New York or Pittsburgh may take the center of the political stage
and be subject to publicity, wide interest, and thorough press coverage; but
news about Siwash has its birth and consummation in the Congressional
wings, unspotlighted and unsung. Hence the smallfry Congressman achieves
in such matters a particular importance denied him in all others. And where
a legislator or official will think twice before antagonizing the correspondent

for a powerful newspaper, he may be highhanded and peremptory with the reporter for a relatively insignificant organ. The correspondent for the small paper thus depends upon one or two men for his information and labors under the necessity of currying their favor.

The decision as to whether to print or not, and with what emphasis, entails a conflict between professional duty and professional discretion. The decision is generally made by calculating the returns. An insignificant item that involves a good news source may be suppressed or written in so perfunctory a manner that it gets little attention. A correspondent dependent upon Representative Simeon Q. Jones may not report the fact that the distinguished solon was arrested for speeding, or for striking a waiter at a night club while in a state of heroic inebriation. But if a story is big enough to overshadow the benefits of suppression, or if it is a story that may have national repercussions and will come to local notice anyway, then the correspondent will send it off. No correspondent would dare suppress the fact that Representative Jones will be tried for criminal malfeasance or was rebuked by the State Department for an insult to the honor of a foreign country. In the refreshing language of one correspondent: "There are stories you've *got* to print, even if they involve your own mother." In minor stories—"Well, it's foolish to sacrifice a first-rate news source for a third-rate yarn."

The degree to which a newspaperman becomes the henchman of a political personage depends upon his own character, the security of his position, and the orders or example of his publisher.

Fortunately, for every story that is killed another is dispatched; where some correspondent tries to play a story down, another may throw his energies into playing it up. In the intangible area of personal discretion, such factors as courage, vanity, asperity, or vengeance play cardinal roles. But this much can be said with assurance: (1) news is suppressed, colored, or played down in inverse proportion to its significance and national interest; (2) the smaller the paper on which a given locality depends for its information, the less independent of pressure can the Washington correspondent of that paper be, and the less *probability* is there that that paper will get complete and unbiased news from "our special correspondent."*

There is neither mystery nor magic in the process of covering Washington. "News," a term about which there has been considerable debate, is essentially the departure from the normal. And events depart from the normal at certain fixed points. In any city, police headquarters, the courts, fire stations, the city hall, the Bureau of Vital Statistics, are focal points at which unusual events

---

* Like all generalizations this is subject to qualification; some small papers have correspondents in the capital who are conspicuously resourceful and courageous.

become overt. Newspapers station reporters at these points to cover such events.

In Washington the places at which events materialize are covered with great efficiency. The press associations have reporters stationed at each government department, each administrative agency, the White House, the houses of Congress, the Supreme Court, and so on. Reporters cover committee hearings and investigations regularly. The movements of high officials are followed. Hotel registrations are often watched. The life of the President is, of course, followed with microscopic care, and visitors to the White House are questioned. Congressional leaders are interviewed when news breaks. Party leaders are always open to questioning. Every major government agency issues press releases about its work. All important officials hold press conferences, sometimes twice a week. The representatives of private pressure groups ("lobbyists") are more than willing to supply information in their field of interest. There is, in short, a definite and systematic method by which events and persons are covered for the newspapers of the country.

The Gossip Column

"Gossip columns" sprang up during the Hoover administration as a necessary device by which correspondents could speculate about news that the government either refused to make public or presented in unreliable fashion. Syndicated columns have soared into popularity largely because of the standardization of news dispatches. There has been a natural demand for a humanized version of the news, for the "inside story." Readers want to know not merely which official plans are being discussed and which Congressmen are voting for what measures; they have an avid interest in what Mr. Borah privately thinks of Secretary Hull, what Mrs. Roosevelt said to the wife of Senator X, how the beautiful wife of an Ambassador made a *faux pas* at the White House, what political deal is being consummated between Mr. Farley and a southern Democratic leader. The flamboyant columns about Hollywood and Broadway whetted the public appetite for a similar type of news from Washington. In the search for a fresh angle on Washington politics, the columns came into vogue. The sensational success of *Washington Merry-Go-Round*, published anonymously in 1931 by Messrs. Allen and Pearson, marked the beginning of a new era in news styles from the capital.

Is Journalism a Profession?

Journalism is often called a "game" in the argot of its practitioners. But many newspapermen like to embellish their status by insisting upon the designation of their trade as a profession. Since the first requisite of a profession is the exclusion of the unfit, "the profession of journalism" is chiefly a convenient term of reference. Newspaper work requires a congeries of skills and techniques, but it is a profession with no professional standards, no professional discipline, no examining or accrediting bodies, no agreement upon norms for testing competence.

The newspaperman in the capital today is faced by the necessity of reporting news that is a compound of economics, political science, monetary problems, constitutional and international law, public administration, social service. The activities of the New Deal range from the field of public works to the esoteric art of encouraging piscatorial copulation. Such responsibilities require intellectual poise, if not specialized competence, in the face of intricate events. A *systematic* approach to the hectic cosmos of Washington would necessitate sophistication in the field of political economy, in all its ramifications; an *impressionistic* approach, which is the approach of journalism, would profit by at least a limited experience in the disciplines of the social sciences.

The correspondents would seem to be in need of a frame of reference within which to orient themselves, and by which to appraise the significance of men, measures, and goals. Without some framework within which competing plans and theories can be related to an inclusive system, or without some analytic viewpoint from which to place social phenomena in a perspective of time and totality, the observer is left with little but an unsystematized bundle of preferences and an incoherent mélange of impressions. His insights may be keen and his sensitivity high, but his ability to understand is limited to the one-dimensional sphere of distilled facts.

This is not an academic judgment, the validity of which newspapermen challenge. It was tested in the anonymous questionnaire submitted to the Washington correspondents. The following statement appeared, to be checked "Yes," or "No," or "Uncertain": "I often feel the need of knowing more economics for my job." 86.6 per cent of those who answered said "Yes." This was a higher degree of agreement than on any other question but one. Extensive interviews with over 150 members of the press corps lead this writer to the conclusion that a majority of the correspondents often feel inadequate to cope with the bewildering complexity of the news they are assigned to cover. Complaints were often heard that "my college work is a dead loss today," and many correspondents regret that they did not have a more thorough training in economics or political science, rather than journalism or the Elizabethan sonnet.

Newspapermen evidence a marked insecurity in the presence of complex theories or political conceptualization. The caustic reaction to "New Deal professors," "crack-pot theories," "The Brain Trust," "Frankfurter's bright young men," etc., suggests the projection of doubts of personal adequacy upon Mr. Roosevelt. Having "betrayed" the objective function they felt they must observe, the conscience of the correspondents acted with doubled vigor. To a situation for which they held the President responsible, newspapermen added those discontents which might more legitimately have been directed against themselves. This was improper, for in inter-personal relations, as in commerce, the admonition *caveat emptor* throws responsibility upon the gullible. A healthy proportion of the antagonism to Mr. Roosevelt was over-reaction by reporters who would have preferred that their earlier exaltations of the man might be removed from the record. They could not wipe out the emotional commitments of the past, but they intensified their efforts to compensate for them.*

Adulation—guilt—debunking. Newspapermen greet the new statesman with a deep hope that here, at last, is the great man incarnate. There is evidence to support this in the traditional honeymoon psychology of the first months. The great man's talents are sung, over-sung, in the struggle for journalistic existence. Then "incidents" occur, a political compromise of not admirable hue, a political setback, attacks from the opposition. The newspapermen begin to see the pedal clay. They have been "taken in." Their faith has been outraged. How did they ever "fall for the stuff"? The demon on the desk in the home office sends them sarcastic reminders of their first euphoria. Other newspapermen, columnists, editors, publishers cry that the press corps was hamstrung by phrases. The correspondents are hurt; they are irritated; and they feel guilty. The breaking of the myth begins, by the men who erected it.

The Concept of News

No newspaper prints *all* the news. A newspaper is neither a chronology, an almanac, nor a history. It is a business enterprise selling a commodity, and it must interest its customers in that commodity. The commodity is news.

The entire process of journalism, from the leg-man on the street to the make-up editor at the desk, rests upon *selection*. This selective process is exercised according to "news judgment." The first test to which any constellation of events is subjected is the test of its news value: "Is it news?" Or, in the parlance of the trade, "Is it a good story?" It is important to notice that the appraisal is not, "Is it significant?" or, "Is it important?"—but, "Is it news?"

---

* The correspondents who yielded to anti-Roosevelt pressure from their home offices should not be ignored. This pressure both buttressed and sanctioned the psychological pattern analyzed above, where it did not initiate an anti-Roosevelt point of view by itself. It has been estimated that 85 percent of the American press opposed Mr. Roosevelt in the 1936 campaign. It can hardly be denied that the editorial stand, and its intensity, influenced newspapermen-employees, where actual policy orders did not.

The concept of news varies with different newspapers, different editors, and different publishers. What is news for Denver is not news for Norfolk; what is news for the New York *American* is not news for the New York *World-Telegram*. By trial-and-error the reporter learns what values his particular paper places on different items.

Newspapers differ among themselves as to what constitutes news because they appeal to different publics, because their editors have different perspectives, because their publishers have different preferences as persons and different motivations as publishers.

Newspapers are published by businessmen whose chief concern, in most cases, is to make profit. Profit comes from advertising revenues. Advertising rates mount with advances in circulation. To increase circulation means to appeal to a wider body of readers; this means lowering the level of attraction to the widest common denominator of interest. This presents a serious limitation to the work of the Washington correspondent.

The Washington correspondents must simplify issues for a public which has neither the background nor the time to analyze what it reads. They must emphasize personalities rather than forces. They must etch those personalities into sharp stereotypes which the reader can find analogous to the ordinary types of his own experience. They must inject into politics the elements of melodrama.

"The newspaper's function is not to instruct but to startle," said James Gordon Bennett, father of the modern conception of news and its first exponent. ". . . and to entertain," adds Silas Bent. The press corps is often obliged to startle and entertain. The realization that the American newspaper, in a competitive commercial society, is an organ of information only in part, will clarify the dilemma in which many critics of the press find themselves. The modern newspaper, with its comics, beauty hints, Daily Romance stories, society pages, radio, sport and entertainment news, is an entertainment sheet, a purveyor of fiction, and a service bureau—as well as a journal of record.

The Washington correspondents, like other journalists, place a premium on conflict, particularly conflict between well-known persons. An attack is news. It does not matter how shallow the grounds, how questionable the motivation, or how meretricious the personality of the attacker. An attack is news. This point has been exploited by politicians and publicity seekers. Congressmen have learned that they can always reach the front page by verbal assaults on the President. The Senator who achieved immortality by referring to some of his colleagues as "sons of the wild jackass" could not make page 1 with one of his best speeches in the Senate.

It is worth noting that the journalistic emphasis on personalized conflict has created a striking coincidence between the language of journalism and

Publisher, said that in the years preceding 1929 financial pages were loaded with " 'inspired' news, press-agent written" and that this "constituted as wicked an exploitation of the reading public as our press has ever been guilty of."

Newspapers are Big Businesses. The character of American journalism has been radically transformed from what the founding fathers visualized. In the eighteenth and early nineteenth century . . . newspapers were published by men to whom journalism was a career. It took relatively little capital for a journalistically minded man to become a publisher. Today the press is an industry and a business, subject to the laws, the problems, and the aspirations of economic enterprise. Newspaper publishing involves enormous investments and expenditures.

Publishing has become an enterprise that is no longer accessible except to the wealthy. This means that, as in other realms of our economy, power has gravitated to few hands, power has tended to multiply itself, economic power has been translated into political power of a magnitude incongruous with the assumptions of a democratic society. Competition, from which the general good of a free competitive society is assumed to grow, has been limited, restrained, and strangulated. Competition has given way to imperfect competition or to near-monopoly. The consequences are far-reaching—perhaps more so in the realm of public opinion, where men have become lords over facts, than in the sphere of finance. For control over the dissemination of the information upon which a democratic society acts, and according to which democratic citizens make political choices, is exercised by men who often recognize no social responsibility, and who may manipulate what is almost a public agency for the sake of private ends.

The newspaper is still "the bible of democracy, the only serious book most people read. It is the only book they read every day." Nor can one dismiss the influence of the press with the blithe statement that people *know* that newspapers are not to be trusted. Charles E. Merriam has made the seminal suggestion that even where readers are skeptical of the reliability of newspapers the repetition of news has a somewhat hypnotic effect. "Journalistic repetition is in some ways reminiscent of the beat, beat, beat, of the drum in the primitive tribe."

One cannot challenge the right of Mr. William Randolph Hearst to utter the most arrant nonsense in his editorial columns, nor the privilege of Colonel Robert R. McCormick to project his personal phobias into the Chicago *Tribune's* editorials, nor the license of the respective publishers and editors of the Los Angeles *Times,* the Philadelphia *Record,* or the *Daily Worker* to stride through their editorial columns breathing hell-fire of their own particular type. Editorials are the soapboxes of journalism. They are approached by readers as recognizable efforts to influence opinion. Their influence may be discounted accordingly. But when editorial opinions are stamped into the news columns, when facts are colored, twisted, suppressed, or mutilated, then a crime is being committed against the society that sanctions journalistic freedom.

For over 150 years the right of American publishers to print what they please has not been challenged. They have enjoyed freedom of expression and freedom of reporting. But they have not been held responsible for the *uses* to which they put their constitutional prerogative. If a doctor falsely or incompetently prescribes strychnine and his patient dies, the doctor is subject to prosecution. If a maniac puts poison into a public-drinking system, he is incarcerated in a stronghold where his possibilities of injuring society are minimized. But a newspaper publisher can give criminal advice, lie to the public, poison its intelligence, and conduct campaigns against civil liberties, decent morals, and the democratic system itself without being held accountable for his conduct, or without having to accept responsibility for the consequences of his action. He is granted legal sanction for behavior which may range from the incendiary to the psychopathic.

The American press is free in the sense that there are no legal or political interferences with its editorial and news columns. But the freedom of the press does not mean the freedom of the *news*. It is the contention of this writer that in abusing the freedom they possess newspaper publishers are strengthening the possibility of political interference with that freedom. The danger of distorted news columns and of colored dispatches lies not merely in the fact that the public is misled (the radio has removed some of the dangers in this direction) but that aspiring demagogues and potential dictators are provided with impressive arguments for controlling the press. A public that has learned to be skeptical of the sources of its news, and that has been given evidence of the falsifications practiced by its newspapers, may be receptive to the oratory of those who ask for the power to "cleanse" the press and "remove" those who pollute the news. This is a danger which few publishers seem to recognize, but it cannot be ignored in a day in which democratic society is being threatened.

The best guarantor of freedom is the intelligent use of it. In no society has license long gone uncorrected: when liberty is used to violate the privileges that liberty confers, men of force and eloquence may win public support to suppress those violations—and freedom with it. It is not academic to suggest to the proprietors of the American newspapers that one of the gravest threats to their freedom lies in the very use they are making of it.

In the final analysis, newspapers get the type of reporting they encourage; publishers get the kind of Washington correspondents they deserve; and the public receives Washington correspondence of a character that newspaper publishers, and ultimately they alone, make possible.

The Free Mind

★

MY LOVED ONES *tell me that I get terribly earnest, even oracular, the minute I face an audience. This may well be true, because I take public speaking seriously—so seriously, in fact, that I feel exhausted afterwards. Few people seem to realize how very much energy goes into thinking on your feet. I say "thinking on your feet" because I have never written out a speech in my life. I hate hearing someone read a lecture and I can't see how the act of reading can avoid a certain didacticism, at best, or an irritating robotitude, at worst. I spend a good deal of time in thinking about what I am going to say, then make notes—the key ideas, key phrases—to which I refer. Whatever sense of spontaneity or excitement one is able to communicate stems, I am sure, from words that are fashioned in a living context and respond to the responses of an audience. The interplay between a speaker and his listeners is most subtle and fructifying.*

I have perpetrated well over a thousand public speeches in my lifetime. I made my first oration at the age of nine, for a Liberty Bond Drive in World War I, and began receiving actual money for talking when I was eighteen. I have inflicted my ruminations upon old and young alike: at luncheons, dinners, forums, conventions; for student assemblies, women's clubs, Rotary lunches; to levies of teachers and herds of Lions. I made several swings through the Middle West lecturing for the League of Nations Association. I have been introduced, eulogized, prayed over and misquoted to audiences ranging from eight to 2,500. During the last war, I hope, I even waxed eloquent before a throng packed into the open promenade of Rockefeller Center, from which I left to drive a gaggle of delinquents into a coma in the cellar of a community center you'll have to go to your grave without knowing the name of.

203

The speech I most enjoyed giving is "The Free Mind," which I presented at the 1962 National Book Awards. I was honored by the invitation and moved by the response. It is a distillation of ideas I had long been turning over in my mind and testing in seminars, conversation, lectures. The speech must have made some impression on those who heard it because the text was printed in full in the Washington *Star, the St. Louis* Post-Dispatch *and other intrepid papers. I edited the prose from a tape-recorded transcript.*

N.B.: If you run across a line that seems to repeat something you already read in this collocation, please don't leap to the phone to dictate a triumphant telegram to me. I know there are certain repetitions, and they don't bother me, because (1) I don't mind repeating something in which I fervently believe; (2) a man should be allowed to indulge his whims once in a while; (3) if you feel like editing my copy, just get a blue pencil and go to it. If these three reasons aren't enough, here is another: Perhaps some things should be drummed into all of our heads; in a society governed by certain ideas, so very much depends on our not forgetting them.

*

We live among madmen. We are surrounded by those who believe in witchcraft. The most critical problem which free men face today is to get some of their co-citizens to listen—to listen to that which seems to threaten them. For the right to talk involves the duty to listen.

We are all raised so that we confuse *a* way of thinking with *the* way of thinking. We must all try—desperately hard—to see things not as *we* are but as *they* are. The function of the thinker, the scientist, the writer, the editor—indeed, the function of the free man and the free mind—is, stubbornly and painfully, to try to find truth—truth as it is, not as we want it to be, or hope it to be, or prefer it to be. The wife at the cocktail party who said indignantly to her husband, "Darling, don't you think you ought to stop drinking? Your face is already beginning to get blurred!" suggests the singular capacity of human beings to project onto the outer world that which might more properly be examined within.

To be free means to have made a deep and incontestable commitment to the self: to love ideas, to examine them, to explore them no matter where they lead; to test what is new, even what is threatening. For wisdom is not much more than the capacity to confront dangerous ideas with equanimity.

Now, there is a special irony in what I am saying. Not so long ago, in these United States, the target of political disdain and political contempt was that pathetic, that unrealistic, that useless person—the egghead. You may remem-

There is the myth I hesitate to utter, so outlandish is it: that men and women are equal. This is madness. The fight for equality under law has led to conclusions that are biologically silly and psychologically insupportable. Men and women belong to different races, as different as Eskimos and Hottentots. I am convinced that it is impossible for any man truly to understand, really to enter the universe of, a woman, just as it is impossible for a woman truly to grasp, sense, comprehend, empathize with the secret and internal structure of the male.

Little Johnny sent this note to a girl in school, a typical masculine note: "Dear Mary, I love you. Do you love me? (signed) Johnny." He got back from Mary this lovely, feminine reply: "Dear Johnny, I do *not* (underlined three times) love you. Love, Mary."

There is the myth that you can explain neurotic behavior by attributing it to an unhappy childhood. But *all* childhood is unhappy; all childhood is charged with uncertainty and fear, with conflict and frustration, with unbearable rage and unattainable desire. It makes little sense to talk about unhappy childhoods unless we ask why some people emerge from childhood with their productive capacities enriched, while others remain paralyzed by unresolved and infantile dilemmas.

There is the myth that it is wrong to spank a child. Well, for about thirty years, I think, we have been bamboozled by this cliché. Now, I assume that civilized people don't say, "Dear, let's have some fun: let's beat up the kids." The relevant question, surely, is this: *if* you are angry enough, for whatever reason, to want to strike a child, what do you do with that anger? I submit that if you do *not* spank the child, the alternatives you leave him are horrible. For the child knows that the parent is angry; and what can the child think? "Oh, he's mad; he's real mad. If I were that mad, I'd hit, I'd kick, I'd bite, I'd chew, I'd knock him down, I'd cut him up. But he doesn't. Oh, how much better he is than I. Will I ever be that good?" What a terrible thing to do to a child. Or, he may think, "He's *mad*. He'd really like to slug me. Why doesn't he hit me? *I* know why he doesn't hit me. Because if he ever let go, he'd kill me—which is what I suspect he's been wanting to do all along!" Or, "*When* will he become human? What do I have to do to make him act like other parents?" And so on. We can only celebrate the insight of our departed colleague, George Bernard Shaw, who once said, "Never strike a child in cold blood."

There is the myth that a child should adjust to its group. Well, is the group worth adjusting to? Are not some children meant to be alone, not to be well-liked, not to be popular? If you want your child to be popular, I'll give you a fool-proof recipe: tell him to ask people for advice. Tell him not to *listen* to the advice, nor take it; just ask. Try it yourself. Everyone will love you and think you wise and good.

There is the myth that a 35-hour week is better than a 40-hour week, that more and more leisure is desirable. But I suspect we have not begun to learn how to handle the leisure we already have. The American week-end has become a prolonged exercise in the destruction of time: frantic drinking, barbecuing, infidelity, reckless driving, all by people conned into thinking that the American way of life means: "Don't ruminate; don't think; never be alone. Fill up every free moment in a crowd, with strenuous relaxation."

There is the myth that every problem has a solution. But some problems will never be solved; they can only be re-shaped and re-formed. Do you want an example of a problem that is insoluble? It's illustrated by Groucho Marx, who once resigned from a country club in these words, "I don't want to belong to the kind of club that accepts people like me as members." There, in a nutshell, is the insoluble dilemma of snobbery.

There is the myth that eloquence means wisdom, that the articulate are able. Some of the most articulate people I know wouldn't know how to operate a newsstand. And I would hate to have our country run by, say, musicians, or even by poets. Wisdom is often found in the dry, non-eloquent analysis of reality.

And, finally, there is that myth to which so many of us are beholden— that the purpose of life is to be *happy*. I know of nothing more demeaning to man than this exaltation of "fun." Where, in God's name, was it written that life can ever be easy, or free from conflict, uncertainty and pain? Those who want the refuge of idiot bliss can find it in tranquillizing pills, or in senility. I have said elsewhere, and with no less indignation, that there was a time when men were permitted the dignity of depression, when we were permitted moods and preoccupations. But under the vulgarized diffusion of psychiatric "insights," we are all made to think that we must never feel depressed. Even worse—you must feel *guilty* about feeling depressed.

I end with a creed, a creed to which, in my judgment, all free men must forever hold fast.

We must forever oppose hysteria, even when it is wrapped in the vestments of patriotism.

We must learn that those we like are not always right, and those we don't like are not always wrong; for the validity of an idea has little to do with who is for it or who is against it.

We must learn to seek change without violence—always change, and never violence, not even in words, much less in deeds.

We must try to understand each other by reconciling ourselves to the fact that most of us never really mature; we simply grow taller.

We must meet fanaticism with courage, and idealism with a dose of caution.

We must be skeptical of that which is promised, but not proved.

We must be strong enough to be gentle.

We must know that life will always contain unbearable stretches of loneliness, of conflict and darkness and pain, and that we can never truly be
understood—even by those who love us. We cannot completely understand
someone else, no matter how much we want to or try to.

We must have the great good courage to live without absolutes, without
dogmas.

We must have the will to seek imaginative escapes from conformity, knowing—with Emerson—"Whosoever would be a man, must be a noncon-
formist."

We must learn to meet life in a series of tentative and impermanent
approximations, knowing that the final goals may never be reached, that the
last truths may be forever unknowable, that life holds nothing more precious
than the process by which, to the fullest reaches of which we are capable,
we stretch the mind and the heart.

Is Fear Destroying Our Freedom?

★

I OFTEN WONDER *how historians will explain those dreadful, foolish, soiled, and tragic few years called "the McCarthy era," or that unconscionable technique of innuendo, half-truths, sneak-punches, red herrings and vicious ambiguities called "McCarthyism."*

Senator Joseph McCarthy, according to those who liked him, was an engaging man. He is said to have housed a hail-fellow-well-met exuberance, a diamond-in-the-rough manner, and a disarming way of flinging his arm around your shoulder to smile (as he did to one newspaperman whose reputation he had just massacred on a national television hook-up), "I'm real sorry I had to do that to you, pal—but you know politics. When this blows over, let's have a drink and laugh it off together."

The Senator was, of course, a demagogue. He knew he was a demagogue. He was utterly cynical and emphatically conscience-free. He had the instincts of a barroom brawler—and a style to match. His astonishing, if short-lived, effectiveness proceeded from a base of what can only be called terrorism. Many a Senator kept quiet about McCarthy because he lived in nightmare fears that the gentleman from Wisconsin, if provoked, might publicize a hotel-room rendezvous with a loose lady, or a son's homosexual proclivities, or the receipt of campaign funds from a questionable character. The patriot from Wisconsin, after all, had the research staff of a Senate committee under his blustering command, and lieutenants who ranged from the prurient to the paranoiac.

All this sets the stage for "Is Fear Destroying our Freedom?" It appeared in the lead position of Look on September 7, 1954, won considerable acclaim, considerable hostility, a certain number of subscription cancellations, a Freedoms Foundation Award, a George Polk Memorial Award, and editorial applause across the nation. What surprised me was that friends, complimenting me on the "courage" it took to write such an article in so troubled a time, implied that I must have shown considerable ingenuity to get the text "past" Gardner Cowles, editor-in-chief of Look, a most staunch Republican. The fact is that the idea for the article was suggested to me by Mr. Cowles and his editor, Daniel D. Mich. I may say that Look had already run several strong anti-McCarthy pieces (at a time when many journals were hearkening to counsel of discretion) despite nasty mutterings and threats from some of the Senator's fuglemen.

Anyone who thought that Gardner Cowles would permit his politics to distort his editorial judgment, clearly did not know either the Cowles character or the Cowles record. And anyone who thought he could frighten Dan Mich from printing an article he believed to be true, never ran into that cantankerous Dutchman either. It is a pleasure to work with such editors. They are, to put it simply, men.

★

You open this magazine to this page and lean back and read.

You are free to read. You are free to think. You are free to talk. You are an American—a citizen of the noblest political system man ever devised. You are free.

But as you read this, an unseen presence breathes down your neck. Your freedom is being crowded. Your schools are being attacked. Your books are under fire.

Before you finish reading this page, some liar or enemy, some hysteric or fool, some perjurer or crackpot, may smear your reputation and question your loyalty. You will be forced to defend yourself—explaining, protesting, denying.

The charges against you may be quite wild, cockeyed, or outrageous. But those who make them need not prove them. They put the burden of proving your innocence on you. You find yourself an object of suspicion. You suddenly become "controversial." And it is not wise to be "controversial" in our land today.

Absurd? Not as absurd as you think.

Farfetched? Not as farfetched as you imagine.

Read the cases below. They are a factual record of recent events in the United States of America.

Let us be clear about one thing: The terrible threat of Russian power hangs over all our heads. The Communist shadow falls squarely across all our lives. Treason and subversion are nightmares to be neither denied nor disparaged. We live in a time of danger and tragedy.

In such a time, we have a right to be vigilant; but we have no right to be hysterical.

We have a right to be worried; but we have no right to scuttle the ideas which keep us free.

We must guard against deadly enemies; but we must not fall into the trap of assuming that (to paraphrase Walter Lippmann) the way to prove you are not red or pink is to act yellow.

The cases below are not, thank God, typical. Most of them had decent endings. But it is worth asking ourselves why and how they got as far as they did—maligning the innocent, subverting our liberties, disgracing the heritage of a land proud of its strength and its freedom.

The Attack on People

Lt. Milo J. Radulovich was discharged from the Air Force Reserve—not because he was a Communist, or disloyal, or dangerous. The Air Force Board that dropped Lieutenant Radulovich said quite candidly that he was of unquestioned loyalty. He was dropped because (1) his father, an elderly worker, had read a Slavic-language paper which was pro-Communist; (2) his sister purportedly had Communist or Communist-front associations.

Lieutenant Radulovich, who was studying at the University of Michigan, said, "It would be senseless for me to continue in physics or meteorology if the decision stands . . . The fact that I have been labeled a poor security risk would nullify my professional qualifications. We have two children to support. I may be forced to look for work in another field."

Edward R. Murrow's television program, "See It Now," presented a documentary record of the Radulovich case. The press of the nation blasted the principle of "guilt by kinship." Americans asked themselves whether American justice had taken on the special Communist-Fascist hue of systems where men and women and children *are* punished for what a father or brother or sister may believe. Air Force Secretary Harold Talbott reinstated Lieutenant Radulovich.

Val Lorwin, chief of a section in the State Department, was accused of having once been "connected with a number of Communist-front organizations." The State Department investigated him, found that, a Socialist, he had been actively *anti*-Communist for years, concluded he was not a loyalty risk —but dismissed him on "security grounds."

Lorwin appealed the decision. He was vindicated and reinstated with full back pay. He stayed on in his job long enough "to show that honest men don't have to run," then resigned to accept a university post.

Several months later, Lorwin was indicted—for committing perjury before the State Department Loyalty Board. When his case came to trial, an assistant attorney general asked the judge to stop the proceedings. For the Department of Justice had found that the indictment of Lorwin was obtained "by outright misrepresentation."

The Department of Justice official who had obtained the indictment against Lorwin had told the grand jury two crucial things that were simply not true:

1. He told the grand jury that two FBI informers would identify Lorwin as a Communist—but a Justice Department witness said "there never was any basis for that statement in the record. . . ."

2. When the grand jury asked why Lorwin was not called to appear before them in person, the prosecutor said it would do no good because Lorwin "would probably claim the Fifth Amendment." But when the prosecutor made that statement, there were on file several hundred pages of testimony which proved Lorwin had testified freely and openly, flatly denied Communist party membership, and made no attempt to invoke the Fifth Amendment.

The case against Lorwin was dropped. It had taken him almost four years and several thousand dollars to clear his name.

In Gregg Township, Ind., William Lewis, principal of the Hall School, was fired because of his religious beliefs. A member of Jehovah's Witnesses, who claim their allegiance is to God, he respectfully declined to salute the flag. He did not try to prevent anyone *else* from saluting the flag. He did not teach his doctrine in the classroom. But he was fired.

In Los Angeles, the directors of the Philharmonic Society denied the use of their auditorium for a meeting to commemorate Bill of Rights Day—because one of the leading churchmen in America, Methodist Bishop G. Bromley Oxnam, was to speak. He was "too controversial."

Three months earlier, the House Un-American Affairs Committee had issued a formal statement that no evidence whatsoever showed that Bishop Oxnam had ever had any dealings with the Communist party.

One of the charges against Bishop Oxnam was his support of a Massachusetts Council for Soviet-American Friendship—in 1943, during the war. Bishop Oxnam proved that in 1945, two years after he had resigned, Dwight D. Eisenhower, along with other Republicans, had praised the objectives of a national council with which the Massachusetts group was affiliated.

The Supreme Court of the State of New York reprimanded officials of the City of New York for using unproved charges of Communist ties to keep men off the police force:

1. The Police Department dismissed Jesse Hubbard for "associations" with Communist causes. A supreme court justice called the action entirely "arbitrary, unreasonable and capricious" and ordered the department to reinstate him.

2. Jervey C. Hamilton, a 26-year-old Navy veteran, passed his examinations for patrolman—but was ruled ineligible because he had once signed a petition for a Communist candidate for City Council. Hamilton testified that he had no Communist links or sympathies whatsoever; that, like many another innocent, he had been fooled into signing the petition. A supreme court justice upheld Hamilton's claim and ordered that his name be restored to the appointment list.

The Minute Women of the U.S.A. conducted a series of intensive "telephone chain" campaigns in Texas, to put pressure on public officials. They ran ads in seven newspapers throughout the nation asking for legislation which would prevent President Truman from sending more soldiers to Korea without the consent of Congress. [The Communists picked up these same ads for their own propaganda.]

In San Antonio, they spearheaded the attempt to ban 600 books in the public library. In Los Angeles and Denver, they attacked books, educators and teachers. In Columbus, Ohio, they had merchants remove U.N. flags from window displays.

The Minute Women were exposed in a series of articles by Ralph O'Leary of the Houston *Post*. The organization which professed so deep and abiding a concern for democracy had no constitution, no bylaws, no elected officers, no parliamentary procedure, no opportunity for motions to be introduced from the floor.

The Attack on Our Schools

The National Education Association studied over 520 school systems in the United States and concluded that American freedom—to study, to think, to discuss—is in danger. Attacks on our schools have increased to the point where most principals, teachers and educators are alarmed.

The NEA circulated questionnaires to its members. The first 700 replies to this year's questionnaires showed: One out of 12 elementary-school teachers, 1 out of 8 high-school teachers and 1 out of 7 social-studies teachers reported that last year they made a special effort to avoid discussing anything "controversial." (A controversial issue is one about which people disagree; otherwise the issue would not be controversial.)

The group leading the attack on education is called the National Council for American Education, an organization run by Allen Zoll, a critic of such

treason and dissent; that it is the Communists who wash brains and demand confessions and persecute those who disagree.

In the midst of troubles no smaller than ours, the thirteen original states adopted the Bill of Rights. There were those who sneered that the thirteen states were weak. But they were strong; they did not fear the free exercise of free minds. "Ideas are dangerous," some said then, as some say now. But the suppression of ideas is worse.

Freedom is not freedom when it is confined to what is popular or inoffensive.

This country was not founded by cowards.

The Intellectual and the Mass Media

★

IN 1958, THE EDITORS of Daedalus (published by the American Academy of Arts and Sciences) and the director of the Tamiment Institute conspired to hold a three-day conference on "Mass Culture" in the smoky blue Poconos. They invited a group of exceptionally cerebral scholars to this symposium, among them Hannah Arendt, Daniel Bell, Ernest van den Haag, Sidney Hook, Paul Lazarsfeld, Arthur Schlesinger, Jr., Edward Shils. To off-set the academicians, the sponsors invited James Baldwin, Stanley Edgar Hyman, Randall Jarrell; and to introduce the hard note of professional experience in debasing our culture, I suppose, they invited Frank Stanton, President of Columbia Broadcasting System, and me.

The Tamiment Conference was about as good as any I ever attended. The papers presented there were published in a book called Culture for the Millions? and sub-titled Mass Media in Modern Society. It is, I think, an excellent symposium—even though the flap of the jacket begins: "In this lively and entertaining book. . . ." How the pure of mind have fallen—into the very vocabulary of the hucksters they correctly castigate for spurious excitation! Culture for the Millions? is often provocative and sometimes profound, but it is not, by even the most charitable verdict, either "lively" or "entertaining." This is what happens when scientists, like paperback publishers or fountain-pen salesmen, try to lure customers into buying their wares.

I made myself miserable during a week on the beach in Florida, brooding over the paper I was to present in the Poconos. I was, after all, tarnished by concourse with "mass circulation" on Madison Avenue. In the end, I simply composed a list of the charges commonly leveled against television, movies,

and magazines—and responded to them as best I could. An introduction and
a coda rounded out the essay you may read below. I hope you will.

★

Most intellectuals do not understand the inherent nature of the mass media. They do not understand the process by which a newspaper or magazine, movie or television show, is created. They project their own tastes, yearnings, and values upon the masses—who do not, unfortunately, share them. They attribute over-simplified motivations to those who own or operate the mass media. They assume that changes in ownership or control would necessarily improve the product. They presume the existence of a vast reservoir of talent, competence, and material which does not in fact exist.

A great deal of what appears in the mass media is dreadful tripe and treacle: inane in content, banal in style, muddy in reasoning, mawkish in sentiment, vulgar, naïve, and offensive to men of learning or refinement. I am both depressed and distressed by the bombardment of our eyes, our ears, and our brains by meretricious material designed for a populace whose paramount preferences involve "fun."

Why is this so? Are the media operated by cynical men motivated solely by profit? Are they controlled by debasers of culture—by ignorant, vulgar, irresponsible men?

Many intellectuals think so and say so. They think so and say so in the face of evidence they either do not examine or cannot bring themselves to accept: that when the public is free to choose among various products, it chooses—again and again and again—the frivolous as against the serious, "escape" as against reality, the lurid as against the tragic, the trivial as against the serious, fiction as against fact, the diverting as against the significant. To conclude otherwise is to deny the data: circulation figures for the press, box-office receipts for the movies and the theater, audience measurement for radio and television programs.

The sad truth seems to be this: that relatively few people in any society, not excluding Periclean Athens, have reasonably good taste or care deeply about ideas. Fewer still seem equipped—by temperament and capacity, rather than education—to handle ideas with both skill and pleasure.

The deficiencies of mass media are a function, in part at least, of the deficiencies of the masses. Is it unfair to ask that responsibility for mental laziness and deplorable taste be distributed—to include the schools, the churches, the parents, the social institutions which produce those masses who persist in preferring pin-ball games to anything remotely resembling philosophy?

Intellectuals seem unable to reconcile themselves to the fact that their hunger for more news, better plays, more serious debate, deeper involvement in ideas, is not a hunger characteristic of many. They cannot believe that the subjects dear to their hearts bore or repel or overtax the capacities of their fellow citizens. Why this is so I shall try to explore later. At this point, let me remark that the intellectual, who examines his society with unyielding and antiseptic detachment, must liberate himself from the myths (or, in Plato's term, the royal lie) by which any social system operates. It is ironic that intellectuals often destroy old myths to erect and reverence special myths of their own. A striking example is found in the clichés with which they both characterize and indict the mass media. Let us consider the principal particulars in that indictment.*

"The mass media lack originality."

They certainly do. Most of what appears in print, or on film, or on the air, lacks originality. But is there any area of human endeavor of which this is not true? Is not the original as rare in science or philosophy or painting as it is in magazines? Is not the original "original" precisely because it is rare? Is it not self-evident that the more that is produced of anything, the smaller the proportion of originality is likely to be? But is the absolute number of novel creative products thereby reduced? Are we dealing with Gresham's Law—or with imperfect observation?

The mass media are not characterized by endless inventiveness and variation. But they are considerably more varied and inventive, given their built-in limitations, than we give them credit for. Consider these limitations: neither life nor truth nor fiction offers infinite choices: there is only a limited number of plots or stories or themes; there is only a limited number of ways of communicating the limited body of material; audiences develop a cumulative awareness of resemblances and an augmented resistance to the stylized and the predictable; and even the freshest departures from routine soon become familiar and routine. Besides, originality is often achieved at the price of "balance" or proportion: the most arresting features in, say, *The New Yorker* or *Time* often incure the displeasure of scholars precisely because these journals prefer vitality to a judicious ordering of "all the facts."

The artist, of course, wrests freshness and new insight from the most familiar material; but true artists, in any field at any given time, are so rare that their singularity requires a special word—"genius."

* For the best general summary, and critical comment, see Chapter XV in *The Fabric of Society*, by Ralph Ross and Ernest van den Haag (Harcourt, Brace & Co., 1957), a work of remarkable lucidity and good sense.

bation, venereal disease, abortion, dope addiction, in ways not so easily undertaken on television or film. The reader reads alone—and this is a fact of great importance to those who write for him.

"The mass media do not give the public enough or adequate information about the serious problems of our time."

Never in history has the public been offered so much, so often, in such detail, for so little. I do not mean that Americans know as much as intellectuals think they ought to know, or wish they did know, about the problems which confront us. I do mean that the media already offer the public far more news, facts, information, and interpretations than the public takes the trouble to digest. I find it impossible to escape the conclusion that, apart from periods of acute crisis, most people do not want to be *involved* in precisely those areas which the intellectual finds most absorbing and meaningful.

Consider these recent authors and subjects in popular journalism: Winston Churchill on the war; Harry S Truman on the presidency; Geoffrey Crowther on United States-British relations; William O. Douglas on Russia; Dean Acheson on Berlin; Joseph Alsop on Suez; George Kennan on Europe; Henry Kissinger on nuclear weapons; Adlai Stevenson on nine different countries and their problems; Nehru on India and the West; Ben-Gurion on the Middle East.

I wonder how many academic journals have been more relevant or edifying.

Do intellectuals find it unnoteworthy that, year after year, four to five times as many citizens in New York City choose the *Daily News* as against the New York *Times* or *Herald Tribune?* Or that for decades the citizens of Chicago have preferred the Chicago *Tribune* to competitors closer to the intellectuals' heart? Or that for decades the people of Los Angeles have voted in favor of the Los Angeles *Times*, at the expense of less parochial competitors?

"The aesthetic level of the mass media is appalling: truth is sacrificed to the happy ending, escapism is exalted, romance, violence, melodrama prevail."

The mass media do not attempt to please intellectuals, on either the aesthetic or the conceptual plane. Some commentators believe that if the media offered the public less trivia, the taste of the public would perforce be improved. But if the media give the public too little of what they want, and too much of what they don't want (too soon), they would simply cease to be mass media—and would be replaced by either "massier" competitors or would drive the public to increased expenditures of time on sports, parlor games, gambling, and other familiar methods of protecting the self from the ardors of thought or the terrors of solitude.

The question of proportion (how much "light stuff" or staple insipidity to include as against how much heavy or "uplifting" material) is one of the more perplexing problems any editor faces. It is far from uncommon to hear an editor remark that he will run a feature which he knows will be read by "less than 5 per cent of our readers."

I suspect that intellectuals tend to judge the highbrow by its peaks and the nonhighbrow by its average. If we look at the peaks in both cases, how much do the mass media suffer by comparison? American movies, for instance, caught in staggering costs (and, therefore, risks), have produced, in a short span of time, such films as *The Bridge on the River Kwai, Marty, The African Queen, Twelve Angry Men, The Defiant Ones, High Noon, The Sheepman, Seven Brides for Seven Brothers*, etc.

Television, beset by the problem of a heterogeneous audience, and submitting to the disgraceful practice of advertisers permitted to exercise editorial censorship, has produced some extraordinary news and documentary programs, and such dramas as: *Middle of the Night, Patterns, Little Moon of Alban, Days of Wine and Roses, The Bridge of San Luis Rey, The Winslow Boy, Requiem for a Heavyweight*. CBS's "Camera Three" recently presented, with both skill and taste, three programs dramatizing Dostoevski's *Notes from the Underground, A File for Fathers* (scenes from Lord Chesterfield, Lewis Carroll, Oscar Wilde), *Père Goriot*, Chekhov's *The Proposal*.

In my opinion, some of the more insightful work of our time can be found in the mass media, for example, the comic strip *Peanuts*, which throws an original and enchanting light on children; the comic strip *Li'l Abner*, which is often both as illuminating and as savage as social satire should be; the movies of, say, William Wyler, George Stevens, Jules Dassin, John Huston, David Lean, Delbert Mann.

Intellectuals generally discover "artists" in the popular arts long after the public, with less rarefied aesthetic categories, has discovered them. Perhaps there is rooted in the character structure of intellectuals an aversion, or an inability, to participate in certain sectors of life; they do seem blind to the fact that the popular can be meritorious. This changes with time (e.g., consider the reputations of Twain, Dickens, Dumas, Balzac, Lardner). And a Jack Benny or Phil Silvers may yet achieve the classic dimension now permitted the Marx Brothers, who—once despised as broad vaudevillians—have become the eggheads' delight.

"The mass media corrupt and debase public taste; they create the kind of audience that enjoys cheap and trivial entertainment."

This implies that demand (public taste or preference) has become a spurious function of manipulated supply. Here the evidence from Great Britain is illuminating: for years the government-owned BBC and the admirable Third Program offered the British public superior fare: excellent music, learned talks, literate discussions. For years, the noncommercial radio defended the bastions of culture. Yet when the British public was offered choices on television, it dismayed Anglophiles by taking to its heart the same silly quiz shows, panel shows, Westerns, melodramas, and "situation comedies" which the critics of daily newspapers deplore both in London and New York.

Or consider what happened in March, 1959, when the Granada TV network, a British commercial chain, presented *The Skin of Our Teeth* with no less a star than Vivien Leigh—and in her first appearance on television. The noncommercial BBC ran, opposite the Wilder play and Lady Vivien, a twenty-five-year-old American movie, *Follow the Fleet*, with Ginger Rogers and Fred Astaire. The English critics sang rare hosannahs for Thornton Wilder's play, its glamorous star, the script, the direction, the production. But for every seventeen homes in London that chose the Pulitzer Prize play, sixty-six preferred the twenty-five-year-old musical. Outside of London, the ratio was even more depressing. Viewers by the millions, reported Reuters, switched their dials away from Wilder and Leigh to Fred and Ginger. The head of the Granada network even castigated the BBC in the press, urging that it be "ashamed of itself" for seducing a public that might have adored Art by offering it Entertainment. (A similar *contretemps* occurred on American television when the magnificent production of *Green Pastures* lost viewers by the millions to the ghastly *Mike Todd Party* in Madison Square Garden.) The final and crushing irony lies in the fact that *Follow the Fleet* put a BBC program among the first ten, in popularity, for the first time in the year.

Doubtless the mass media can do more, much more, to elevate what the public reads, sees, and hears. But the media cannot do this as easily or as rapidly as is often assumed. Indeed, they cannot get too far in front of their audiences without suffering the fate of predecessors who tried just that. There is considerable evidence to support the deflating view that the media, on the whole, are considerably *ahead* of the masses—in intelligence, in taste, in values; e.g., the vocabulary in almost any popular journal, not excluding fan magazines, is often too "highbrow" for its readers.

It seems to me a fair question to ask whether the intelligence or taste of the public is really worse today than it was before the mass media came along.

*"The mass media are what they are because they are
operated solely as money-making enterprises."*

Publishers and producers are undoubtedly motivated by a desire for profits.
But this is not *all* that motivates them. Publishers and producers are no less
responsive than intellectuals to "ego values"; they are no less eager to win
respect and respectability from their peers; they respond to both internalized
and external "reference groups"; they seek esteem—from the self and from
others.

Besides, producers know that a significant percentage of what they present
in the mass media will not be as popular as what might be substituted—but
it is presented nonetheless. Why? Partly because of nonpecuniary values, and
partly because of what critics of the crass profit-motive seem blind to: the
fact that part of the competitive process involves a continuous search for
products which can win favor with audiences not attracted to, or satisfied by,
the prevailing output. New and minority audiences are constantly courted
by the media, e.g., the strictly "egghead" programs on television, the new
magazines which arise, and flourish, because they fill a need, as *Scientific
American, American Heritage.*

Whenever profits, used as either a carrot or a stick, are criticized, it is
tacitly assumed that reliance on other human impulses would serve man
better. Is this so? Do virtue, probity, self-sacrifice guarantee excellence? It
seems to me that most of the horrors of human history have been the work
not of skeptical or cynical or realistic men, but of those persuaded of their
superior virtue.

To replace publication for profit by publication via subsidy would of
course be to exchange one set of imperfections for another.* The postal system offers scant support to those who assume that non-profit enterprise is
necessarily better than private competition (I hasten to add that in some fields
e.g., public health, it clearly is).

It should be noted, parenthetically, that anyone who enters the magazine
or newspaper field in the expectation of high profits is either singularly
naïve, extremely optimistic, or poorly informed: few areas of American business show so high a mortality rate, are plagued by such unpredictabilities,
promise so many headaches, and return so low a net profit. Successful magazines earn as modest a profit as three percent on invested capital. To the

---

* It is unthinkable, for instance, that any open competitive system would have barred
from the air someone like Winston Churchill—who was not given access to BBC, for his
then-maverick opinions, from 1934 to 1939. Nor is it likely that a government-controlled
network would be able to withstand the furor that followed CBS's initial interview with
Nikita Khrushchev. Nor would a governmentally supervised program dare to present a show
such as *The Plot to Kill Stalin.*

purely profit-minded, business has long offered innumerable opportunities outside of publishing which far surpass it in profitability, security, or potential.

"The mass media are dominated—or too much influenced—by advertisers."

The influence of advertising is often too great—even if that influence is one-tenth as potent as many assume it to be. The editorial function should be as free of non-editorial influences as possible.

But publishers, producers, and editors would respond to power or influence *even if all advertising were abolished*. It is an inescapable fact of human organization that men adjust to power (that, indeed, is one of power's attributes); that men consider, or try to anticipate, the effect of their acts on those who hold most of whatever is most prized in a society.

There is a reverse and paradoxical angle to advertising: when a newspaper or magazine, a radio or television station becomes successful, the advertiser needs it as much as the other way around. Revenues from many advertisers increase the capacity to resist pressure from individual advertisers. Organs which can be "bought" nearly always decline in prosperity and influence.

Purely professional calculations often override vested interest. Some news or stories are so significant that it is impossible to prevent their publication.

The instance of the cigarette industry, mentioned above, is worth notice. Tobacco companies represent one of the largest and most consistent sources of national advertising revenue. Yet within an hour after medical reports appeared linking cigarette smoking to lung cancer, they were fully and dramatically presented to the public—not only on the front pages of newspapers but in radio and television reporting as well. The news was simply too big, too "newsworthy" to be suppressed (even though several discussion programs shied away from the subject). The deficiencies of automobiles, where safety is concerned, have been analyzed in magazines which receive huge advertising revenues from automobile companies.

This is not to say that all truths which threaten power—in business, in the arts, even in the groves of academe—always gain as swift and public an airing as they deserve. They often do not. They do not because men, even men in power, are often timid, or weak, or frightened, or avaricious, or opportunistic, or unwise, or short-sighted. Some media operators, like some politicians, some clergymen, some labor leaders, some economists, are overly sensitive to the side on which their bread is buttered.

There is another and telling body of evidence about advertising on which no one, so far as I know, has commented: motion pictures accept no advertisements, never did, never depended on it, and were never "at the mercy of advertisers."* Yet of all the mass media, it is the movies which have been most parochial and timorous. Is it because movies do depend entirely on box-office receipts, and have no advertising revenues to subsidize independence?

Advertisers seem to me to exercise their most pernicious influence in television. For in television, advertisers are permitted to decide what shall or shall not appear in the programs they sponsor. This seems to me insupportable. An advertiser in a newspaper or magazine buys a piece of space in which to advertise his product. He does not buy a voice on the news desk or at the editorial table. But the television advertiser buys time both for his commercials and for *the time between commercials*; he becomes a producer and publisher himself. I am convinced that this is bad for the public, bad for television, and (ultimately) bad for the sponsors.†

"The mass media do not provide an adequate forum for minority views—the dissident and unorthodox."

Producers and publishers give more space and time to minority views (which include the *avant-garde*) than numerical proportions require. They feel that it is the function of specialized journals to carry specialized content. The popular media carry far more material of this kind than anyone would have predicted two decades ago. They hunger for the *interesting*.

The democratic society must insure a viable public forum for the dissenter—in politics, morals, arts. That forum will never be as large as the dissenters themselves want. But I know of no perfect way to determine who shall have what access to how many—at the expense of whom else—except to keep pressing for as free a market as we can achieve.

It may seem to some readers that I have substituted an indictment of the masses for an indictment of the mass media; that I have assigned the role of villain to the masses in a social drama in which human welfare and public enlightenment are hamstrung by the mediocrity, laziness, and indifference of the populace. I hope that detachment will not be mistaken for cynicism.

I should be the first to stress the immensity of the social gains which public education and literacy alone have made possible. The rising public appreciation of music, painting, ballet; the growth of libraries; the fantastic sales of paperback books (however much they are skewed by *Peyton Place* or the works of Mickey Spillane), the striking diffusion of "cultural activities" in

---

* Some movie theaters show advertisements on their screens before and after a feature, but advertising is not to be found *in* movies.

† When I wrote a similar criticism in *Harper's Magazine* in 1958, certain television executives hotly denied this. That was eighteen months before the recent and sensational revelations of advertiser-control over quiz shows.

communities throughout the land, the momentous fact that popular magazines *can* offer the public the ruminations of such nonpopular minds as Paul Tillich or Sir George Thomson—the dimensions of these changes are a tribute to the achievements of that society which has removed from men the chains of caste and class that hampered human achievement through the centuries. I, for one, do not lament the passing of epochs in which "high culture" flourished while the majority of mankind lived in ignorance and indignity.

What I have been emphasizing here is the inevitable gap between the common and the superior. More particularly, I have been embroidering the theme of the intellectual's curious reluctance to accept evidence. Modern intellectuals seem *guilty* about reaching conclusions that were once the *a priori* convictions of the aristocrat. It is understandable that twentieth-century intellectuals should dread snobbery, at one end of the social scale, as much as they shun mob favor at the other. But the intellectuals' snobbery is of another order, and involves a tantalizing paradox: a contempt for what *hoi polloi* enjoy, and a kind of proletarian ethos that tacitly denies inequalities of talent and taste.

The recognition of facts has little bearing on motivations and should surely not impute preferences. The validity of an idea has nothing to do with who propounds it—or whom it outrages. The author is aware that he is inviting charges of Brahminism, misanthropy, a reactionary "unconscious," or heaven knows what else. But is it really heresy to the democratic credo for intellectuals to admit, if only in the privacy of professional confessionals, that they are, in fact, more literate and more skillful—in diagnosis, induction, and generalization, if in nothing else—than their fellow-passengers on the ship of state?

Perhaps the intellectual's guilt, when he senses incipient snobbery within himself, stems from his uneasiness at being part of an elite, moreover, a new elite which is not shored up by ancient and historic sanctions. For intellectualism has been divorced from its traditional *cachet* and from the majesty with which earlier societies invested their elites: a classical education, Latin or Greek (in any case, a language not comprehensible to the untutored), a carefully cultivated accent, the inflection of the well born, the well bred, or the priestly. One of the painful experiences spared intellectuals in the past was hearing Ideas discussed—with profundity or insight—in accents which attest to birth on "the other side of the tracks."

It may be difficult for shopkeepers' sons to admit their manifest superiority over the world they left: parents, siblings, comrades. But the intellectual who struggles with a sinful sense of superiority, and who feels admirable sentiments of loyalty to his non-U origins, must still explain why it was that his playmates and classmates did not join him in the noble dedication to learning and the hallowed pursuit of truth. The triumph of mass education is to be found not simply in the increment of those who can read, write, add, and subtract. It is to be found in a much more profound and enduring revolution: the provision of opportunities to express the self, and pursue the self's values, opportunities not limited to the children of a leisure class, or an aristocracy, or a landed gentry, or a well-heeled bourgeoisie. The true miracle of public education is that no elite can decide where the next intellectual will come from.

Each generation creates its own devils, and meets its own Waterloo on the heartless field of reality. The Christian Fathers blamed the Prince of Darkness for preventing perfectible man from reaching Paradise. Anarchists blamed the state. Marxists blame the class system. Pacifists blame the militarists. And our latter-day intellectuals seem to blame the mass media for the lamentable failure of more people to attain the bliss of intellectual grace. This is a rank disservice to intellectuals themselves, for it dismisses those attributes of character and ability—discipline, curiosity, persistence, the renunciation of worldly rewards—which make intellectuals possible at all. The compulsive egalitarianism of eggheads even seems to lure them into a conspicuous disinterest in the possible determinism of heredity.

Responsibility increases with capacity, and should be demanded of those in positions of power. Just as I hold the intellectual more responsible than others for the rigorous exploration of phenomena and the courageous enunciation of truths, so, too, do I ask for better and still better performance from those who have the awesome power to shape men's minds.

"We Hold These Truths . . ."

★

THIS APPEARED as the lead article in an issue of Look that was devoted to one theme: "Where We Stand." I had often thought of trying to reduce the ideas on which a democratic order really rests to as concise, precise, and irreducible a set of propositions as possible. I am still, you see, a nag, driven by the need to try to reduce concepts to formulae, or at least to cut the fat and fluff of thinking away from the meat. I also admire the epigram.

"We Hold These Truths . . ." was awarded a gold medal from the National Conference of Christians and Jews.

★

H. L. Mencken used to delight in describing these United States as "a mob of serfs" whose average intelligence is so low that any citizen who has read a dozen books and does not believe in hobgoblins is sure to be a roaring success. No phase of American life escaped the merciless fusillade of Mencken's mockery: the church, women, the home, the YMCA, the press, mother love, patriotism. He lambasted the courts, the Congress, and the clergy. He named judges he considered crooked, politicians he considered scoundrels, reformers he considered frauds, and ministers he considered morons. He had the sharpest eye since Mark Twain for anything that partook of the phony or that threatened to tread on that holiest of holy ground: individual freedom.

It is a testimonial to the American way of life that Mencken was neither tried for treason nor lynched. You may wonder how he escaped it. Yet there is no real cause for wonder. The secret lies in that consensus that is at the heart of what we mean by freedom: We defend the rights of those we hate or fear or despise.

231

The greatest political invention known to the race of man is the idea that men shall be protected in their right to criticize the state itself: that every man shall be free to think what he pleases, read what he pleases, say what he pleases—so long as it is within the bounds of decency and does not incite others to violence.

The entire structure of our freedom rests on political ground rules that separate opinions from crimes, the unpopular from the subversive, the disturbing from the dangerous. To distinguish ideas from deeds, what a man says from what he does, is something tyrants, lunatics, demagogues and Communists cannot understand. Being too fanatical to tolerate argument, the political barbarians punish men for asking questions and slaughter them for raising doubts.

It is one of the crowning ironies of politics that the far Left and the far Right have more in common with each other than either does with the middle. For both the radical Left and the reactionary Right are enemies of moderation. They talk of freedom, but are driven by fanaticism. They may espouse democracy, but do not begin to understand its very heart: civil liberties. If we visualized politics not as a straight line, with a left and right, but as a circle—the far Left and Right would meet, as they should. For they have this in common: They would use force to enforce their prejudices. They feel threatened by diversity. They would, if they could, beat up, imprison, deport, or kill a good many of us.

Democracy is the only political system that makes it possible to effect *change without violence*. Under no other form of government is it possible to rearrange the structure of power without killing off some people, disenfranchising others, jailing or exiling a good many. (The British can legislate more sweeping changes on shorter notice than we can, since Parliament is not hobbled by constitutional chains; we may all thank God that Congress is.)

We govern ourselves by rules that describe the ways in which we can even remove our governors. And a society of maximum liberties works only because we accept the obligation to check the natural human impulse to beat up those we dislike, imprison those we fear, or murder those we hate. Democracy works because of ten central ideas we have made sacred:

1. Political power is power over others, and power over others must always be watched, guarded, circumscribed.

2. No man, no group, no sect, no party ever has a monopoly on truth, virtue and competence.

3. This means that no man, no group, no party is wise enough *and* good enough *and* sane enough to be entrusted with too much power. For good men are often silly, and competent men are often wicked, and even the combination of virtue and ability in no way guarantees judgment or reason

The artist is driven by the demon of his talent—always, incessantly, often beyond his capacity to understand, much less control. He is driven by the need to express that talent and, through it, to express himself. He is enslaved by the compulsion to communicate, to say something, to make a personal statement, to share his feelings, his insight, his visions, his sense of revelation. Above all, he is beholden to the necessity of *creating* something (it may be beautiful, it may be horrifying), something that did not exist before. He can create it only out of his own inner and insistent universe . . .

We find ourselves impressed by the endless richness of art, the miraculous singularity of an artist's visions, the astounding variety of ways there are of seeing the world around us. Most of all, we marvel at what painters have created out of their own unconscious universe, to make it a new part of ours.

The simple but startling fact is that painters *see* differently from the rest of us. This process we call "seeing," which we all take for granted, is unbelievably complicated. We see not what is "real" (a phantom seems real enough to one terrified by it), but what we have been conditioned to think of as "real." The human eye is a lens, to be sure, but that lens only receives images; and these images are referred back to the brain, where they must be patterned and given meaning. And meaning is a convention; it stems from our education and our expectations.

Constable once said that seeing is itself an art and that even seeing nature is an art that must be learned. Degas, that irascible genius, declared: "Drawing is not what one sees, but what others have to be made to see."

Does this idea seem preposterous? The brilliant art authority, E. H. Gombrich, reminds us that ancient artists used to draw eyelashes on the lower lids of horses. There are no lashes on the lower eyelids of horses. Still, the artists "saw" them there, because they were so accustomed to seeing lashes on men's lower lids. A great painter, as skillful a recorder of "reality" as you could ask for, made certain mistakes in drawing the heart, from cadavers opened for examination, because he had been reading Galen—and Galen was wrong. Even so impeccable a draftsman as Dürer made certain errors in drawing the human eye because his own vision was skewed by the fallacious stereotypes of his day.

What we call "reality" is not much more than those perceptions that pass through the filters of our conditioning. We all live, in part, within the conceptual past. It is the great, revolutionary role of the artist to liberate us from the strait jackets of the too-familiar.

Does all this seem unreal to you? Do you believe in a realness, an absoluteness of things visible to anyone and everyone alike? Perhaps you are thinking, "All this is intellectual quibbling. Reality is simple enough. Just set a camera down and press the trigger—and *that* will record exactly what is 'there'!"

Well, let us test that out. Suppose you take a camera and set out to photograph, say, a house. Any house. You want "just a picture of a house." Now consider the decisions you will have to make—consciously or unconsciously, intuitively or by default. From what distance shall the house be photographed? From far away? From near? From the middle? Then at what angle? How high? How low? All these depend, of course, on what kind of picture you want—indeed, what kind of house you want to portray. And that depends on what impression or mood or detail you want to present. If the house is seen from a low angle, that will emphasize its height. If seen from a hill looking down, it will look different. "Just straight on," you say? Very well, is the sycamore to the left to be included? The azalea on the right? The ridge beyond? Will you include the rail fence there, the rock here, the curving path? You will soon notice that each position, each view, changes the total field of vision, and each contains its own cluster of characteristics.

"Enough!" you cry? But you have much more to decide. Do you want to make this house crisp-clear in all its particulars—shutters, windows, shingles? That will also make sharp a mass of unpretty and disturbing objects around. Do you want the scene made pastoral, scary, sad? Shall the sky be ignored or brought forward? A filter can make the clouds leap toward the eye. Even moonlight need not be the prerogative of the moon alone; infrared film can transform the sun into its sister.

Well, suppose you take your picture, whatever it is. You are in the darkroom now. You have your negative. You are about to print your picture. Now a new army of possibilities marches before you. You can print any part of the picture. You can "crop" out the top, the bottom, either side or both. You can magnify a detail to achieve a quite unexpected effect. You can take that innocuous house you recorded on film and endow it with shadows or highlights, make it saccharine or sinister. You can change the visual impact by selecting different papers on which to print your image. You can—but perhaps this is enough.

No two photographers take precisely the same picture of the identical subject, even if they try to, because there are different emotions and mentalities behind the different lenses. The difference between a photograph taken by an amateur and one taken by a master is as great as the difference between a jingle and a sonata.

If what we have said here is true of photography, consider how much more powerfully it applies to painting. Any camera, lens, film, or filter contains certain mechanical limitations, none of which confines the painter. An artist can draw what no camera can photograph. No camera can record the images in a man's mind. No camera contains the flexibility and resourcefulness of the human hand, to say nothing of the immense imaginative possibilities of the human brain.

It is the multitudinous differences in vision and visual sensitivity; in the sensing of arrangement and accident; in the apprehension of line, light, color, form, mass, space; in recognizing unsuspected attributes of beauty, power, grace; in opening new windows of perception to surprise—it is the wonderful variations in these, to say nothing of differences in sheer skill, that distinguish the creative artist from his fellow men.

As Leonardo put it: "If the painter wishes to see beauties to fall in love with, it is in his power to bring them forth, and if he wants to see monstrous things that frighten or are foolish or laughable or indeed to be pitied, he is their Lord and God."

The artist, we have said, frees us from the bonds of tradition. He gives us new eyes, eyes with which we can see "reality" anew, aspects of reality we did not dream were there. They were not, in fact, "there," until he created them. A Japanese master was once asked, "What is the most difficult part of a picture?" He answered, "The part that is to be left out."

Was ever a woman's face as mysterious, as cool and lovely, as Botticelli painted it in "Primavera"?

Where, in any garden on earth, are there flowers so close to visual music as those from Redon's hand and heart?

Is deformity ever as final and as harsh as that which Bruegel assigned his "The Beggars"?

We have all been taught, through the eyes and minds and artistry of such men, to extract fresh meaning from the confusing, unstructured plenitude of objects, details, impressions, distractions that clamor all around us. We have all been led to find beauty where previous generations did not dream it lay concealed. There is truth, no less than mischief, in Oscar Wilde's aphorism: "Nature imitates art."

The moral to all this is perhaps best found, as it so often is, in an anecdote. A woman who "knew what she liked in art" was visiting Matisse's studio. She studied the painting on his easel for a while, then said, "You have made the arm on that girl much too *long*." To which Matisse made this shattering rejoinder: "Madame, that is not a girl; it is a picture."

The Scientist: The Creative Idea

★

THE LINKAGES BETWEEN ART *and science began to surprise and intrigue me about ten years ago. I started lecturing on the creative process and the creative personality not because I knew very much about them, but because it gave me a chance to structure my ideas. I also started asking psychologists and psychoanalysts how much they knew, or could guess, about the extraordinary way in which original minds, in science no less than art, counterpoint discipline and imagination, order and invention, system and insight. The late Ernst Kris urged me to commit some of my own guesses to print, as did Warren Weaver, that rare amalgam of clarity and sophistication.*

Today, of course, research projects on The Creative Process *or* The Creative Afflatus Amongst Kurds and Serbo-Croatians *crowd the catalogues of the best foundations and jostle one another on campuses as far as the human eye can see.*

In 1960, by an act of God, I was invited to spend a year in the Berkeley colony of the University of California, as a Visiting Professor. My duties involved no heavy lifting; I was required only to be in residence and pursue whatever researches engaged my interest. Well, I happen to be able to reside with great ease, and I spent a marvelous year in reading, ruminating, and palaver. "The Creative Idea," which follows, is a by-product of that year in Berkeley. It was first unleashed as a lecture at Columbia University, as part of the festivities commemorating the seventy-fifth anniversary of Teachers College. I edited the speech for publication in the Teachers College Record *(May, 1963) and have reluctantly omitted many passages here. Certain themes may echo certain trumpets sounded on earlier pages of this miscellany. Too bad.* ★

238

The history of man's politics is a shameful chronicle of violence, greed, hate, vanity, foolish ambitions and parochial fears.

The history of man's beliefs is an absurd story of ignorance, credulity, superstition, infantile terror, and magical beguilements.

The history of man's ideas is a story of incredible stupidity, relieved by the occasional, sparkling eruption of gifted or original minds.

It is impossible to spend twenty-four hours on this planet without encountering, in ordinary life, several hundred examples of folly, irrationality, lunacy, self-deception, buncombe, or idolatry. Common sense is certainly not very common. *Non sequiturs* seem to be dear to the human heart, and preference or wish-fulfillment seem to be the most powerful of human drives.

I sometimes think that the central fact about our race, the one commanding generalization, is this: We see what we want to see and hear what we want to hear, for we flee from the necessity of re-structuring our cherished models of the universes we have conceptualized. We feel threatened by truly new ideas.

The ideas of Newton, which baffled all but a handful of men in his time, are quite easily understood by high school students today. And the ideas of Einstein, which you and I find so difficult to comprehend, will not be difficult for the next generation to take for granted.

Every day in the United States, in some home with a child of, say, six or seven, a parent is asked, "Why is two and two four?" And every day the answer is given, "Now, Johnny, don't be silly. It just *is*." In fact, the question is a terribly interesting one, to which many answers can be given—not the least important of which is that two and two make four in *one* system of counting, but we might devise others in which this is not necessarily the answer.

Every day in the United States, children are brought right up to a moment of great importance in the human experience, but are not told how exciting and fruitful this moment can be. This moment comes during multiplication table drills. "Johnny, how much is two and two?" "Four." "Mary, how much is two times three?" "Six." "Jack, two times *what* equals ten?" Jack says, "Five," and the lesson proceeds and the precious moment is passed. The teacher or parent could have said, "At this moment you are standing before one of the great inventions of the human mind—the concept of x. 'Two times *what* equals ten?' can also be asked this way, 'Two x equals ten.'" X, the unknown, can be taught at a very early age, not deferred until that frustrating, exasperating subject called algebra, which is not mentioned until high school.

Over and over, our fallacious customs lead us to teach a convention as if it is an irrevocable truth. As parents, as teachers, as citizens, we go on teaching one way of thinking as if it is the only proper way of thinking. We all cling to the familiar, to the conventional, because it is safe, because we are uneasy in the presence of ambiguity. What lies beyond convention is precisely that wonderful ambiguity in which the artist, the scientist, the theoretician finds himself most at home. It is in this area that creative men play their great and commanding role, for it is the creative mind that *dares*—whether in the arts, or science or philosophy. It dares to look freshly. perception—or, better, orthodox distortions of perception. The original mind *dares*—whether in the arts, or science, or philosophy. It dares to look freshly.

It wasn't until the nineteenth century that adults had the nerve to do with paint what children have always done—put color into shadows, paint metaphors, as it were—that is, paint a face green because that is the face of envy, or a face red because that is the face of rage. Have we not chastised the freshness of children all these centuries by saying, "Now, Johnny, that's perfectly silly! That isn't the way a face (or an apple, or a tree) *really* looks!" Isn't it?

Now if we must re-learn so simple a thing as seeing, think of how much more we must re-learn those areas where theory, complexity, abstractions are involved. Physics, for instance, is a science that moved along clumsily, slowly, crudely, and through models that were built by bright men, in their minds, to clarify the phenomena they were observing. These models were patched up, reinforced, revised, made to work—until someone came along who had the courage to ask a simple question, a question that challenged, and in so doing destroyed, the prevailing model—to replace it with another.

Not until Newton did someone ask himself *not*, "Why does the apple fall?" (they knew about gravity in those days) but, "Why does the apple fall straight down, towards the center of the earth, even though the earth itself is moving?" Newton proceeded to ask a series of questions which could be answered in a way that seemed absolutely fantastic: that the planetary system can be understood if all the great bodies act as if their entire gravitational pull, their entire mass, is *concentrated in one hypothetical pinpoint* at the center. Newton proceeded to work out the laws by which to support this hypothesis.

It was Darwin who asked himself, among other things, "Where does the human race come from?" Was it Riemann or Lobachevsky who asked, "But *is* a straight line really the shortest distance between two points— for instance, on a curved surface?" It was Rutherford who asked, "Can it be that inside the atom, this tiny, tiny, supposedly irreducible core of matter, is another universe—with a center and whirling bodies that duplicate the structure of the universe itself?"

But let us pause. None of these men really asked these questions in the way I have put them. I just think we can better understand some of the problems they raised and solved if we formulate them in the kinds of questions I have suggested. (Rutherford, for instance, discovered the nucleus of the atom in 1911—but didn't know it. He wrote Hahn in 1913 about the surprisingly large angle at which particles bounced off a thin metal screen or foil; he was absorbed in the relationship of these angles, and the distances to the imaginary center of the atom; and apparently it wasn't until Niels Bohr told him what he had uncovered that Rutherford fully realized what was going on.)

Or consider Einstein, who asked such questions as, "But what do we really mean by 'simultaneous'?" Are two things happening "simultaneously" if simply observed so? Then what about observers in different positions? What about an event witnessed from the position of a man on a train that is speeding *towards* the event, as against a man on the ground, who is not moving?

It wasn't until Sigmund Freud that men really asked, "*Why* do people make mistakes—in spelling, writing, talking? Is there a reason—a reason they do not themselves suspect?" Or, "What do dreams mean?"—not what do they predict; not what possible magic or prescience is in them; but what is this particular person, in this dream, trying to *say* to himself? Is there a special, secret, symbolic language in dreams? Or, "Is it possible that men love and hate the same object?" Or, "Can it be that someone does not know that he knows something?" Can one part of the self be cut off from the remainder; and can it become known—not through reason, analyzing, deliberate effort, but through the deliberate avoidance of reason, in a process of free and random associations, a process of undirected, foolish, irrelevant, uncensored verbal productions? Can man ever *not* be relevant?

Some years ago, in a talk to a group of psychoanalysts, I commented on the fact, so striking to me, that it has taken so very long for the human race to come upon, much less incorporate, ideas of this kind; and I read the following passage to them, a passage I am sure you will all easily recognize:

Every man appears to have certain instincts, but in some persons they are subjected to the control of reason, and the better desires prevailing over them, they are either wholly suppressed or reduced in strength. I mean particularly those desires which are awake when the taming power of the personality is asleep; for it is in sleep that the wild beast in our nature stands up and walks about naked, and there is no conceivable folly or shame or crime, however unnatural, not excepting incest or parricide, of which such a nature may not be guilty. In all of us, even in good men, there is a latent wild beast that peers out in sleep.

I said to the psychoanalysts, "Of course you recognize this as coming from Sigmund Freud's *The Interpretation of Dreams*. . . But, alas, it was not written by Freud at all. It was written in the year 320 B.C.—by Plato." Does it not seem remarkable to you that since all educated men in the past read the same few books (there were not so many books to read), surely thousands of them read Plato; yet hundreds of decades went by, and these words passed before how many eyes—but did not, to use a modern term, "register."

As long ago as the twelfth century, bread mould was being used to cure inflamed abscesses. The Chinese used ephedrine five thousand years ago. The Hindus used snakeroot for tranquillizers long, long before we had Miltown. And among some primitive tribes in Africa, it has long been customary, when moving from one place to another, to take along some dirt—dirt from the floor of the old shelter, to be placed inside the new one to serve as— an antibiotic. You may protest that these Africans could know nothing of micro-organisms, but are only propitiating their gods. Quite so. And yet, was this propitiation, by any chance, linked to someone's observation that there was something about old dirt that protected them against certain diseases, that gave the community protection against certain infections?

Our educational system does not teach people very well; it certainly does not teach us how to think very well, how to handle new concepts, how to solve problems. This is so not only because our educational system is poor in imaginative techniques of pedagogy, but because even the wisest of us must make a very hard effort to revise the models with which we work, the only models we have.

We like to think of scientists as men who quickly respond to facts, to evidence, to new, promising clues to the future. Nonsense. Copernicus' heliocentric model was strongly opposed not only by non-scientists, but by the greatest astronomer of his time, Tycho Brahe, who could not break with the tradition about the earth's lack of motion, and it confounded him all his life. The great Leibniz criticized Newton for omitting "providential destiny" from his model of the universe.

Nineteenth-century scientists resisted the wave theory of light, enunciated by Thomas Young, because they were so completely wedded to the notion of the corpuscular form of light.

Biologists resisted Pasteur's discovery that fermentation is not just a chemical process, and chemists scoffed at it as well. Scientists opposed Lister's germ theory of disease. They resisted Mendel's theory of genetic inheritance from 1865, when it was first announced, until the end of the century.

When Waterston suggested that gases have molecular aspects, his paper was rejected by the Royal Society as "nothing but nonsense." When Poincaré, one of the great mathematicians of his day, examined Georg Cantor's theory of sets, an historic turning point in mathematics, he (Poincaré) said, "Later generations will regard this as a disease from which one has recovered."

When Karl Pearson in 1900 used statistics to analyze a problem in biology, a resolution of the Royal Society requested that, in the future, papers on biology should not contain mathematics. When Roentgen announced X-rays, Lord Kelvin passed it off as a hoax.

People tend to assume that science can solve all problems, which is certainly not true. It is my conviction that the problems of human behavior are infinitely more complicated than any problems the physical sciences have thus far had to deal with. Here are some: How do we think? Where does an idea come from? How is an attitude formed? How can a prejudice be changed? What *is* love? What *is* aggression? What *is* insight? What *is* imagination?

It is the creative mind that can leap over obstacles and complexities—to find, through insight or intuition or imagination, surprising solutions to problems that resist systematic inquiry or orderly solution.

Now, I know no one more inept than I am about many of the things I have been discussing here. I have no aptitude whatsoever for mathematics or the physical sciences. Everything in me groans when I see an equation, flinches before the simplest device in a laboratory. But I have one characteristic it may be relevant to mention here: I am prepared to believe almost anything. I may not *understand* it, but I seem to have no anxieties about believing it, for the sake of where that belief may lead. I enjoy the game of, "Let's suppose . . ." or "Let's pretend . . ." or "Just for the fun of it . . ."

Lest you think these are trivial formulations, may I point out that these are precisely the techniques (call them "hypotheses") that are involved in scientific investigation—and surely in what we call the creative process. The capacity of the self to entertain (if only for a moment) absurd, irrational, outrageous, illogical, silly possibilities; the capacity to get pleasure out of symbolic explorations: these lie at the heart of the creative process—these plus plain daring, the *daring* to ignore what you have been told is true, to ignore past rules and reasoning and logic; the boldness to court the apparent chaos that seethes below the surface of consciousness, to plunge into the undisciplined unconscious without fear (though perhaps with anxiety, and often with ambivalence), the courage to suspend sense in the cause of provisional freedom of the mind.

Creativity, to me, is a shuttle between fancy and discipline, between imagination and system, between intuition and control, between fantasy and reason, between reverie and evidence, between imagination and analysis. It is a counterpoint, a kind of a roaring internal dialogue in which one part of the self tries to communicate with other parts of the self, in which the self breaks out of the restraints, the conventions, the crippling restrictions of what is "proper" or "reasonable" or "sensible."

The history of science, or the arts, or philosophy, is the story of those high points that are reached by men who had the rare capacity to be direct, to be infantile, stubbornly to seek the simplicities behind complexity.

The operation of the mind in creative endeavor involves an incredible amount of loneliness, and long stretches of what non-creative people are terrified of—uncertainty. I have suggested that ambiguity always lies beyond what is known, what is *safe*; and I believe that the creative personality derives pleasure out of playing there, pleasure in fantasy, in the wild guess, the sudden hunch, the glorious "But what if . . . ?" The most powerful displeasure, to the creative person, is boredom. Imagination, which is a leap into the unknown, is, I think, a defense against boredom.

Now you may think all this too abstract. You may think that the counterpoint between reason and fantasy is something men should try only after learning how to add, subtract, spell, etc. But we seem to forget that we are all *born into a symbolic universe*, and we must begin thinking by thinking symbolically. Our first and only equipment for making sense, for locating regularity, for trying to understand form, sequence, identity, meaning, is itself inchoate, wordless, pre-verbal.

Some years ago, I suggested that the world of the child is much closer to the world of Einstein than the world of Einstein is to the world of adults. (Piaget, by the way, confirms this.) I remember conducting a curious experiment one Sunday afternoon on my three children. "I want to read you something," I said. It was a passage from Eddington's *The Nature of the Physical World*, describing what happens, according to nuclear physics, when you take a step. You are stepping from emptiness into emptiness; solidity is achieved by the bombardment of billions of electrons, and so on. So I read this passage—it wasn't more than 200 words—and asked, "What do you think?"

My son, who was then twelve, said, "That sounds nutty!" My daughter, who was then nine, said, "That upsets me." My younger daughter, who was five, said, "But, of course, Daddy: *I play that game all the time.*"

Copernicus offended men by daring to say that man is not the center of the world. Darwin came along and robbed us of the illusion of the uniqueness of our species. Freud deprived us of control over our own souls. Harlow Shapley deflated the human race by locating our galaxy, the last hope of our egocentrism, way out, billions of heaven-knows-how-many-light-years away from the center of the universe. And now some people think that machines threaten to usurp or replace the uniqueness of the human mind. I am not among them.

We used to think that men could never devise machines that would do what the human brain can do; today, some think that we already possess machines that will do, or do better, whatever men can do. Both views are silly. As Ulric Neisser says in *Science*, ignorance about machines accounts for the optimism, and ignorance of human behavior accounts for the pessimism.

Machines certainly can solve problems, store information, scan and correlate and play games—but not, let me remind you, with either excitement or pleasure or the chill of discovery. And machines can't stop; they don't get bored; they don't dream; they have no feelings. Machines don't grow as men grow; they don't change as men change; they don't doubt. Machines can be set for single purposes. There is almost no human activity that doesn't contain several goals, often in conflict.

We know less about human behavior than we know about animal behavior. We still have no satisfactory general theory of human intelligence, much less of human behavior.

To unlock the awesome power of the atom was as nothing, in my judgment, compared to what will happen when we mortal men unlock the power, the beauty, the daring, the infinite imaginativeness that still reside, in secret and untapped recesses, within the human mind and spirit.

On Communication

I STILL MARVEL over how little we know about the ways in which we try to communicate with one another, and how poor, how imprecise, how fumbling are the efforts we make to capture meaning, much less convey it, in the numberless words we utter. The following fragment formed one part of "The Creative Idea," but it may be read for itself and as a stab at clarification. I have played with the puzzle of communication in many talks, especially to teachers and to writers; what surprises me is the liveliness of their response to these unresolved observations.

★

WE KNOW ALMOST NOTHING ABOUT SOME SEEMINGLY SIMPLE THINGS WE DO every day: for instance, try to communicate with someone else. We know very little about the dynamics of the process by which you can get an idea from one head into another. We do know, from preliminary investigations, that this process is far from simple, and far from as simple as it sounds. We don't know why some people are effective communicators (speakers, teachers, writers, executives) and why others (speakers, teachers, writers, executives) are not.

I have a rather disturbing theory about this interplay of selves we call communication: Most men have great and deep resistances to being communicated with. Don't go away. Consider, for a moment, what it means to listen. Not "hear," but really *listen*.

Truly to listen means to surrender control of the self. And to surrender control of the self, even for a moment, represents danger. It arouses deep anxieties, vague memories of a helplessness, a terrible vulnerability, we have all known once. To be passive may mean to be impotent, not in the sense of adult genitality but in the sense of an incapacity to prevent brutal violations. That such dangers may be unreal, foolish, absurdly exaggerated, has nothing at all to do with their power to influence or govern us. We are all, one way or another, driven by symbols. It is a delightful and tormenting paradox of human behavior that symbols are often much more "real" to us than a resolute inspection of reality would warrant. Where to draw the line between symbol and reality is, of course, one of the oldest and most perplexing problems in philosophy.

Now, the good communicator—that is, the effective communicator—is someone who, I am sure, first communicates within himself, to himself, very rapidly, before uttering a sound or scratching a letter. He tests out his content and his formulations in an exceptionally swift "dry run" within himself. He tries to make sense to himself; he alters, discards, replaces alternative distillations of meaning. He conducts elaborate internal experiments in "talking to himself."

The good communicator succeeds in conveying to us the feeling that it is safe to let him communicate with us, that it is safe to let him enter our inner world. He creates the confidence in us that he knows what he is doing, that he knows his purpose and direction, that it is safe to place our fantasies under his momentary command, that he may be trusted to take control, that it will all come out right because he will deliver us back, enlightened or delighted, pleasured or enriched, to our autonomous cerebrations.

No more powerful words have ever been invented by the human race than these four: "Once upon a time." This phrase, "Once upon a time," puts the listener into a passive, accepting, receiving frame of mind. It says, "This is only a fable. . . . Remember the time when you were happier than you are now. . . . Don't worry, I know what I'm doing. I'm going to tell you a story . . . but it may have a meaning . . ." And there is a promise, in those first four words, that four equally welcome others will come at the end: "lived happily ever after." Communication is partly an activity of the communicatee.

The communicatee, when properly courted and skillfully controlled, experiences the excitement of entering the world of someone else, of having his imagination freed, used, focused—and returned to him. We surrender our fantasies to those who somehow reassure us that they can accept responsibility for the curious ambiguity that must be created, and the necessary tension that will be resolved, in a magical process.

The effective communicator must have a capacity for multiple identifications, for he establishes rapport with disparate personality structures. He must be able to carry on his internal dialogues with electronic speed, dialogues in which another is encapsulated and in which he, the communicator, tests out various and intricate ways of bridging the gap between himself and the other.

Even the length of a word, the number of its syllables, is crucial in a sentence that registers high communicative impact. Alter one word, change it from two to three syllables, or the other way around, and see how the rhythm, the momentum, the force of the content change.

Just as good style in exposition is not much more than clear thinking, so good communication ultimately depends on the communicator's really knowing what he wants to say. You would be surprised by how rare this is. Most people spray out a large number of sounds in speech, or scribbles in writing, and hope that some meaning will somehow congeal to convey something—somehow. The good communicator makes himself clear to himself before he tries to make himself clear to others.

This puzzle, communication, is not limited to words. It operates in the paint on a canvas, in the symbols of the mathematician, in the marvelously ingenious models of scientists, in the interrelations of human beings who try to escape their loneliness, to share their experience, to communicate their feelings—feelings common to the human race, yet so different in each of us and so very difficult to convey—as we would really like to.

To understand is one thing; to make oneself understood is another—a tribute to the empathy and technique which are imbedded in that orchestration of interactions we call communicating. Few men understand themselves. Is it a wonder that fewer still understand one another? Insight into the self is rare; insight into someone else—?

Communication is a problem in creativity.

VIII

CAPTAIN NEWMAN, M.D.

Captain Newman, M.D.

★

ONE MORNING in 1955, I started working, around 9 A.M., to complete a melodrama I had been hacking away at it for months, stymied by the non-Aristotelian problem that plagues every writer of a whodunit: "Why don't they just call in the police?"

Suddenly, without thinking, I shoved the manuscript aside and began writing a story I had told some friends the preceding night. It was a tall tale about a boy in the army who drives his officers crazy by refusing, quite sweetly and politely, to make his bed. I had heard about this enchanting anarchist from Dr. Ralph Greenson, my closest friend, and as I had warmed to my theme, encouraged by the others, I elaborated an entire fable.

I now wrote like a fury, everything falling into place easily, even the names of characters (ordinarily the product of so many trials and errors) dropping off my pen by magic. I heard myself laughing as I worked, for Coby Clay, as I dubbed my hero, seemed to "write himself." Words, twists of plot, phrases gushed out of me in an uninterrupted cascade. When, exhausted, I looked at my watch I saw that it was past five. I had been writing for eight straight hours, without food, without water, without a moment's hesitation or a moment's rest.

That story, "The Happiest Man in the World," set me off on a prolonged creative frenzy. I wrote ten stories in one straight spree. Never, before or since, have I felt so euphoric: people sprang full-grown from my head; dialogue poured out of their mouths; what I call the "leverage-points" of narrative tumbled out in a torrent. I wrote for six, eight, ten hours a day; I could not, in fact, stop. I took a sedative one night, utterly spent, fell into a deep, mar-

251

velous sleep—and found myself at my desk writing like a happy idiot, four hours later. In one month I wrote 70,000 words without bothering to re-read a page—and I usually re-read until I am green around the gills.

Now, I must tell you that no material really appears by magic. For twenty years I had been interested in psychiatry; I had read many a technical journal, attended many a psychoanalytic meeting, often visited St. Elizabeth's Hospital in Washington, when my good friend Dr. Zigmond Lebensohn graced its staff, visited other mental hospitals through doctor-friends, made their rounds with them, interviewed patients, sat in on clinical seminars. In 1942, I was approached by the Office of the Surgeon General about writing a training film for army doctors, designed to initiate them into psychiatric therapy. I had visited N.P. (neuro-psychiatric) wards in Air Force hospitals —never, I should make it clear to the unkind, as a patient. The stories were also built upon fragments of my own wonderings about men I had seen on a four-month tour of duty for the Secretary of War's office in France, England, and Germany, six weeks after the shooting stopped.

I had vaguely determined to write a novel into which I could pour the richness and range of these experiences. I had begun to pattern a book, in my mind, around a psychiatric ward in an army hospital—not in a theater of war, but on a desert base in the southwest. I had spent many a holiday in the Mojave, and near Phoenix, Arizona, and in Palm Springs, and from the time I first entered the strange and special world of the desert, I knew that someday I would use its beauty and its desolation as a setting. . . .

I lived in an agitated writing trance for another month, until one night, without warning, the inner excitations ended. I had run dry. The "divine seizure," as it is fancily called, had stopped as abruptly as it had begun. I felt wonderfully content, and confident.

I went back to other things. I wanted to get distance between myself and what I had, in such an orgy of exuberance, written. Some weeks later, I picked up the manuscript proudly and began to read. My heart damn near stopped: it was awful. Dear God, the work that waited—the chopping out, the shoring up, the patterning of pace and point, the need to focus, the strengthening of motives, the sharpening of conflicts, the search for exact words and crisper images, the dosages of humor and heart-pulls, the manipulation of tone, nuance, catharsis, muting some moments and extending others, the "planting" of clues like land-mines to be exploded in surprises, the substitutions of dialogue for description—oh, God, oh, God.

I worked on the book from 1955 on—not daily, not always, dropping it,

to that. Man, oh, man, that's mighty fine stuff." He was entirely at peace with the world and at home with himself—his body, his reveries, his Maker, his soul. His moods ran an exceptionally narrow gamut, being bounded at the lower end by pleasure and at the upper end by bliss. The only thing he was sensitive about was his height, which he reported, in rueful confession, as "five foot seventeen."

On the post we always knew when Coby was about to materialize; we could hear, in advance, the whistling or humming or chuckling which accompanied his running colloquy with his beatific self. Hear it? No; overhear it. For his contact with any of us, with the unhappy universe beyond his own fantasies, was fragmentary, and oddly compassionate. I think he felt sorry for everyone who could not join him in the idyllic past with which he chose to replace the irksome now.

Coby was an exceedingly amiable soldier, but he was most oddly co-ordinated. His long, far-flung limbs seemed to live a life independent of his torso. When Coby drew those six feet five inches to attention, for instance, he did it in sequence—as if his brain were sending messages to the outlying provinces of his bodily empire; naturally it took more time for a foot to respond than, say, a hand, since the one was so much farther from headquarters than the other.

Coby had immense biceps and looked strong, very strong, which I'm sure he was; but he did not feel strong. And a man who does not *feel* strong simply is not able to lift heavy loads, or move burdensome objects, or heave, haul, toss or carry things which much weaker men manage to do because they want to be strong. This was an illusion Coby did not entertain. He did not care a fig about physical strength; he wanted harmony, not power.

At an early age, he had found himself in a world where men competed—for jobs, for money, for women, for promotions—and he had long since come to the conclusion that he did not care to compete for anything. He was content with himself, encouraged himself, enjoyed himself, and admired himself. "His ego," Captain Newman wrote in the confidential report on Coby Clay which Colonel Pyser requested, "appears to be inaccessible to conventional appeals."

It certainly was. For Coby was the only private in the United States Army who never made his bed; his sergeant made his bed for him, each and every morning. I think Coby was the only soldier in military history whom neither sergeants nor lieutenants nor captains nor majors nor colonels could prevail upon. They tried—all of them; Lord knows they tried. They tried command and cajolery, blandishment and bluster and threats of reprisal, but Coby would not make his bed. He would hear out the orders, the coaxings, the reasoning, the threats; he would gravely consider the appeals to sense, to teamwork, to *esprit de corps*. Then all he would say, with the utmost kindliness, was: " 'Tain't fit for a grown man to make his own bed."

All this broke upon our collective awareness the very first dawn after Coby was shipped to our unsuspecting installation, when his sergeant came into quarters to find Coby gazing out of the window happily, humming a roundelay. His bed was unmade.

Sergeant Pulaski, an uncomplicated Polish boy from Chicago, called, "Clay!"

"Yes, Sarge," Coby beamed.

"Clay," said Sergeant Pulaski sternly, "you didn't make your bed."

"That's right, Sarge."

Sergeant Pulaski wrinkled his brow. "Why not?"

Coby said, " 'Tain't fit for a grown man to make his own bed."

Sergeant Pulaski, who had a gift for unvarnished command, put his fists on his hips at once and barked, "What the hell kind of double-talk is that?"

"Back home," said Coby, "my maw always makes up my bed. Ever since I been born, my maw always made up that there bed."

"In the Army," said Sergeant Pulaski slowly, "there ain't no ma's to make no beds. In the Army, soldier, everyone—everyone except officers—makes his own bed!"

Coby took thought and clucked his tongue.

"Inspection is in ten minutes."

"That's *nice*," said Coby.

"Now, boy, make that bed."

Coby sighed and shook his head with regret. "I ain't hankerin' to make no trouble for nobody, nohow; but I jest cain't do it."

"And why 'cain't you just do it'?"

"Why, I jest couldn't look my maw in the eye again if I made up my own bed."

Sergeant Pulaski stared at Coby in amazement, tightened his lips, declared, "A guy asks for trouble he's gonna get trouble!" and stalked out.

Coby lay down on his bed and sang himself a song. In less than five minutes, Sergeant Pulaski returned with Lieutenant Bienstock. I had briefly met Bienstock, a second lieutenant with fuzz on his cheek but not on his chin. He was an enthusiastic exponent of that Come-on-fellows-let's-all-put-our-shoulders-to-the-wheel attitude which never failed to puzzle military observers from abroad, who expect an army to be divided simply into those who command and those who obey.

Lieutenant Bienstock now hastened into the barracks with shining eyes, alert ears, and palpitating disbelief. "Which one? Where, Sergeant? Which one is it? That one? On your feet, soldier."

As Coby undulated himself upward, part after part, until all of his five foot seventeen assembled more or less at attention, Lieutenant Bienstock paled slightly.

"Mornin', suh," Coby smiled.

Lieutenant Bienstock glanced uneasily at Sergeant Pulaski and said, "Now listen, Clay. Sergeant Pulaski has been very patient with you, I must say. You don't want to get into any trouble, do you? And we certainly don't want to make you any trouble. Now, what's all this nonsense about your refusing to make your bed?"

Coby looked down at his superior from bland, unruffled heights. "Oh, I don't aim to make no trouble for nobody, nohow. I *like* it here, suh. But it jest ain't right, suh. I couldn't look my maw in the eye again if I made up my own bed."

Lieutenant Bienstock stared at the kind, forbearing face above him and, in a strained voice, asked, "Do you realize what you're *saying*, Clay? Do you know what this means? Why—you are deliberately refusing to obey an order from a superior officer!"

"Oh, no, suh," Coby drawled. "I ain't refusin' t'obey no one, nohow."

"Then you'll go ahead and make that bed!"

"Cain't," said Coby.

Lieutenant Bienstock glanced at Sergeant Pulaski nervously, wetting his lips, and said, "Sergeant, take this man to Captain Howard's office."

"Right." Sergeant Pulaski saluted and nodded to Coby, who regarded Lieutenant Bienstock in the kindest possible way before ambling out. Bienstock lighted a cigarette and inhaled deeply, organizing his thoughts. There were a great many of them. Then he hurried out and headed for Captain Howard's office in Building Two.

Coby was sitting on a long bench, one foot drawn up, his elbow on it, his hand dangling loosely, moving in lazy rhythm to his humming. Sergeant Pulaski was standing next to him in the correctest possible military fashion. Lieutenant Bienstock regarded Coby sententiously, giving him one last chance to reconsider or recant. Coby started to mobilize his bodily ingredients for ascent; Lieutenant Bienstock turned on his heel and strode into Captain Howard's office.

I disliked Captain Howard. He was a knuckle-cracker and a mint-sucker— efficient, crisp, hard-working, and mean. An automobile salesman from Wichita, Herbert Howard was a stern believer in fair play, cold showers, and clean thoughts. His thoughts were so clean that he spent most of his evenings at the Officers' Club boring us with his plans for a five-minute car-washing service he was going to open up as soon as the war was over. He was the kind of incomplete personality known as "a man's man." He had few friends and many doubts. When he thought no one was watching, he bit his nails. I am sure that when he slept, he looked puzzled.

He was tallying up some requisition forms when Lieutenant Bienstock entered. Bienstock saluted smartly, accepted Captain Howard's cursory "Proceed," and, while the latter continued to add and carry over, recited the details of Private Coby Clay's defiance of the simplest and most universal requirement of military life.

Captain Howard lifted his head with an expression of incipient outrage. "He won't make his *bed?*"

Lieutenant Bienstock cleared his throat. "Yes, sir."

Captain Howard scrutinized Bienstock as if he had just told him the sun had risen in the west that morning.

"He says it's against his principles, sir," Bienstock quickly added.

"His principles?" Captain Howard echoed. "What the hell is he, a Mohammedan?"

"No, sir. He's from the South."

"So what? Halfa this little old installation is—"

"He says his maw always made his bed for him and 'tain't—it isn't fit for a grown man to make his own bed."

Captain Howard leaned forward, hunching his shoulders like a fullback plowing through the line, and cried, "His '*maw*'? What the hell's the *mat*ter with you, Bienstock?"

"Nothing, sir," said Lieutenant Bienstock with a pained expression. "I was just *quoting.*"

"Well, stop quoting and talk sense! He calls his mother 'maw'?"

"Yes, sir."

"Is he a hillbilly or something?"

Bienstock hesitated. "I think he's from Alabama, sir."

"I don't care if he's a thirty-plus-three *de*gree Mason! Do you mean to stand there and tell me you let a damn dogface pull a cockeyed gag like *re*fusing to make his own bed on you?"

"Sir, I explained and insisted and argued with him. I even—"

Captain Howard's face assumed various variations of impatience as Lieutenant Bienstock proceeded. This made Lieutenant Bienstock more nervous, and he began to stammer. This made Captain Howard's lips thread themselves so that contempt replaced impatience. This made Lieutenant Bienstock blush. This made Captain Howard slap his desk with his open palm and snap, "You *argued* with him? What the hell's the *mat*ter with you anyway, Bienstock? You are an *of*ficer in the *U*nited States *Ar*my! This isn't a debating society. We're at war! Get the marbles out of your head and throw that nogood gold-bricker in the little old guardhouse!"

"Sir?"

"You heard me. Throw him in the can!"

"I thought—"

"That's not smart of you, thinking. Give him to the MPs, Bienstock, to the MPs. Twenty-four hours in the little old cooler will cool off that joker. It's as simple as that. Won't make his bed! 'It ain't fit for a grown man.'" Captain Howard's expression was a masterpiece of disgust. "Holy Moses, Bienstock, even the Communists make their own beds. Dismissed!"

Lieutenant Bienstock wiped his brow the minute he got outside the door, signaled to Sergeant Pulaski, and strode out as Sergeant Pulaski told Coby, "Up!"

When they were fifty feet from Captain Howard's office, Lieutenant Bienstock took Coby under a tree and made a last earnest effort to save him from his fate. Coby listened with the utmost consideration. Anyone could see that he wouldn't want to hurt Lieutenant Bienstock's feelings for the world. But what he said, after Bienstock's moving appeal to reason, was, "'Tain't fit for a grown man to—"

"Sergeant," said Bienstock petulantly, "take this man to the guardhouse! By order of Captain Howard."

Coby spent that day and night behind bars. He spent most of the day singing and all of the night sleeping like a particularly contented lamb.

When Coby returned to the barracks from the guardhouse the next morning, Sergeant Pulaski was waiting at the entrance with a superior smile.

Coby was delighted to see him. "Man, oh, man," he chuckled, "I caught me up on plenty of snoozin'."

Pulaski said, "Okay, Clay. Let's us have no more trouble from you, huh?"

Coby's eyes moved serenely around the barracks, coming to rest on his own bed in the far corner. It looked as neat, tight, and oblong as a coffin.

"We got commended for neat quarters at inspection this morning," growled Sergeant Pulaski defensively. "Okay, okay, so I made up your bed. But no more trouble from you, huh, Clay?"

"No, Sarge," said Coby. "I ain't aimin' to give nobody—"

"—no trouble nohow," Pulaski finished. "I heard you. Now get the lead out of your tail and fall in with your squad."

Coby spent the day training with his company, went to sleep that night, responded to reveille nobly the next morning, helped his comrades mop the floor and sweep the porch, lent a cheerful, helping hand to one and all— but he did not make his bed. Sergeant Pulaski looked hurt as he went out to find Lieutenant Bienstock.

Bienstock gave Coby a ten-minute lecture on military discipline, Captain Howard's cold heart, Major Forman's nasty temper, and the reputation of

Colonel Pyser, an absolute Caligula in disciplinary matters. Coby could not have been more interested in these novel insights into the military organization of which he was so small a part. But he would not sacrifice his principles; he would not sully his mother's image of him; he would not make his bed. He returned to the guardhouse. And, back in the barracks, Sergeant Pulaski made his bed again, while Coby sang for his colleagues in the can.

The next day Coby was back with his fellows. That night he slept in the bed which Sergeant Pulaski had made that morning. The next morning he declined to make his bed, with genuine affection and regret, and went to the guardhouse again.

This went on for a week, Coby spending alternate nights at the guardhouse, sleeping alternate nights in the bed which Sergeant Pulaski, hamstrung and desperate, made for him. When it seemed clear that Coby Clay was willing to spend the rest of his days in this idyllic double life, Sergeant Pulaski appealed to Lieutenant Bienstock, and Lieutenant Bienstock reported to Captain Howard with an unmistakable note of panic in his voice.

Captain Howard cracked his knuckles, studied Lieutenant Bienstock with disgust diluted only with disbelief, and, between his fine, well-brushed teeth, said, "Bring that mother-loving soldier in to me." He had never laid eyes on Coby Clay.

When Coby presented himself, Captain Howard was on the telephone, tilted far back in his chair, his back to the door, reading aloud acidly from a report and bawling out a lieutenant in Quartermaster's. Captain Howard was feeling especially curt, concise, and complete that day. He slammed the phone down, swiveled around to his desk, deliberately keeping his eyes on the report, and waited for the familiar: "Private —— reporting, sir," from the soldier awaiting his dispensation. He did not get it, because Coby saw no reason to give it.

Captain Howard put his pencil down slowly, exactly parallel to the blotter pad, assumed an expression of icy foreboding, then slowly lifted his eyes up the height of the erect body before him. This calculated maneuver of the eyes had always before served Captain Howard's purposes; it effected a slow deflation of the other's ego; it smothered hope or illusion; it was a shrewd tactical gambit which made it crystal-clear who was standing and who was sitting, and who was going to continue standing at the sole pleasure of who was sitting.

But Lieutenant Bienstock had forgotten to tell Captain Howard that Coby Clay was six feet five. By the time Captain Howard's gaze reached the unexpected altitude of Coby's chin, Herbert Howard, who was only five feet eight, had his head far back in the socket of his neck and his eyes bugged in an involuntary bulge.

Coby blushed sheepishly, as he always did when people first comprehended his eminence. "I come right over, suh, like that there other fellow told me."

"Who?" asked Captain Howard.

"That there other fellow. The one brought me here before."

Captain Howard could feel his neck getting hot. "That 'other fellow' is an officer, an officer named Lieutenant Bienstock, and you will re-fer to him hereafter by name."

"He never told me his name," said Coby.

"Well, I am telling you his rank and name!" Captain Howard retorted, slamming his fist on the desk. "And even if you didn't know his name, you could call him 'lieutenant.' You understand that much, soldier, don't you?"

"Yes, suh!" Coby was always grateful for increment to his store of knowledge.

Captain Howard turned sideward and poured himself a glass of water, noting with approval that his hands were steady. He sipped the water slowly, lowered the glass, studied it, placed the glass on the table, leaned forward, put his palms together, and said in an even voice, "Soldier, I want you to listen carefully to what I am about to tell you. I'll say it slowly, so there is not the slightest chance you'll misunderstand. It involves your making a decision that may affect your whole life! Are you ready?"

Coby furrowed his brow, concentrating on every word Captain Howard had uttered, and nodded.

Captain Howard took a deep breath and let it out, word by word. "Either you make your bed, every morning, without a single beef, or I will throw you in the little old guardhouse for ten days." He fixed Coby with his deadliest I-take-no-nonsense-from-anyone stare. "Is that clear?"

Coby nodded.

"You understand it?"

Coby nodded again.

"Any question you want to ask?"

Coby shook his head.

"Fine. Now, boy, which will it be?"

"How's that again, suh?" asked Coby.

Captain Howard gritted his many teeth. "Which—will—it—be? Make your bed in the morning, every morning, or go to the cold, cold jug for ten days?"

Coby sighed, regarding the man seated before and below him with infinite compassion. "I don't want to make no trouble for no one nohow, suh, but 'tain't fit for a grown man to—"

The blood drained out of Captain Howard's face; all sorts of evil thoughts welled up in him and had to be denied. He placed a mint in his mouth and pressed a button on his desk. "Goodbye, soldier!"

Coby spent the next ten days in the guardhouse. It was, according to the reports that Corporal Laibowitz brought to the hospital and that raced through all the wards with the speed of a forest fire, the happiest ten days of Coby's life.

The MPs and Captain Howard and Major Forman—to whom Captain Howard brought his problem, confessing defeat—simply could not believe it. They could understand it, but they could not believe it. Or perhaps it was the other way around.

For Coby Clay was behaving in such a way that the entire theory of punishment as a deterrent was endangered. Every day Coby spent happily in the guardhouse clearly demonstrated that the punitive could be made rather pleasant, and this challenged the very foundations of law enforcement. For the whole idea of a guardhouse, or any place of confinement, rests on the assumption that detention is hateful to man's free spirit and crippling to man's free soul. But now the American Army was confronted by a man for whom detention held no terrors, confinement meant no deprivation, discipline represented no threat. The awful truth, which was beginning to confound our brass, was this: Private Coby Clay *liked* the guardhouse. He slept like a king and sang like an angel. In fact, he preferred the guardhouse to the barracks. There was something about that bounded, ordered microcosm that appealed to Coby no end; there, life was reduced to its simplest form—devoid of conflict or the perplexities of choice.

The fact that Coby declined to make his bed in the guardhouse, too—politely, but definitively—presented its own special problem to the MPs: after all, there was no other guardhouse to which you could send a man to punish him for not making his bed in the guardhouse in which he was. "What in hell can I *do*?" Major Inglehart, commanding MP, often moaned to us. No one knew what to tell him.

Nor was this the worst of it. The other prisoners, who regarded Coby with the awe of apprentices to master, were beginning to be converted to Coby's unique philosophy of life; the insidious idea began to germinate in their delinquent brains that perhaps they could get away with not making their beds, too. To nip this frightful prospect in the bud, Major Inglehart swiftly transferred Coby to a cell with one Lacy Bucks, a young enlistee from Louisiana who could not endure Yankees but felt kin to anyone south of Tennesee. The major interviewed Private Bucks personally and, after a certain amount of shilly-shallying, bribed Bucks ("double rations") to make up Coby's bed every morning. "And don't tell anyone you're doing it!" Inglehart warned him darkly.

Bucks seemed contented to be silent for the Major, and the rations. Coby, of course, had no reason to tell anyone that Bucks was making his bed for him. He never felt the need of initiating any discussion of the bed problem;

diagnostic genius of our society could discern, Coby Clay was a healthy, responsible, wholesome, brave, reasonable, well-adjusted (though slowly co-ordinated) specimen of American manhood. His schooling was not all that might be desired; his vocabulary was far from impressive; his spelling was atrocious—but then, so was the spelling of most of our armed forces. Coby's IQ was 96—not high, to be sure, but you must remember that 50 per cent of the GIs in the Army ranked between 95 and 105.

"How," Captain Newman asked me, with rather bated breath, "would you summarize all this? If you had to describe Clay in one word, what would it be?"

"Delightful," I said.

Captain Newman put his head between his hands. "Okay, Barney, bring him around."

Captain Newman interviewed Coby Clay for an hour and returned him to the unhappy jurisdiction of Sergeant Pulaski.

The report which Captain Newman wrote on Coby for Major Forman and, through him, for Colonel Pyser, was something to treasure. There was not a note of irony in it, nor a smidgen of levity. It was precise, technical, thorough, and—to someone like Colonel Pyser—infuriating. Francie showed it to me, smiling. "If you want to see the great psychoanalyst at the top of his form, cast your youthful eyes on this." I copied parts of it for posterity:

Clay's reflexes are good, though not particularly rapid. He shows excellent psychological equilibrium. He has balance, proportion, and a good sense of humor. He sleeps well, eats well, and (aside from the particular problem for which he was referred to the undersigned) performs his duties in a responsible fashion. He may be classified as "Oral, passive." . . .

He discusses his convictions about bed-making (rather, about not-bed-making) without anxiety, ambivalence, or hostility. He appears to have deeply encapsulated opinions about the masculine and feminine roles, placing some things firmly in the former category and others (such as bed-making) in the latter. . . .

I do not believe his opinions on this subject can be altered by therapy. Clay may be described as having an unusual character structure. His aggressions are well in hand. His views about certain aspects of military discipline are unique, but not subversive. His ego appears to be inaccessible to conventional appeals.

(Signed) J. J. NEWMAN, Captain, M. C.

When Colonel Pyser called Captain Newman to his office, that report on Coby Clay lay on Colonel Pyser's desk. Major Forman and Captain Howard were present. They looked terribly serious: Pyser kept biting his mustache, Major Forman kept drumming his fingers, and Captain Howard kept sucking mints.

Colonel Pyser opened the conference bluntly: "Captain Newman, do you regard Clay as a mental defective?"

"No, sir."

"Do you regard him as a queer—I mean *as* queer, in any shape, manner, or form?"

"No, sir."

"I take it, from your report, that you insist on considering Private Clay well adjusted?"

"Yes, sir."

"You couldn't find *any* signs of neurosis, psychosis, or any other incapacitating factors?" asked Pyser almost plaintively.

"No, sir."

"What about moral turpitude—or *antisocial behavior?*"

Newman shook his head.

Colonel Pyser studied him hatefully. "So you won't recommend a Section Eight hearing for this son-of-a-bitch?"

"No, sir."

Pyser put his hands on the arms of his chair and looked as if he might spring at Captain Newman any moment. "Goddamit, Newman, you have recommended men for a Section Eight-ing who never gave us half the trouble this soldier has put the post through! And now, when we really need and can *use* an N.P. diagnosis, you get more conservative than Herbert Hoover!"

"But apart from not making his bed, Colonel, Clay has created no difficulties—"

" '*Apart* from not making his bed'?" Pyser echoed, his cheeks going gray. " '*Apart* from not making his *bed*'? What more do you want from a nut than refusing to make his bed and *enjoying* the guardhouse, for the love of Mike? I ask you again, Newman. Do you mean to sit there and tell me that you will not recommend this gold-brick or screwball or whatever-the-hell-he-is for a Section Eight?"

Newman met Colonel Pyser's glare steadily. "I *might* classify him as neurotic, phobic type—a bed-making phobia, but that would only go with a recommendation for a C.D.D."

"Medical discharge?" shouted Colonel Pyser. "Give that bastard a pension—on half-pay—for the rest of his life? Over my dead body, Newman!" He leaped to his feet and paced back and forth furiously, then wheeled on Newman. "The real test is—do you think this soldier is fit for combat?"

"Yes, sir."

"God," Pyser groaned. "Look; if we send him overseas, do you think he's going to change his opinion about making his bed?"

"No, sir."

"Right!" cried Pyser. "Then who the hell do you think *will* make his bed overseas?"

"Someone else," said Captain Newman.

Colonel Pyser stared at Newman bitterly. Newman said he could hear Major Forman's chair trembling, and Captain Howard sucking on a mint as if it were an oxygen tube.

"One final question, Newman. If Clay finishes his training, and if I send him overseas with his outfit, when the chips are down—is this joker going to fight or is he going to wash out?"

"This boy will never wash out," said Captain Newman.

"Oh, Christ," said Colonel Pyser.

And so when Coby Clay, that fine and delightful soldier, returned from his latest stretch in the guardhouse, rested and unruffled as of yore, and appeared before Sergeant Pulaski, smiling and considerate, that product of the West Side of Chicago studied him in silence for a long, long moment before inquiring, "Coby, you learned your lesson now? You want solitary and bread-and-water next? Or you gonna be a good boy and make your bed?"

Before Coby could even finish shaking his head, Sergeant Pulaski threw his head back, crying, "Oh, hell! Okay! All right, I give up! You win! A couple million guys in the whole screwy American Army, from North and South and East and West, and I have to draw you! So okay, soldier. That's the way God wants it, that's the way He's gonna have it! I'll make your goddam bed from now on."

And he did. Every morning. Every single morning, an American sergeant made a private's bed for him. It was the talk of the post—except at Headquarters, where no one dared mention it. Not a day passed but what Sergeant Pulaski got kidded and razzed and needled about this basic transmutation of the established order. Pulaski began to get mighty edgy.

Then one day Private Clay loomed over Sergeant Pulaski and said, "Say, Sarge, can I ask you somethin'?"

"Come on, come on," said Pulaski crossly. "Talk fast."

Coby scratched his head. "Well, I been thinkin' out about this bed-makin'. 'Tain't fit for a man to make his own bed, like my maw says. But I been thinkin' an' scratchin' aroun' an' all, an' I don't see no right reason why a man cain't make up someone *else's* bed. Like you been doin' for me. I figger my maw wouldn't hardly mind if I jest did that same little thing for you."

The kidding of Sergeant Pulaski stopped after that. For from then on, until that whole contingent of brave men was flown into action overseas, while Sergeant Pulaski made Coby's bed each morning, Coby—humming of dark glades and promised lands—made Pulaski's.

Little Jim

CORPORAL LAIBOWITZ OFTEN MADE SOJOURNS AROUND THE POST AS A SELF-appointed confidential agent. A careful and accomplished student of scuttle-butt, he had established grapevines to Headquarters, Hospital Administration, Colonel Pyser's office, and Lieutenant Colonel Larrabee's staff conferences. He sometimes used Pepi Gavoni as a research assistant ("Make a pass at that typist who stencils the travel orders") or Hammerhead as a trial balloon ("Doc's giving a paper at the A.P.A. next Christmas. Spread the word. Start with the waiters").

Laibowitz's espionage network sometimes brought him quite rare nuggets of intelligence. He discovered that a lieutenant in Quartermaster's was meet-ing a WAC secretary every Friday night in a diner on the highway twelve miles from camp; they were shacking up in a motel named Fifty Palms. He found out that an imaginative bar boy at the Officers' Club was diverting the top three to four ounces on each bottle of gin to a container he kept handy under the counter, adding tap water to the original bottles and selling the diverted fire water at $2.50 per canteen. He knew, a week before Major Wicker-sham did, that Wickersham was being transferred to Alaska, and why—which Wickersham never did find out: He had been making too many passes at other officers' wives.

The product of Laibowitz's personal reconnaissances whom I shall never forget was Little Jim.

It was one of those afternoons when the sun was mercifully veiled by clouds. I was in Captain Newman's office, going over some case histories with him, when Corporal Laibowitz entered, carrying a tray. As he removed tea and Fig Newtons from the tray, he took the occasion to declaim without warning, as was his wont, "In Ward Four is a guy you should take into Ward Seven."

Captain Newman groaned. "Can't you ever find a man in Ward Seven who would be better off in Ward Four?"

"Games," said Laibowitz acidly, "are for children."

"So is sarcasm, you once said."

"Correction. On children, sarcasm is wasted altogether."

We sipped our tea. It was piping hot.

Captain Newman winced. "Dammit, Laibowitz, you know I prefer iced tea!"

"Ice freezes the muscles. Heat relaxes the same."

"Medicine will be indebted to you forever," said Newman. "But tomorrow, just to indulge the foolish whim of your rapidly aging Captain—"

"Do you want to hear about this guy from Ward Four?"

"I don't see how I can avoid it."

"I'm glad you brought up the subject," said Laibowitz. "Well, last night, late, maybe one, one-thirty, I happen to pass the Rec Hall and I hear something like music, very soft. It's dark, not a light on, but the moon is in business and I make out someone in one of the wicker chairs—near the windows. I go in and turn on a lamp and spot this guy huddled in the chair. He's holding a guitar and he's loaded: I can smell the booze a yard away. It's in a beer bottle on the floor. I tell him he's got to get back in the sack or he's in for trouble. He begins to mumble. 'Okay, Big Jim, let's cream them tonight.' I get him up on his feet and he blubbers, 'Okay, Big Jim . . . Little Jim's comin'. . . . Let's kill us some Germans . . .' I get him back to Ward Four, where the nurse on duty is plenty ticked off. It's the third night in a row this guy snuck out and got plastered. I tell her she's got a disturbed personality on her hands, not an ordinary lush, and advise her to send the guy down to see you. His name is Tompkins. James Bowie Tompkins."

Captain Newman nodded wearily. "That's fine. That's just dandy."

"I'm not *done*."

"Excuse me."

"I checked on this boy this morning. The doc on duty up there is some chiropractor named Beshar. I told him, in my opinion Tompkins ought to see a psychiatrist—you. An hour later Tompkins came down."

"I didn't see him," said Captain Newman.

"How could you? You were giving Lissner a Pentothal. I asked Tompkins to wait. He gave me a 'What-do-you-think-I-am-a-patsy?' look and said he's got to get some chow. So I start shooting the breeze with him to keep him there—casual, like you do, but watching him, like a hawk. He made a dirty crack about you and said no one is going to slip a needle into him, and pfft!—

he's up and gone!" Laibowitz pursed his lips sagely. "This boy is in a bad way, Doc. Cocky, but tense. He didn't fool me. My diagnosis is 'Depression: Agitated. Troublemaker.' "

Captain Newman rubbed his forehead. "I hope you didn't tell him that."

"Fresh, maybe I am; stupid, no. A patient I treat like he's made of eggshells. All I told this kid was for his own good he should positively come back to see you and take the load off his emotions, which are ready to pop."

"Jackson," Captain Newman sighed, "may I remind you for the hundredth time that it is *not* part of an orderly's duties to go around the hospital drumming up business?"

"From such business, who except the sick can profit?" Laibowitz left with a look that suggested what a prophet has to go through in his own country.

Captain Newman resumed his comments about the new cases. As I got up to leave, he said, rather apologetically, "Oh, if you happen to be around Ward Four—see what the story is on that boy."

The head nurse in Four told me Tompkins was a waist gunner who had flown into Colfax from North Africa two weeks earlier, with thirty-four missions behind him, a Purple Heart, a citation for courage, and a battered guitar. He had been grounded for insomnia and severe gastrointestinal pains. He was a quiet, co-operative patient—except for the times he slipped out of the ward and got drunk. No one knew where he was getting liquor, or where he kept hiding it.

I wandered into Ward 4.

Corporal Tompkins was stretched out on his bed, fully and neatly dressed, puffing on a long, thin cigar. He could not have been more than twenty-one or twenty-two, but he had an old man's face. His guitar was on the chair next to his bed.

"Hello, Corporal."

He sat up. He was short—just over five feet five—wiry and compact. He eyed me craftily. "Howdy."

"How are you?"

He smirked and tapped his cigar ash into a waste basket.

"Mind if I sit down?" I asked.

He shrugged. "The chairs ain't reserved."

I sat down. "Where are you from, Corporal?"

"Kaintucky."

"Whereabouts?"

"You wouldn't know, Lieutenant. Right from the hill people an' sour mash. Brung up with mud on m' feet an' rot-gut in m' belly an' now I'm a heero for Uncle Sam."

I could not tell whether he was pulling my leg. He kept a sly grin on his lips.

"I see you play the guitar," I said.

"You see, but you ain't heard," he snickered. "That there ol' gee-tar scared more guys in m' outfit than all the Jerries an' the JUs an' MEs put t'gether."

"How are you getting along here?" I asked.

He shrugged. "I been in worse places."

"Is there anything you need?"

"Sure. Cheaper booze an' juicy broads . . . Don't knock yourself out, Lieutenant. I'll git me outa here afore you do." He touched his forehead with one finger, picked up his guitar, and walked away. He walked with a swagger, a bantam cock's bravado.

I spoke to Captain Beshar about Tompkins. He made no effort to pretend that he liked him. "Cocky little bastard," he said. "He wouldn't help a blind man cross a street. He's just another one of those hot-shots from combat who hates all us feather-merchants."

Tompkins neither liked nor disliked the pleasant, unhurried world of the convalescent ward. He had won no friends, made no enemies, shared no secrets, offered no portion of his self or his past to the others. Several nights a week he would steal out of the ward with his knowing, insolent smile and would cat-foot it into the Recreation Hall or behind the PX, where he would strum on his guitar and drink whiskey from a long-necked beer bottle until he slid into insensibility. Once Captain Beshar had seen him pull a bottle out of the water tank in one of the toilets, and confiscated the bottle. Tompkins simply made new arrangements with his bootlegger, whoever he was.

"I hear he got a citation," I said.

"Sure," said Beshar. "He's probably a brave little punk. They usually are."

"May I see his chart?"

"Go ahead."

I made some notes out of Tompkins' history and left—to find Tompkins leaning against the wall just outside Captain Beshar's door. He gave me an ironic glance and walked away. I wondered if he had been eavesdropping.

When Captain Newman entered his office next morning, Corporal Tompkins was waiting for him—sitting in his chair, tilted far back, his feet on the desk, a panatela at a cocky angle in his mouth. "Come on in, Captain. I been waitin' for you."

"You've been doing more than that," said Captain Newman.

Tompkins grinned. "I jest like to put m' feet up." He got up abruptly. "I ain't stayin'. You want me to talk, you don't need no flak-juice. Jest come to Rec Hall. At night. When I'm swacked. I ain't promisin' nothin'. No one is gonna slip me no needle and shoot me full of flak-juice. I'm wise to the way you hook 'em—git 'em talkin', then slip 'em the needle. Right?"

"No," said Newman. "No man ever gets flak-juice unless he's willing to—"

"Well, Little Jim ain't askin' for it! The way I hear it, that flak-juice gives you a jag an' you start gabbin' an' gabbin', an' when you git up you don't remember a thing. Right?"

"Something like that."

"I knew I had you taped."

"That isn't hard. If you really want to know, flak-juice puts you to sleep, in a kind of twilight sleep. It helps you remember."

"Remember? Remember what?"

"What you can't forget," said Newman.

Tompkins scowled. "Nuts. That's for psychos. I ain't one of your goof-balls, y'know."

"Who said you were? Hold out your hands, please. . . . Come on, I won't touch you."

Tompkins put his hands out slowly, smiling. "Stiddy as rocks!"

"Sure. Now turn them over."

Tompkins turned his palms up. They were glistening with sweat.

Captain Newman said, "Thanks, Jim," and turned away.

Tompkins studied his hands thoughtfully, then wiped them on his shirt. "Some things ain't purty, Doc. Some things jest ain't purty!" He broke the cigar in two and flung the parts on the floor and hurried out.

In a moment, Laibowitz materialized in the doorway. "What's your diagnosis, Doc?"

"It is customary," said Captain Newman, "to greet an officer by saying, 'Good morning, sir.' "

"I said 'Good morning, sir,' yesterday."

"How time flies."

"You don't have to hide your emotions from me, Doc," said Laibowitz cryptically and left.

"Between Dr. Laibowitz and myself," Captain Newman told me at lunch, "Tompkins is going to ask for Pentothal."

"Are you going to see him? In the Rec Hall, I mean?"

He gazed at his plate abstractedly. "I don't know. He loads himself up with booze. He's getting barbiturates upstairs. I can control the Pentothal dosage, but the combination of flak and alcohol and barbiturates—hell, no. He might go wild. He might die."

Captain Newman returned to his office after dinner that night and left the door wide open. He waited until long after "Lights Out," but Tompkins did not appear. He did not appear the next morning either, nor the next night, nor the next.

But three nights later, at eleven, just as Newman was about to leave for his barracks, Tompkins appeared in the doorway. He looked unsteady. He was clutching his guitar.

"I ain't even drunk. Wait." Tompkins began to strum some chords on the guitar. "Hell, Doc, that's a lie. Little Jim's tanked up good—afore I come in. That's a fact. Oh, Jeeze. Oh, Jeeze, Doc. I feel it acomin' on. *It's gonna come out!* An' it ain't purty. I want to fergit it. I jest got to fergit it!"

"But you can't, Jim. Not really. It's like I told you: Some things you can't forget, until you've remembered them."

"Hey, that's purty good. Man, that's purty damn good. Well, I ain't gonna tell you, see—not the whole thing. Only . . . About Jim de Silva; that was his name. Big Jim everyone called him, an' one hell of a flyer. Man, could he handle that crate! Only guy in the whole goddam squadron knew how to bounce a B-24 around real good." He gave the foolish, vacant laugh of inebriation. "I'd git me loaded every damn night, hidin' in different places every night afore we had to go up. Know what it means if you don't show up for a mission, Doc? Court-martial. No foolin' around neither . . . But Little Jim Tompkins here always showed. Yup. You know why? 'Cause *he'd* make me. That's right. Big Jim. He'd find me. No matter where I'd hide, I'd feel this big paw shakin' me an' hear that big bastard's voice saying, 'Come on, buddy boy, time to go. This is Big Jim. Come on, Little Jim, we got to take us a ride. We got to kill us some nice, rosy-cheek Jerries.' An' I'd open my eyes and see that big Portagee bastard grinnin' at me, an' I'd say, 'Yeah, man. You're Big Jim an' I'm Little Jim an' no one's ever gonna kill us two!' An' he'd pull me to my feet like I was a bag o' hay an' hustle me out that field an' get me in that goddam crate. . . . Only buddy I ever had, Doc. Only guy ever took care of Little Jim real good. An' I—I—" The tears began to course down his cheeks. "Don't let me talk no more, Doc. Please. Stop me. If I remember, I'll blow my top. I'm tellin' you, I'll *blow-my-top!* Stop me, Doc. Please stop me—'fore I smash up that lamp an' throw around them chairs an' push m' fists through all the goddam glass in the friggin' windows!"

"Sure," Captain Newman cut in harshly. "You'll smash up the lamp and throw around them chairs and push your fists through all the goddam glass in the friggin' windows—and it won't help one bit, boy. Not one damn bit! And you know it. You've done it before, and it didn't help, and it won't help now."

Tompkins looked at Captain Newman with bleary and imploring eyes. "That's where the flak-juice comes in, don't it?"

"Yes."

Tompkins moaned. "I'm in a sweat. I don't want to think of it. I got to stop thinkin'—"

"But you *are* thinking of it—all the time, day and night, week after week, month after month after month. You play the guitar—to use up your thoughts. You fight off sleep—so you won't dream. You get swacked—to run away from memory." Newman changed the timbre of his voice abruptly. "What a stupid way to live, boy. What a goddam stupid way to *live!*"

Tompkins' body was racked by terrible sobs.

Captain Newman turned away, letting the boy cry unobserved, and when he heard the weeping soften and the sniffing begin, he said quietly, "When did it happen? Come on, Little Jim. Why don't you spill it? Why don't you get it off your chest, once and for all? What happened? When?"

"November 17. We take off, 18:05. Me an' Buck in the waist, an' Lieutenant Bates with Big Jim—" He caught himself and cried, "Yeah! Like hell! I'm no good. I'm a yellow-belly who let—Oh, Jeeze, Doc, gimme the flak-juice. You win. *I'm askin' for it.* Give it t' me! Please. Now, right *now!*"

Captain Newman got to his feet slowly and stretched. "Okay, Little Jim. If you lay off the booze for two days, not a *drop*, understand, and I tell them to stop medication—no pills to help you sleep—I'll give you the flak. Thursday morning. In my office. Ten o'clock." He forced a yawn.

"Not now?" cried Tompkins in consternation. "You ain't gonna do it now? When I'm askin' for it?"

"Nope," Newman yawned. "It'll hold, boy. Jeeze, I'm bushed. I'll see you tomorrow. Why don't you hit the hay?"

Tompkins wiped his eyes with the back of his hand. "Sure, Doc. Anything you say, Doc."

Captain Newman started for the door. Tompkins was not following him. He was nestling down in the chair, working his shoulders like a cat. Newman paused, frowning, then he pushed his voice into a shout. "Tompkins, what the hell's the matter with you? Haven't you beaten yourself up enough for one night? *Don't you have any pity?*"

Corporal Tompkins gave a cry, leaping out of the chair. "Okay, okay, don't blow a gasket! Jeeze, they sure picked the right guy to boss the loony squad!" He staggered past Captain Newman with a clutter of elbows and knees and unguarded emotion.

He was halfway to Ward 4 when he reeled, retching, stumbling, trying to use the guitar as a crutch, sinking at last to the floor.

Captain Newman hurried to the boy and kneeled beside him. "Little Jim . . . Get up. . . ." But Little Jim could make no more than foolish, vacant sounds. Captain Newman lifted his head and slapped his cheeks gently. "Come on, boy. You've got to make the sack. . . ."

Little Jim began to whimper, "I don' wan' go up . . . not this one . . . please . . . scairt, I'm so scairt . . ."

Captain Newman raised his voice, calling: "Wardman! Orderly! Here!" But no one answered his call.

the kind of service we give around here." He stepped to the window and put it down. "Okay, Jim. On the cot."

"You—gonna squirt the stuff in me?"

"Yep." Captain Newman picked a syringe out of the tank with a forceps. Little Jim sat down on the bed. "Kin I take off m' shoes?"

"Sure."

"I sleep better without. That's what I'm gonna do, right? Jest sleep?"

"Uh-huh. Roll up your sleeve."

"Man. Ten in the mornin' an' I got me two officers puttin' me t' bed!" His heavy shoes dropped to the floor. He rolled up his left sleeve and stretched out on the cot. "You want me t' think of somethin' special?"

"Nope. Just relax. This shot won't hurt. It's just like all the others you guys get."

"I'll bet. Will it knock me right out?"

"Practically. You'll get drowsy. When I tell you to count, start counting —but backward, from one hundred. Got that?"

"Hey, that's sharp."

Captain Newman got two tiny, sealed ampules out of the cabinet and set them on the night table. One was labeled "Sterile Water." The other label read: "Pentothal Sodium (Sodium Ethyl—1 Methyl-Butyl—Thiobarbiturate— 0.5 Gm. With 30 mg. Anhydrous Sodium Carbonate)." He took a nail file and cut a ring just below the tip of each ampule. He put a tourniquet on Tompkins' arm, to make the cubital vein larger. Then he got a large hypodermic syringe. He knocked the tip off the ampule which contained sterile water, sucked about ten cc. into the syringe, knocked the tip off the Sodium Pentothal ampule, sucked the white powder into the syringe, went back to the sterile water ampule, filling the syringe up to the twenty-cc. mark.

Tompkins watched all this. "Holy Jesus, that's big enough for a horse!"

"All right, boy," said Newman gently. "Here we go." He rubbed a swab of alcohol on Tompkins' arm.

It was hot in the room. The small clock on the cabinet said 10:04.

Tompkins waved to me like a kid going on a trip. There was a ring of sweat on his neck.

Captain Newman sat down in the chair and jabbed the needle into the vein, depressing the plunger with his left thumb, very slowly. He had a pencil in his right hand, poised over a notebook. "Okay, Jim. Count. Backward . . . one hundred, ninety-nine . . ."

Tompkins emitted a brief "Oh!" then a sigh, "Mm . . . feels good . . ."

"One hundred, ninety-nine . . ." Newman whispered.

"Hundred . . . ninedy-nine . . . ninedy-eight . . . seven . . . six . . ." His voice fell away, roused. "Hey, where am I? . . . nine . . . ten . . . How about—

havin' drink—on me? . . . oh . . . good . . . fordy-seven . . . Ma . . ." His breathing was getting slower and slower. By the time the calibrated plunger showed sixteen cc. had gone into Tompkins' vein, the boy's eyes were closed and he was tossing his head and making faint sucking sounds. His mouth opened; his breathing changed, deepening, devoid of apprehension. "Ooooh," he moaned, then was silent.

Overhead, far away, far, far above us, I heard the planes throbbing in the sky.

Captain Newman leaned over, his mouth close to Tompkin's ear, and began to talk, softly, gently, his voice infinitely reassuring, imitating the accent and inflection of the boy on the cot: "Okay, Jim . . . we're goin' up now . . . gonna take us a ride. . . . It's Tuesday, November seventeenth—eighteen-oh-five. Come on, Little Jim. Got to kill us some Jerries. We got to cream them. . . . Man, that crate's all warmed up . . . climb in . . . that's it . . . motor's revving. . . . Let's go, boy . . . come on . . . come on. . . ."

His tone was coaxing, wooing, and it seemed to promise, in its very hushed ease, that all would be well, that this was not an end of days nor a floodgate to punishment and horror, that though pain was agonizing it was not fatal, that it was safe to enter the past again.

Tompkins began to mumble: "Oh,—Jeeze . . . no . . . Don' wanna . . . This's a sweat-job. . . . This one's a piss-cutter. . . . Sonvabitch, okay, Big Jim! Here we go. . . . Hot . . . friggin' hot. Hey, Buck, we get us swacko minute we get back, huh? . . . Goddam them motors. . . . Up—up—*up*. Go—Jim—*up!* Jeeze, pull this goddam coffin off the groun'—*up*—yih! We're up! . . . This is a cinch, sure. Hey, Buck, Buck, hommeny fingers up? An' pig's-ass t' you. Nothin' comin' at us, nothin' shootin'. Give em' a bust. 'Waist gunner to pilot; waist to pilot: Okay I take a practice blast? . . . Roger.' "

Tompkins' hands came up as if he were clutching a machine gun, and his voice imitated a burst of gunfire. "P-r-r-r! P-r-r-r! . . . Waist workin'. Over . . . Shoot the breeze. Hey, Pete . . . Cinchy . . . Hey, Buck, let's get us some broads when we get back—a tomato with a big bazoom. . . . Like hell y' will. Remember the dame with the big knockers? Ha, ha. Let's— *What's that?* Down there, Buck! Four o'clock! Oh, Jeeze, comin' at us, from four—three! Go back! Jim, please, get away. *Flak!* Two o'clock! M.E. 109! Dirty—German —" His whole body shook as, holding the imaginary gun, he rattled off a burst of fire at the Messerschmitt that was once more coming in at two o'clock. "Prr! Prr! Got him! Look't 'im bust open! Fry! He's goin' down! Burn! Yellow bastard! Burn! Fry—Jeeze, three more—oh—" He screamed. "Us—*hit!* . . . Oh, no! Omigod! Oh, Jesus! The *oil!* Dear Jesus, save me, please, holy God, I'll be good. I promise—Ma, I'll be a good boy. . . . Number-three eng—We're goin' down! *Paw!* Oh, Paw, please, help me! *Gonna crash!* Big Jim, you sunvabitchin' crud—*up!* Pull 'er up, *up*, please—Ooooh—Look *out!*"

A long, attenuated "Aaaah!" of terror came from him, the sound pulled out like taffy, then a wailing ululation. His face was pasty, dripping sweat; his head was tossing, turning, a bubble of foam trickling out of the corner of his mouth.

Captain Newman depressed the plunger he had never removed from the boy's vein, sending another cc. into the vein, whispering: "C'mon. Okay. C'mon. You're down. It crashed. You're in that plane." He withdrew the needle. "Tell it—spill it."

"Yeah . . . plane . . . smoke . . ." Tompkins' hands flew up over his head and grabbed the iron rung of the cot. "*Smoke!* Lemme out! Oh, Christ. We're *burnin'!* Out—*out!*" He pulled himself against the frame of the cot furiously, his arms bulging, his whole body quivering, trying to repeat an earlier escape through a hatch. "Oh, Buck. *Buck!* Oh, no, no, no, *no!* Mother o' God, where's his *head?* He got no head! Buck! Oh, God, *put back his head.* Please —someone—he don't look right. . . . *Fire!* The tanks. Out . . . Pull . . . up . . . *up* . . ." He began to sob, the tears pouring down his cheeks now, his teeth rattling. "Out—*out!* I'm out! Yay! Jump! Bang, run, run! Hey, Big Ji— . . . What? Yell?! *Who's yellin'?*"

His face and arms and body froze, just as a voice from the burning plane had frozen him that morning as he had run away. "Big Jim—where—in *there* —callin' me. 'Little Ji-i-m!'" Tompkins' voice shrilled out in a thin, high wail. "'Help. Save me. Little Ji-i-m.' *Go back!* No! Run! I got to go back! I got to pull him out! No! *Run!* The hell. Get away! No! Pull him out, you yellow bast—The *gas!* . . ." From the boy's mouth came a whoosh and a hollow roar, like the roar of a plane catching fire. "Run, run, run, run, run, ru—"

His head fell to one side; a groan rattled in his throat and died away, and he lost the consciousness he had lost once before.

I heard Newman's heavy breathing. Perspiration ran down his face. He was watching Tompkins. I glanced at the clock. It was 10:18.

I remembered something Newman had told me one night in his quarters, when we were having a drink together after working very late. He was a little high. He had been sounding off on insulin shock therapy. "Now, take Pentothal. It's dangerous. Not for the patient, who won't remember a thing you don't remind him he said; but for the doctor. It plays into your omnipotence fantasies. It feeds your illusion you've got magic. Oh, it's easy to feel omnipotent; what's hard is to know what's right. . . . You inject twenty cc. of a hypnotic drug and you're behind all the symptoms, all the resistances, all the defenses. You're face to face with all the soft spots, the weakness, the doubt, the guilt, the undifferentiated rage. . . . Sometimes, when I hear the things these boys say when they go under, when I really let myself know what they've gone through, I wonder how much we expect a man to endure. God! . . . No, not God." He had gotten up to pace back and forth in the small room.

"God won't give you a clue. For a moment, you're that boy's god. I hate that —part of me hates it, at least, the part that knows you can be corrupted by so much power. That's one reason I don't use hypnosis. I hate having someone put his will at the mercy of mine. Still—I use Pentothal, the agency of a drug, for access to the trauma, to what men can't tell you or can't bear to face. . . . They all feel good after flak-juice; they think they've had a wonderful sleep. . . . Then *your* problems begin. How much do you tell them? How much do you hint? How fast can they take how much? What do you never let on they said? When do you get tough? How long do you hold their hand? When do you confront them with the rough stuff? What role do you play? Above all, what's *right*—not for you, but for him? What's right *for the rest of his whole life*? And who has the right to decide? The Army? Pyser? I have no one to turn to. I have to decide. . . . I give myself a hard time. Maybe I don't have to. But what am I supposed to be, anyway? A judge? A priest? A miracle man? Am I the one to decide between good and evil? Do I set boundaries for guilt, or administer dosages of pain and penance? . . . Hell, I'm a doctor—that's all. I'm supposed to heal, not judge. But they *want* you to judge. They want you to punish them, absolve them, sentence them, release them. . . . Consider what the patient projects onto me: hope, faith, infantile trust. But you're alone, all alone. You're his last straw, his last hope. He turns you into his loving mother, his feared or forgiving father, his final court of appeal. You're all he's got to cling to—a raft in the sea in which he's drowning. He thinks you can save him —from death, from hell, from madness. The books don't help you—this is all too new. You're in some damned, dark arena—another man's unconscious —where unimaginable horrors roam." He had refilled his glass. "These boys have to go up and hang in the air and get shot at. We ask too much of them; they ask too much of me. I think of all these things beforehand, sure, one way or another, and I try to balance them out before I give flak-juice. . . . And when it's over they lie there, peaceful, sleeping like a child, and I feel like an empty bag—dry, drained out—no, that's not right. I feel weighted down, tired, carrying a goddam mountain on my back. And a little scared. I'm safe— hell, no one ever got shot down in a psychiatric ward. You don't crash behind a desk. But the boy on the cot? Should you send him back? . . . Well, the Pentothal begins to wear off, and the boy on that cot begins to come around. And now I'm the one who has to stand between his sanity and the merciless forces—panic, guilt, conscience—that put him there. Do you still wonder why I keep a bottle of whiskey in the bottom drawer of my desk?"

All this came back to me as I saw Captain Newman bending over the cot, staring at the sleeping Tompkins. I still heard that frightful wail: " 'Help . . . Save me . . . Little Ji-i-m . . .' "

I shall never forget the expression on Newman's face. He passed his hand across his mouth, like a man emerging from shock, then sighed and straightened up, turning away from Tompkins, and unbuttoned his collar absently. I don't think he remembered that I was there. His shirt, under his arms, was dark with sweat. He opened the window. A hot breeze drifted across me. The sun was hammering on the drum of the sky. Captain Newman stood at the window, gazing blankly into something that was not there. After a moment, he roused himself and opened his mouth wide and took some long, deep breaths. It was 10:20.

Captain Newman wiped his throat with his handkerchief, glanced at Little Jim, turned to the sink and turned on the faucet. He splashed water on his face and got a towel and dried himself. He fumbled for a cigarette and was about to light it, but put it down, frowning, when he saw me. It took him a moment to realize I had been hunched up on the floor all the time.

Tompkins began to mumble something. Captain Newman tossed the towel into a bin. Tompkins gave a massive, arching yawn, stretched his arms, rubbed his eyes. "Doc . . . Musta dozed off."

Captain Newman leaned against the wall.

"Jeeze, feel good. Best I slept in months." He sat up, yawning, scratching his head, and put his feet on the floor. He noticed stains on his trousers. "Christ, I'm leakin', sweatin'. Like a pig. That's what I'm sweatin' like—a knocked-up pig . . . Hey, Lieutenant. Whaddaya know? You been here all night?"

Captain Newman held the pack out and Tompkins took a cigarette. "Man, musta got me ten, twelve hours' hushaby." He rubbed his eyes again. "Hey, Doc, d' I gab a lot in m' sleep?"

"Uh-huh." Newman struck a match.

Little Jim hesitated. "What d' I say?"

"Omigod!" Newman affected disgust. "Every one of you jokers thinks he blabbed out the secret that's going to lose the war or something! Every one of you thinks he's the worst. I'm not passing out any prizes for suffering, boy. And if I did, you wouldn't have a chance! Hell, I was expecting stuff would blow me right out of that chair. You're not even in the running. I've got guys in the ward make you look like Little Orphan Annie."

"But I—Big Jim—"

"I know, I know, I know all about it." Captain Newman dismissed it with an impatient gesture. "It will hold. Tomorrow, same time, same station. Up, boy, off your can. Get some coffee from Laibowitz, run around the track, play some volley ball. I've got *work* to do."

Little Jim grinned with his old impudence. "So that was flak-juice? Big deal!" He winked at me and waved a finger toward Newman cockily. "Best shot I ever did git from ol' Uncle Sam. Beats booze." As he left, he was whistling. But he walked unsteadily, not yet returned from Pentothal's euphoric haze.

I struggled to my feet.

"Wait," said Captain Newman. "Give him time to get out."

After a few minutes, during which he stared at the floor and did not utter a word, Captain Newman said, "All right," and we left the treatment room.

Francie unlocked the iron door to let us out. Her eyes searched Captain Newman's countenance. "Oh, Joe! . . . That boy. It wasn't 'pretty,' was it?"

Captain Newman handed her his cigarette to stub out. "No, Francie. It wasn't pretty."

The next day, Corporal Tompkins came strutting into Captain Newman's office five minutes late, a thin cigar stuck in his mouth. "Howdy, Doc!" He plumped himself on a chair, tilted far back, braced his feet against the desk, blew a smoke ring into the air, and grinned, "Man, I feel perky this mornin'. You talk, I'll jest listen. I got nothin' more t' say—nothin'! Gimme the gospel."

Captain Newman surveyed him frostily. "Take your feet off my desk, soldier."

Little Jim looked flabbergasted.

"You heard me!"

Tompkins slammed his feet down to the floor.

"Sit straight up in that chair!"

The front legs of the chair hit the floor.

"Take that cheap cigar out of your mouth!"

Tompkins' chin began to tremble.

"Go on! Put it out!" said Newman harshly.

Tompkins broke the cigar between his fingers and ground the pieces into an ash tray.

"Don't you ever pull that kind of crap on me again, Tompkins. When you're in this room, you'll show respect—for me, and for yourself. . . . I'm not going to let you cheapen any guy who did thirty-four missions and wears all that spinach on his chest. Do you understand?"

Tompkins glared at him, his lips white.

"Okay, buster. Act tough. Clam up. Sure, I'll do all the talking. You just listen. I'm going to help you—even if you fight me every inch of the way. I can be just as rough on you as you are on yourself. So let's take the gloves off and give James Bowie Tompkins a real good shellacking."

Tompkins' eyes burned hard as beads.

"Attaboy," said Captain Newman. "Be real stubborn. Keep it up. Keep torturing yourself. Keep blaming yourself. Rub your face in it. . . . For what? Because you ran away when you heard Big Jim yelling—"

Newman had not phoned out for anything. She seemed to be waiting outside
his door each night, and when they went to the Officers' Club she made him
leave early. I sometimes saw them walking around the pool together, around
and around, he gesticulating or stopping short with some wild, impulsive
gesture, and she listening, always listening, grave and calm. Once he flopped
into a beach chair wearily, and she took her shoes and stockings off and sat
down, not far from him, her feet playing in the water. The moonlight ran
down her hair like quicksilver. After a while she stood up and went toward
the club, barefooted, and called to one of the Filipino boys to bring Captain
Newman a drink.

Each night, as he lay in bed, Captain Newman told me months later, he
went over the next day's requirements: he would have to present Tompkins
with the naked image of his own self-hatred, his own unreasoning harshness.
And when punishment had run its course, when pain cried out for surcease,
Captain Newman had to offer the boy a chastened conscience, a conscience
which could diminish its unyielding and symbolic demands.

What was harassing Captain Newman, I think, was the knowledge that
if Little Jim stayed sick, he could live on in the hospital until the war was
over. But if Newman succeeded, Little Jim would be sent back into combat.
And then—?

"We protect the sick ones," Newman blurted. "We feed them and love
them and keep them safe. But the healthy, the strong, the brave—those we
send out to be killed. Our job is to make men well—well enough to go out
and kill. All right. But, well enough to go out and *be* killed—oh, God, that's
where it's hell."

One morning, Little Jim came in to Captain Newman's office and said,
straight off: "Think I can git back overseas, Doc?"

Captain Newman searched for some matches. "Why?"

"It figgers, that's all. I been doin' lots of figgerin'. I didn't kill Big Jim. The
Nazzies did. So I want me another crack at 'em, Doc. To kinda even up the
score. Whaddaya say? You going' to fix it for me to git back to some shootin'?"

That, I think, was the moment Captain Newman had hoped for, and
dreaded.

"I hear the missions are getting rougher and rougher over there," he said
gruffly.

"Bound to."

"A lot of our guys are getting shot up."

"Sure are."

"There are no more milk runs, boy! You can get your head blown off in
one of those raids."

"You sure can, Doc."

Captain Newman took a moment to pour himself some water. "You know you can stick around here a little longer."

"Nope, Doc. I got to git me out of here. A couple more missions, Doc, that's all I want."

"You sure?"

Tompkins hesitated. "If I ain't sure of that, I won't never be sure of nothin'. I jest *owe* it, I guess. I let Big Jim down. I guess I owe it to him, an' to them other guys went down with us, too."

Ten days later, Corporal James Bowie Tompkins, USAAF, gunner, was shipped out, out of the hospital, off our post on a desert palpable with heat, to an Eighth Air Force squadron somewhere in the green and mist of England.

He came to see me before he left. His hair was pasted flat, slick and stiff and wet. He was loaded down with a duffel bag, a B-4 bag, and that ungainly guitar. "Got a minute, Lieutenant?"

"Certainly."

"I jest come to say good-by."

I stood up and put my hand out. He wiped his hand on his trousers, like a country boy, and pumped my hand three times. "I thank you for what y' done, Lieutenant."

"I didn't do anything," I said.

"Oh, yes, you did. That first time you come to see me, up in Four, you talked to me jest like I was edjicated. An' when I took the needle, you was in my corner, like they say."

"I think you deserve all the credit, Jim. You and Captain Newman."

"That ol' Doc," he grinned, shaking his head. "Say, could you leave this on his desk sometime?" He unbuttoned the left pocket of his blouse and pulled out a letter. "I ain't got time to go battin' m' gums around with him, bein' m' plane's about due to take off. . . . Good-by, Lieutenant. Say good-by to ol' Laibowitz—and that there salami boy, Gavoni. Tell 'em I'll see you all in church."

I watched him go down the hall, the duffel bag on his shoulder, the B-4 bag bouncing against his shank, the guitar hanging down his back from the cord he had slipped over his head. I had forgotten how short he was. I thought of his Purple Heart and his citation. He had the special courage of the small or the weak: the courage of necessity.

The letter he had left with me was addressed:

DOC NEMAN
Pers.

When I gave Captain Newman the letter, he opened it, read it, turned

scarlet, glanced up quickly, read it again, folded it, and put it into his pocket
without a word. He turned away, reaching for his clipboard. "How about
running some tests for me on the kid in bed Nine?" he said. "He's just simple-
minded enough to be up your alley."

The war in the Pacific took a turn for the better—Tarawa, Kwajalein,
Eniwetok—and the victories of MacArthur's island-hopping began to lighten
our hearts. Tokyo Rose sounded hollow for a change. The Russians held at
Stalingrad and encircled two German armies. Everyone was talking about a
second front in Europe. Churchill glowered more jauntily. The President
seemed strong—stronger than De Gaulle or Chiang Kai-shek or Stalin himself.
Our Navy swept across the seven seas. Day and night, our armadas smashed at
Germany from the air, and England became the assembly point for an invasion such as the world had never seen before.

Easter came to Colfax, the nights cool and sweet now, and our desert burst
into color, blazing with wildflowers I had never dreamed could grow in the
barren sand. In the sometime river beds, the smoke trees flamed purple.

Captain Newman threw a party for Francie at the Officers' Club. It was her
birthday, a good, gay party, with lots of laughter. There were seven of us in all.
Captain Newman was in fine form, reminiscing about his intern days at Cook
County Hospital in Chicago. Francie was radiant that night.

We were swapping jokes, some old, some new, waiting for the birthday cake
to be brought in, when a courier from the Message Center came into the club
and handed Captain Newman a telegram. He signed for it, excused himself,
read it—and reached for the Scotch. His hand was trembling.

"What's the matter, Joe?" asked Francie from the head of the table.

"Nothing. Where the hell is that cake?"

Francie stood up without a word and came around the table and took the
telegram out of Newman's hand. She read it.

"Oh, Joe," she said, and handed the telegram to Captain Jarvis.

He read it and said, "Oh, Christ," and passed it across the table—not
to his date, a pneumatic nymph from town, but to Captain Mathieson, who
read it and put his pipe down.

"Bad news?" his wife whispered.

Mathieson handed the telegram to me. I read:

> THE SECRETARY OF WAR DEEPLY REGRETS TO
> INFORM YOU THAT JAMES BOWIE TOMPKINS . . .

I suddenly heard Little Jim's voice again, as clearly as if he were standing
beside me: "I got no kinfolk: none livin', I mean—" and I realized what he
had put into that letter to "Dr. Neman" he had asked me to deliver that last

time I saw him, the last time any of us would ever see him: "Inform next of kin . . ."

We never had Francie's birthday cake. She excused herself, and took Captain Newman under the arm. He mumbled some vague apology as she led him out.

I tried to finish my coffee, but it was cold and sour.

When the Filipino boy brought the birthday cake in, I told him to take it over to Ward 7, and I went to the bar. . . .

The next morning the staff seemed singularly quiet, and Ward 7 somewhat subdued. Then Laibowitz burst into Captain Newman's office. "My God, Doc, you *saved* that kid!"

Newman turned away.

We learned the details a week or so later, in a letter Captain Newman got from a friend, an air surgeon with the Eighth Air Force: Corporal James Bowie Tompkins, of Boonefort, Kentucky, waist gunner in the lead plane on a massive blockbuster raid on Berlin, had shot down two Focke-Wulfs, they thought, and was last seen going down with nine comrades, in the doomed, riddled, flaming pyre of his Flying Fortress.

I thought of the terrible lines in *Paradise Lost*:

> Him the Almighty Power
> Hurled headlong flaming from the ethereal sky
> With hideous ruin and combustion, down . . . down . . .

Mr. Future

IT WAS RAINING, *mirabile dictu*, RAINING. FOR THREE DAYS THE COLFAX *Courier* had no headline problems. Ten miles from our installation a rancher and his wife were drowned—drowned on the desert, when a flash flood roared down a bone-dry *arroyo* to sweep their car into the terrible inundation.

The rain began with a cloudburst, so sudden and so violent that no one thought it could last. But it lasted. It lasted and it fattened and it turned into tropical torrents. Rain sluiced down our tin roofs, raced across the sandy stretches of the post, hammered on a thousand coffee-colored puddles between the gates and the flying field, deserted and silent now. Across our grounds, only apparitions in ponchos scurried; in our barracks, the GIs played nonstop poker, shot craps, communed with sleep. In the B.O.Q., the officers fretted and wrote letters and read the same magazines three times a day. In our ready rooms, the pilots grumbled over the skull sessions that replaced aerial maneuvers.

But I loved that rain, that blessed armistice with the blinding sun. The earth dared breathe again and gave us sweetness in reward: the fragrance of wet sagebrush, ironwood, palo verde. The mesquite danced with droplet bells and the Spring Deer Horn Cactus wore filigreed liquid jewels. The entire baked, seared land was magically transformed: grays enveloped the world now, and against their unaccustomed monochrome all the strident colors of the desert went muted. It was as if a Van Gogh had been repainted by Corot, or Matisse softened by a Chinese hand.

It was oddly fitting, I think, that out of that sovereign rain the man with the red beard first appeared.

It was quite early, I remember. I had hung up my poncho and shaken the water off the plastic cover of my cap. I was standing at the window, my back to the door, gazing with contentment into the falling sea.

I did not hear the door open behind me. I heard nothing, indeed, until a musical voice murmured, "You may terminate your reverie, Lieutenant."

I jumped.

Leaning against the door, which he had closed noiselessly behind him, was a figure who might have stepped out of Dostoevsky: a tall man with a red beard, a shock of red hair, baby-blue eyes, a thin blade of a nose. On the left breast of his maroon bathrobe a colonel's eagle was pinned. He looked about fifty-five. "Sharp now, lad. Sharp!" He waved a swagger stick and seated himself with a flourish that swirled the bathrobe around himself tightly, poking the stick into one of the folds to carry it across the arm of the chair. "You may be seated." Those blue eyes—very bright, mocking, vaguely maniacal—gleamed with piercing clarity. "Proceed to interview me, in the customary fashion, antecedent to my admission into your woebegone ward. Close your *mouth*, Lieutenant! I am quite aware that you can breathe. You resemble an imbecile."

I opened a drawer nervously and rummaged around for an admission form, stalling for time, saying, "Quite a rain we're having, Colonel."

His eyebrows formed inverted "V"s. "Colonel? Colonel? I see no colonel in this dreary chamber. What evidence warrants your absurd attribution of rank?"

"The eagle, sir," I said in astonishment. "On your robe."

"Correction!" he barked. "There is *an* eagle on *a* bathrobe."

"Oh. Isn't it your eagle?"

"No."

"Nor your bathrobe?"

"No!"

I cleared my throat. "Sir, would you mind telling me—"

"*Delighted!*" He threw his head back and exploded in laughter. "One encounters similar contretemps with the cluttering, clamorous clods in the unmedical corps upstairs. Oh, that the Army of the United States should come to this! Selective service, inductees! I wrote an exposé of the farce for the Chief of Staff, an old friend. It upset him deeply. But of course it was too late. *Millions* of incompetents had already contaminated our ranks. Well, I did my duty, that I did. No man can aver that Mr. Future did not his duty do."

"Is that your—name, Colonel?"

He jerked his head from side to side owlishly. "You are clearly hallucinating." He pointed that blade of a nose at the ceiling and shook with glee. "Bravo, Mr. Future, bravo!"

I found myself hoping that someone would enter the room. I started to excuse myself, to step across the hall, but remembered that Captain Newman and Stacy Mathieson were at Lubbock Field for a two-day conference. Captain Jarvis would be starting on morning rounds. My hand wandered to the phone. The man with the red beard leaned forward. "I detest stupidity," he murmured. "There is no need to seek reinforcement. Fear not; I am un-homicidal."

I remembered something Captain Newman had said a long time ago: "Never show you are afraid of a patient. Even a violent one. Your fear is more dangerous than his hostility. He wants the reassurance that you are not frightened by that in himself which frightens himself and threatens to over-whelm him." I arranged the admission form in front of me. "May I ask how you got here?" I tried to sound brisk.

"You may ask; I may not answer. Remove the ambiguity, sir."

"Who—sent you here?"

"A malignant M.D. upstairs, one Captain Robling. He is perbophoric."

"I beg your pardon."

He winked slyly. "You do not understand the word?"

"No, sir."

"Neither did that idiot Robling. He would not know how to track a hippo-potamus through the snow!"

"Did he give you permission?"

"He? Give? Me?" The desk shook under the blow of his fist. "It is *I*, sir, who gives permission. I informed Dr. Rhubarb of my destination. Get on with your *questions*, man."

I poised my pen. "Name, please."

"Mr. Future."

I cleared my throat. "First name?"

"Objection! Immaterial and irrelevant. Put down any name you wish. Yes. Any-name Future. Next."

"Date of birth?"

He leaned forward. "The day he left."

"Who's he?"

"A friend," he whispered, "a very close and special friend. Mr. Past. Would you like to know about him, where he went, why he will never return?"

I leaned back in my chair. "All right."

"Ah . . . You restore yourself in my good graces. Mr. Past is gone, sir, far from these primitive, puerile purlieus. You have observed, I trust, my skill in alliteration. Where is Mr. Past? I gave him my word, as an officer and a gentle-man, never to reveal his whereabouts. Lips sealed. Ozymandias." He winked again. "Ergo. Your hospital has me, Mr. Future, about whom they know nothing; but in their files rests a dossier on Mr. Past, who is nowhere to be found. One patient with no case history; one case history, but no patient. What a paradox! What a triumph! . . . At this point you should inquire about my age."

"How old are you?"

"How gullible you are. . . . Why must I be surrounded by dolts—dupes, drones, depressive dumbbells? I am excellent on 'd's today. Decidedly. There's another." He put both hands out in supplication. "Do not be deceived by my façade. I have been diagnosed as psychotic: paranoid-schizophrenic. I do not mind. I do not *agree*, mind you, but mind I do not, though I detest psychiatric jargon. *I* put it to you simply: I am sick, sir. Sick of the Army to which I gave my life and my brilliance; sick of this panatropical pesthole; sick of being questioned, probed, doused, spied on; sick of the disgusting charlatans who masquerade as physicians—at least two of them upstairs are latent homosexuals; be on guard, lad, on guard. I am also sick of you!" He reached across the desk, picked up the admission form, tore the page down the center, turned the parts, tore them across and, rising, holding his arm out high above his head, let the fragments flutter down from his hand in a paper snowfall. "Now, sir, you have my permission to escort me to Ward Seven!"

"But I can't—Captain Jarvis will have to authorize it."

"He will," whispered Mr. Future, "he will. Swiftly, swiftly, for I feel the fearful furies closing in." He drew himself up to his full height and lifted the swagger stick, signaling me to follow him. As he strode out, even in that drab and shapeless robe, he looked majestic.

Captain Jarvis, after a sardonic lecture from Mr. Future on dementia praecox ("which, sir, I warn thee, may at any moment turn into three-dimensional postcox"), assigned Mr. Future to Room E.

An hour later, Jackson Laibowitz slouched into my office to growl: "It's some democratic-type army that puts the privates in public and the officers in private."

The case history I got from the files of Main identified Mr. Future as Colonel Norval Algate Bliss. A professional soldier for almost thirty years, he had seen service under Pershing in Mexico and France, and had completed tours of duty in the Philippines, the Canal Zone, Guam. After Pearl Harbor, he had been an executive officer in the Fourth Interceptor Command, San Francisco. He flew to Australia on a liaison mission in the spring of 1943.

In Port Moresby, New Guinea, his aide found him in his quarters one morning, entirely nude, cursing and ripping the sheets to shreds. In the base hospital, said the psychiatrist's report, he developed a peculiar facial tic and "onomatomania," dwelling on certain words compulsively, as if they contained hidden meanings or were endowed with magical powers. He often invented words, words entirely without meaning. During a hurricane he had become homicidal, almost choking an attendant to death. He was put in a strait jacket. "E.C.T." was initialed under "Treatment." After six sessions of electroshock in a general hospital, he was shipped back to the States. . . .

The ward was proud to have a full colonel in Room E—at least Arkie Kopp was proud of it: it added luster to his responsibilities. Laibowitz's favor was not won so lightly; he regarded "the Moses with the red beard" as a telling example of the well-known dictum (well known only to him, it turned out) that the regular Army turns out more psychos than what he called "the civilian lifeblood." Gavoni was overawed by Mr. Future and offered him no salami. Hammerhead Lawrence hated him.

When Captain Newman returned from Lubbock he made me repeat every word I could remember from that extraordinary first interview with Mr. Future. He did not seem impressed by the *bizarreries* which had made so vivid an impression on me. He asked me whether Mr. Future had referred to himself in the first person or the third person, if he had perspired much, if he showed spasmodic tremors. Then he brooded and paced back and forth. "Did he identify the two doctors upstairs—the ones he called queer?"

"No. He didn't, by the way, say they *were* queer; he called them 'latent homosexuals.' "

"I know. Overt homosexuals are rare among M.D.s."

"Why is that?" I asked.

He grinned. "Someday I'll try to find out if that's really so."

Captain Newman went into the ward, where he got Mr. Future's chart from Francie. "How's he doing?"

Sergeant Kopp said, "Doc, we'll have to watch out for him. He *hates* Hammerhead."

"What do you mean?"

"Hammerhead was doing the old man's room this morning, real nice, like he likes to. The Colonel watched him, then grabbed a pillow and began beating him on the head. Laibowitz and me had to jump him."

"What had Lawrence done?" asked Newman.

"*Nothing.* I asked him what did Hammerhead do? He gave me a hundred-proof octane glare and yelled, 'It's in his eyes! Can't you see what's in that little swine's eyes?' "

Captain Newman frowned. He entered Room E. Mr. Future was propped up in bed, the sheet drawn up under his beard, a book in his hands. "I granted no appointment for this hour!" he snapped. "Dismissed!"

" 'Dismissed'? Before I've even come in?" Newman sighed elaborately. "That's not very friendly, is it? I'm Captain Newman."

The book lowered in Mr. Future's hands. "*Ahhh* . . . the perceptive one of whom I hear the baboons babble brightly. At last. Come in, sir, *do* come in." He waved regally. "Forgive the antiseptic aroma and the dreariness of the décor. Neither, of course, did I choose. . . ." His crystal eyes were dancing. "Making observations on the patient, eh, Captain? You should learn to control your expressions. I await your first question with the keenest anticipation."

"How do you feel?" asked Newman.

Mr. Future winced. "Tsk, tsk! Standard opening. You disappoint me. Have you no imagination?"

"I'm holding it in reserve. You've got enough for both of us."

"Clever, clever . . . Consider: First, you bestow a compliment on the patient, to establish rapport; then you attempt a tacit alliance—with that oh-so-innocuous 'both of us.' A lesser man than I would walk into your trap." He indicated the wicker chair. "Do sit down, Captain Boo-man, *do* sit down."

"Thank you, Colonel," said Newman wryly.

"Colonel? Colonel?" The red head bobbed from side to side. "Where?"

"What do you prefer I call you?"

"It is a matter of fact, not preference!" he glared. "The name is Future, not Colonel."

"And mine is not Boo-man."

"Excellent, Captain, *excellent!* I underestimated you. But you are beset and beleaguered by blockheads—brainless, benighted blockheads. I am in a mood that bursts with 'b's this morning."

"Brilliant!" Captain Newman got his cigarettes and held the package out.

Mr. Future's eyes gleamed as he murmured, "Are you mad, sir?"

"Not at the moment."

"Offering a cigarette—in a psychiatric ward? Matches, sir! Damnably dangerous in the hands of demented men."

Newman nodded. "I was going to light it for you."

"You were not going to let me hold the matches?"

"Certainly not."

"Bravo! I commend your candor. I believe I shall like you."

"That shouldn't be hard; I'm a likable type."

Mr. Future grinned. "I believe we shall understand one another."

"You'll understand me, all right," said Newman. "I'm not so sure that you want me to understand you."

"Then we understand each other already!" The head went back; a laugh boomed out; the red beard shook. "Capital, sir! You are shrewd in appraising my resistance, and canny in trying to effect a transference. My insight takes you by surprise, eh? You *must* learn to control your expressions. I happen to be a student of psychiatry, sir. By necessity, not inclination. It is child's play for me to use your silly mumbo-jumbo. Oh, what a pity Mr. Past is not here! He would be amused by you and enchanted with me. Enchanted, sir, beguiled. No, I am tired of 'b's; they contain 'boring' and 'banal.' I shall favor 'e's for the remainder of our talk. Elementary, my un-dear Watson! I feel euphoric."

Captain Newman looked at his watch ostentatiously. "We have thirty minutes before my next patient. You can use it up trying to show me how skillfully you play with words, how cleverly you produce verbal smoke screens —and waste my time and yours; or you can lower your guard a couple of notches and tell me a few things which might—just possibly—help me alleviate some of your misery."

"Misery, sir? Mr. Future? Bah! You are considerably more miserable than I!"

Newman shook his head. "I'm only impatient. You—" He stopped.

"Yes? Go on, go *on*." Mr. Future leaned forward eagerly.

"Nothing."

"You must be fair, sir! You are deliberately inciting me. It is *I* who am impatient, not you. What were you going to say? I have certain rights; I insist upon them. Complete your thought!"

"You," said Captain Newman, "are afraid."

Hate flared up in the blue eyes; then they widened in a parody of dismay. "Afraid? Bless my soul, O penetrating pharmacist of the psyche: of what?"

"Of what you may reveal."

"Careful!" Mr. Future whispered. "Do not overplay your hand."

Captain Newman groaned. "Can't you stop being clever? This isn't a fencing match. We're not trying to score points, or win—"

"But you are!" cried Mr. Future. "You *are* trying to win."

"What?"

"My confidence!" The head shot back; the whole body shook with glee.

"Hooray. Hooray for Mr. Future," said Newman. "How cunning he is. If it's flattery you want, here's a bushelful. You are an extremely intelligent man. You are erudite. You have an excellent brain and a remarkable sense of words. Now—can we go on from there?"

Mr. Future was beaming, nodding, chuckling into his beard, stroking his mustache in vast self-satisfaction.

Captain Newman sighed. "But what a pity that such intelligence, such energy and skill should be wasted on such trivial gestures. For what? To impress an Air Force psychiatrist you hardly know, in an obscure Army hospital—"

"You flatter yourself!" laughed Mr. Future. "I am not trying to impress *you!*"

"No? Then you must be trying to impress him."

Mr. Future's features went dark. "Do not meddle, sir! You will never understand certain things!"

"I think I understand; but I don't agree."

"That which exists between Mr. Past and Mr. Future is sacred! You want to destroy it!"

"Change it," said Newman.

Mr. Future licked his lips. "How?"

"I want to put Mr. Past where he belongs, in the past. And all your ingenuity and pyrotechnics—do they really change anything? Do they really help you? You're so miserable, Mr. Future, so very miserable. Running, twisting, turning, fleeing—from what?"

"Goddam your eyes!" Mr. Future shouted. "God shrivel your heart and consume your monstrous brain. You are vile, vile, vicious and contemptible. I scorn your solicitude!"

Captain Newman nodded. "Most people talk in order to express themselves. But you—" He stopped.

"Continue," said Mr. Future. "Go on. Finish your thought! How do *I* talk?"

"You," said Captain Newman, "talk to conceal yourself."

Mr. Future's eyes burned. He spat on the floor.

"Maybe you're right." Newman tapped a cigarette on the back of his hand and struck a match, observing how greedily the man in bed followed the flame as it came up to light the cigarette.

"One day," Mr. Future whispered, "I will show you what I can do with fire. Ectomorphic ectonesia. The triumph of spirit over matter . . . But we digress, sir. You were asking me to describe Mr. Past."

"I was not," said Newman.

"How direct you are."

"You *want* me to ask you."

"Excellent, Captain! You are not one to be ambushed." Mr. Future grinned. "Ask me."

Newman shrugged. "Would you care to describe Mr. Past?"

"I care very much. But to care is not to comply."

"Can you describe him?"

"I can, but shall not. . . . Do not be discouraged."

"How old is he?"

"That's better. He is as old as Mr. Future."

"How tall?"

"As tall, too."

"What does he do?"

"Be more specific."

"You showed me the triumph of mind over matter."

"And you think me mad. Do you not?"

"Well, you certainly *act* mad," Newman replied.

"And am I not?"

"What do you think?"

Mr. Future punched his pillow in exasperation. "A cheap device! You evade the point. I asked what *you* think, sir. Am I not entitled to direct response? I repeat: Is Mr. Future mad or is he not mad?"

"Mr. Future," said Newman, "is an invention."

Mr. Future smiled. "Is he incurable?"

"I'm trying to decide."

The red beard waggled. "At least you are honest. Not like the others. They persecuted me."

"Who are 'they'?"

"The doctors."

"Oh, come now. Doctors don't go around persecuting patients."

Mr. Future grinned. "Your equanimity does not deceive me, sir. You are simply maintaining professional detachment. Oh, you do it quite well, that I grant you. Yet someone *is* persecuting me!"

"I agree."

The eyes filled with astonishment. "Yes? Then you see it? Who?" Mr. Future whispered. "Who is persecuting me?"

"You."

"No!"

"Part of you is persecuting the rest."

"No. Oh, no." Suddenly tears welled into the pale blue eyes. "Oh, if Mr. Past were only here. If you could but know him."

"But he *is* here," said Captain Newman.

"Where? Look—search—examine every nook and cranny of these ghastly quarters! Where can anyone conceivably find Mr. Past?"

Newman pointed at Mr. Future without a word.

"You lie, sir!" Mr. Future shouted. "Mr. Past is gone—far from here. I sent him away."

"Not entirely. You can use the past, learn from it, build on it. You can reshape it, even surmount it. But you can't abolish it, not even you; and even with the most powerful will in the world, you can't will it away."

"Mr. Future can," whispered the man with the red beard. "Mr. Future did."

"And is this where you wanted to end? In a mental ward?"

"It was not I who consigned Mr. Future here!"

"This is where men end who split themselves in two."

Mr. Future was silent for a moment, lost, for the first time since he had come to Ward 7, in sadness. "Shall I tell you a story, Captain? It was years ago. I was on extended leave, in mufti, which permitted me to indulge my fancy and grow this hirsute badge. I was walking through a long tunnel in Central Park, one cold winter day, and as I emerged, the sun struck my hair, my beard. A little lad, perhaps five, perhaps six, saw me, astonished, open-mouthed, his eyes like china saucers. 'Santa Claus!' he cried. 'Are you Santa Claus? Are you?' I hesitated not one moment, sir, and bowed: 'That, son, is who I am.' The lad caught his breath: 'But you are so *tall*; you are so big and *tall*. How will you ever come down my tiny chimney?' The question gave me but slight pause. 'Watch,' I said, and lighted a cigarette and blew out a cloud of smoke. 'This smoke, son, is like the smoke in your chimney. Watch.' I puffed and puffed and blew out smoke. 'See? The smoke gets larger and larger, but the cigarette gets smaller and smaller. And that's what I do, too, on Christmas Eve. Part of me turns into smoke, so I can come down your chimney.' . . . Then I heard someone cry out—and *she* came along. Slut. Nurse. Slut. Like all the rest. She clutched that little golden lad, and tore him away, jabbering, 'Naughty! Bad, bad boy. Talking to that filthy, crazy man!' " Mr. Future's head dropped to one side, and though he made no sound, no sound at all, the tears gushed down his cheeks.

" '*Reach*' him? How the hell can I? How does anyone 'reach' a psychotic?" Captain Newman looked tired that staff meeting; his voice had that irascible edge I had come to recognize, the edge of discontent—with a colleague, a patient, above all, with himself.

"What about trying Pentothal?" asked Captain Jarvis.

"Pentothal breaks down the defenses. And that's the one thing Mr. Future doesn't need. He needs all the defenses he's got—and more. He's afraid to lower his defenses, even for a moment. Why else his inability to tolerate silence? Why his fantastic barrage of words, his obsession with letters, alliteration, puns? He has to obliterate an internal threat, drown it in symbols, suffocate it with words. He has to escape from the terrible temptation to perversity by compulsive preoccupations—with verbal games, puzzles, rituals. He's afraid to listen. He's afraid to relax. He's afraid to reverie, to sleep, even to be quiet. To be quiet is to be passive, too. To be passive spells danger; in his mind, it invites attack. Remember his rage about Private Lawrence. . . . He even has anxieties about taking sedation. He'd have more violent fears of a hypodermic needle. That can represent an invasion of the body. . . . No, Bill, to accept flak-juice means to surrender control. And every move he makes shows us that he is overorganized around that one threat. He must keep control. By the way, has he had any surgery?"

"He had a lot of dental work upstairs," said Francie. "His teeth were in pretty bad shape when he got here."

Captain Newman grunted. "Bill, suppose you find out what happened."

At our next staff meeting, Captain Jarvis reported, rather sheepishly, that when Mr. Future had seen the hypodermic needle in the dentist's hand he had gone wild. It had taken three men to pin him into the chair. Then he sat through hours of drilling for a week in a row, without any anesthesia, not even Novocain, his arms folded defiantly.

One day Captain Newman asked me to come to Room E with him. Mr. Future was standing before the window, staring out. His back to us, he exclaimed, without turning: "Halt! It is useless to try to catch me unawares. I have exceptionally acute hearing. There are two of you: Captain Know-it-all and Lieutenant Bewildered. I have made a lifelong study of footsteps." He threw his head back, turned to face us, and laughed. "Gentlemen, your questifications. Bequest them, I beseech you. I always burst with 'b's before breakfast."

Captain Newman did an odd thing. He sank into the wicker chair and gazed at Mr. Future steadily, saying not a word. Mr. Future cocked his head to one side. Newman did not move. Mr. Future frowned. The moments passed. Mr. Future shot me a glare of suspicion, then glanced back to Newman. He had not stirred. I think he wanted to see what Mr. Future would do if offered no comment, no cue, no foil, no words to turn against their user, no distractions to seize upon as respite from an insupportable self. As the silence spun itself out, I saw a bead of sweat form on Mr. Future's brow; he put on a smile, but it was a ghastly grimace and I could see it was an effort; his eyes were anxious. Suddenly a sly, sidelong expression formed on his features; recognition tried to allay anxiety as the self mobilized itself against betrayal. "Careful, Captain," he murmured.

Newman waited.

"Who is playing games now?" cried Mr. Future.

Newman did not stir.

Mr. Future shouted, "You, goddam you! You think you're smart because you make the rules, don't you? It's you who's mad. You!" He towered over Newman's chair and his hand slashed through the air, back and forth, as if wielding an ax, a few inches from Newman's head. He began to sob, like a child in a temper tantrum, enraged and thwarted, then sank to the bed and buried his face in his hands. "You bastard," he cried hoarsely. "You dirty, scheming, clever bastard."

At last Captain Newman said, "How do you feel now?"

"You know how I feel. You won't meet Mr. Past this way. Never." He glanced up. "You know, I presume, that Mr. Past once floated for thirty-seven hours in a sea of burning muck before they rescued him."

"When was that?"

"After a certain troopship was torpedoed. I will also tell you this: He can do anything Jesus did."

"Can you?"

"You mean, 'Can *he*'?" rasped Mr. Future.

"No, Mr. Future, I mean 'you.' "

Mr. Future grinned. "I, sir? Why, at this very moment am not I, like our blessed Saviour, being crucified—between two thieves?"

This is a copy of the report Captain Newman submitted that afternoon:

TO: Lt. Colonel Michael Larrabee,
Commanding Officer, Colfax A.A.A.F.B. Hospital
FROM: Josiah J. Newman, Capt., M.C.
Ser. #0-1-785-902
In re: Norval Algate Bliss, Colonel, U.S.A. (0-169-621)

(1) The undersigned requests the summoning of a Retirement Board meeting to authorize a medical discharge for the patient named above.

(2) The patient is a 52-year-old male in an acute psychotic phase of schizophrenia, paranoid type. He exhibits pronounced homicidal drives.

(3) The patient has received maximum hospital benefits and requires custodial care.

(4) The patient should be committed to a veterans' hospital.

(5) Insulin-coma therapy, under competent supervision, may be indicated—in more doses than attempted in previous E.C.T. (see attached).

Diagnosis: Schizophrenia, paranoid type; acute, severe.
L.O.D.: No. E.P.T.S.
Prognosis: Requires prolonged hospitalization.

(signed) JOSIAH J. NEWMAN

Mr. Future's appearance before the Retirement Board was brief but memorable. He strode into the room like an emperor, head high, carriage superb, left hand on hip. He had brushed his beard carefully. A braided *fourragère* encircled the upper left sleeve of his dress jacket. On his breast were pinned four theater-of-war ribbons, three battle decorations, an oak leaf with palms, a rosette on a bar (from a foreign government). He had demanded the return of his swagger stick, which, he insisted, he had a right to carry, but Captain Newman had talked him out of it.

Mr. Future nodded to me, and with a slightly superior air bowed to the officers behind the green table.

Colonel Pyser, presiding, tapped his gavel on its wooden base. "This board is now in session. . . . Colonel Bliss, will you please state your name, rank and serial number?"

Mr. Future gazed at Colonel Pyser stonily.

Captain Newman said gently, "Mr. Future . . ."

"*D*elighted! Alonzo Archimedes Future, United States Army, World Victory II. Expert on tactics, tautology, logistics, semantics."

Colonel Pyser's brow furrowed. Major Wyzanski coughed. Major Durant examined his pencil.

"The patient's name is Bliss, Norval Algate. Colonel. Serial number—" Newman read it off.

"Proceed with the medical report," said Colonel Pyser.

Captain Newman rose. He gave a résumé of Colonel Bliss's medical history since the episode at Port Moresby. He read passages from a case folder. To all of this, Mr. Future listened with the keenest interest, his head moving in birdlike movements to indicate approval. Captain Newman said, "I should now like to question the patient before you, gentlemen."

"Proceed."

Captain Newman turned to face Mr. Future, who donned an expression of mock gravity. "Mr. Future, I think you understand the nature of this hearing, and its purpose?"

"I understand your purpose." The bearded figure smiled. "You do not understand mine."

"I want to ask you some questions."

"Permission granted. Caveat: the right not to answer is reserved."

"Mr. Future, how do you feel these days?"

"*Feel*, sir?" Mr. Future beamed. "My mood may be described, in technical jargon, as hypomanic." He winked at Colonel Pyser. "You, sir, realize I am here through a gigantic hoax. It is Mr. Past you seek, of course. He spurns your invitation and invites your inquisition. These proceedings are patently illegal—"

"One moment," Colonel Pyser interrupted. "What do you mean, you're here through a hoax?"

"The hoax is mine," smiled Mr. Future, "on you."

Colonel Pyser cleared his throat. "We will dispense with sarcasm. You mention a Mr. 'Past'? To whom were you referring?"

"To Mr. Past, you silly ass."

"Mr. Future—" Newman cut in quickly (only Colonel Bliss's rank spared him Pyser's reprimand)—"would you tell these officers a little about Mr. Past?"

"I will not."

"It is important that they know."

"It is important that they be befuddled!"

"Was Mr. Past's legal name—formerly, that is—Norval Algate Bliss?"

Mr. Future braced his shoulders and stared straight ahead.

"Was Mr. Past a patient in this hospital?" asked Newman.

Mr. Future snickered.

"Are you not taking Mr. Past's place because he—'left' here?"

No answer.

Captain Newman placed the folder on the table. "Do you think you are mentally ill, Mr. Future?"

Mr. Future cocked his head to one side. " 'Do you think you are mentally ill, Mr. Future?' Do you think *you* are mentally ill, Dr. Boo-man?" It was extraordinary how he mimicked Newman's voice and inflection. He turned to address his peers. "You are losing the war, gentlemen. Mark these words. You are pawns in a putrescent conspiracy, persecuting professional soldiers, driving them from the ranks, breaking will and reason on the rack!" He raised his hands in a travesty of supplication. "More need not be said. Duty has been done."

"You think these officers are persecuting you?" asked Captain Newman.

"Of course."

"Why?"

"Because I am intelligent and they are ignorant. Because I know what they fear and do not fear what they know."

"Is anyone else persecuting you, Mr. Future?"

"All the psycho-pseudo-psychiatrists—excluding you. You merely wish to trap me."

"How do you think I wish to trap you?"

Mr. Future pointed that thin blade of a nose toward the ceiling and laughed. "Trap, trap, clap-trap."

"Do you have any physical complaints?" asked Newman.

"None."

"Is your appetite good?"

"Too good for the culinary crimes committed in these kitchens!"

"Do you suffer from any diseases you know of?"

"I suffer fools and frauds you know not of."

"Do you feel any pains?"

"Only in the ears—from the prattle of idiots."

"How do you sleep?"

"Miserably."

At this point, Colonel Pyser, who had been listening with amazement and discomfort, suddenly leaped forward, glad, I suppose, to intervene. "You say that you sleep miserably? Why?"

"How would *you* sleep, Colonel Numbskull, in a room full of howling maniacs?"

Colonel Pyser's cheeks went livid. "You will refrain from—"

"I will quote you Samuel Johnson!"

Pyser's gavel came down sharply. "You will respect the dignity of this board—"

"I will quote the learned doctor!" shouted Mr. Future. " 'Boy, let us be grave; here comes a fool!' " He wheeled on Captain Newman. "Why was I exposed to this tristomic farce? That man is a fraud, sir, a *fool!*"

Colonel Pyser was rapping his gavel on the table insistently. "The hearing is concluded!"

"No!" roared Mr. Future. "Coward! Craven!"

Captain Newman stepped to Mr. Future's side. "Norval . . ." he said quietly.

"They shall not rob the worthy, nor act Ahab to the whale!"

Colonel Pyser signaled the MPs and strode out of the room. Mr. Future shouted scornfully after him. But all he said to the MPs who led him out was: "Lads, do not quote scripture to the heathen, for he will eat you alive."

No relatives were listed in Colonel Bliss's file—no wife, no children, no parents. The only name cited under "In case of emergency, notify . . . " was a Mrs. Leslie Orkum Cluett. The address was a small town near La Jolla, California.

It took several hours before Captain Newman's call went through. A soft, pleasantly husky woman's voice answered, "Mrs. Cluett's residence."

"May I speak to Mrs. Cluett, please?"

"And who may I say is calling, please?"

"My name is Captain Newman. I'm calling from the hospital at Colfax Army Air Force Base."

"Oh? . . . One moment, please. I'll see whether Mrs. Cluett is in." A moment later the same unmistakable voice said, "Hel-lo. This is Mrs. Cluett."

"Mrs. Cluett, I'm sorry to bother you, but I don't know whom else to call. It's about Colonel Bliss."

"Who, please?"

"Colonel Norval Bliss. Your name is given in case of emergency, and—"

"Norry? Norry Bliss—gave *my* name? Are you sure?" The mellow voice quickened, almost girlishly.

"Oh, yes. I've got his file in front of me."

"How strange. Did you say you were calling from an Army hospital?"

"Yes, Colonel Bliss is my patient."

"Are you a doctor?"

"Yes. Mrs. Cluett, are you related to Colonel Bliss in any way?" There was a moment's silence, so dead that the connection seemed to have been broken. "Hello . . . Mrs. Cluett . . . are you there?"

"I heard you, Captain. No, Norry and I are in no way related. We were married, many years ago. It was annulled."

"Oh. I called because I hoped someone, perhaps you, might come here, to the hospital, I mean, to see him. It's not too far, and I thought that if someone he knew, a friend, someone he cared about, showed an interest in him—"

"What is wrong with him?"

Captain Newman said carefully. "He's in a psychiatric ward, Mrs. Cluett. He's going to be committed—"

"A mental ward? Norry?" The charming, husky voice rippled. "Oh, that *is* rich, really. That's too good to be true. That's certainly where he belongs."

"What did you say?"

"You heard me, Captain. I said he belongs in a lunatic asylum, and I hope he stays there! I hope you never let him out! I hope he goes through the same torture he put me through—"

"Mrs. Cluett—"

"Don't 'Mrs. Cluett' me, Captain whoever you are. You telephoned *me*, didn't you? Why that filthy swine had the gall to put *my* name down there I'll never know. If my husband were alive I'd send him to your camp—with a pistol, so he could blow that smutty brain out of Norry's head. Who are you to judge? What's your first name? St. Francis? Is that it?"

"Good-by—"

"Don't hang up. I want to know your name!"

"Josiah," he said impatiently.

"What?"

"Joe."

"Joe? Joe Newman? And you want me to rush out to a hospital and hold poor Norry's filthy hand—"

"Not any more, Mrs. Cluett—"

"I'll tell you what you can do. Just go out and dig a grave and throw Norry in, and save the taxpayers all the money you Jews and Democrats are wasting in Roosevelt's lousy war—"

Captain Newman put the phone down. His hand was shaking.

The day before they were to put Mr. Future on a train for the veterans' hospital in Canandaigua, New York, Captain Newman went to Room E. Mr. Future was seated in the wicker chair, facing the window, his arms folded rigidly, staring out at the cottonwood trees and the parade ground. It was a dank, oppressive day, the sky gray and leaden, and all the flags hung limp and spiritless. Mr. Future made no sound as Newman entered, no movement when Newman came beside him, not the slightest response when Newman greeted him. The blue eyes were fixed, hard and cold, with no light in them.

"This may be the last time I'll see you," said Captain Newman.

Mr. Future might have been a statue.

"You understand, don't you, that they're going to take you to a veterans' hospital now?"

Silence.

"I chose the one nearest to where you were born and went to school. I thought—you can be sent to another, if you want. You've got that privilege. If you'll tell me, I'll arrange it."

No response.

Captain Newman sat down on the bed. "I'm sorry, Mr. Future, I'm sorry as hell I couldn't help you. . . . More hospitalization might help you. I've recommended it. There have been some surprising recoveries in cases like yours. . . . Maybe I wasn't the right doctor for you. Maybe I didn't really understand. I couldn't get through to you, could I? But maybe another man . . . I just hope that you won't give up. You're an officer. You've had a brilliant career. You've got a lot to be proud of."

Not a muscle stirred.

Captain Newman lighted a cigarette and held it before Mr. Future's lips. "We could have one last smoke together. . . ."

Nothing.

"Are you angry with me?"

Silence.

"Well, I want you to know that I respect you—for the fight you're putting up. . . . Yes, you are. If you weren't, if you had just surrendered to what has put you into this terrible conflict—" He paused, waiting.

No sound, no movement.

Captain Newman rose. "This is good-by, then." He felt inept and defeated. "Good luck, Colonel Norval Algate Bliss."

The arms stayed folded, the head high, the eyes frozen.

Captain Newman was halfway out of the room when he heard a whispered, "Captain. . . ." Quickly, he stepped back to the chair. "Yes?"

Mr. Future did not shift that frigid pose by so much as a hair as, in a monotone, he whispered, "Tell her—I tried."

"Who?"

"The one—whose name is written."

Captain Newman forced a cheerful note into his voice: "Sure. I'll telephone her. Maybe she'll come—"

"I am now entering a state of catatonia. These are the last words that shall ever pass my lips."

"Wait! What about Mr. Past?"

There was no answer.

"Don't do this to him!" exclaimed Newman. "He's part of you. Where can he go if you leave? Where? To whom?"

A shield, glazed and impenetrable, covered those blue, blue eyes.

"Think, Norval! Mr. Past—he has *no place to go*, no place on earth, except to you. He understands you. He needs you. You need him. Together, you can be whole—"

Not even a tremor touched the lips or eyes or beard.

Mr. Future had entered the future, and would not return.

I was asleep, restlessly, tossing, vaguely aware of the heavy, stifling air, of wheels of thunder rolling across the heavens, when my ears were split by a thunderbolt. I leaped out of bed. My room, for a startling moment, seemed on fire, then blacked out, then lighted up again in a flash of lightning. I heard something crash overhead and voices cursing in the next room.

I yanked my trousers over my pajamas. There would be trouble in the ward; there always was during a storm, especially with lightning, worst of all with thunder.

I could hear windows slamming all around me. Thunder cracked out close to the barracks, and, as lightning serrated the sky, the post became a surrealistic set on some strange, forbidding stage, lighted up and blacked out in a flash.

I ran down the porch steps, cut across the corner of the parade grounds. Clouds—muddy, restless, angry—churned across the moonless firmament.

Phantoms were hurrying to the hospital, a looming presence in which patches of light were popping. I heard the agitation inside, the wails of fear, the whimpers of pain reawakened.

As I went through the swinging doors, even before I hit the ramp, I heard the screaming in Ward 7.

No one was at the iron door. Through the bars, I saw the ward in turmoil. Nurses and orderlies were hurrying from bed to bed, trying to calm the men. Some had pulled sheets over their heads, several had covered their heads with pillows. Carbo Wilkes was sprawled on the floor, face down, hands clapped over his ears. Nick Ives was running around, babbling and laughing. Nasty Nevers was standing on his bed, shaking his fist, howling about the avenging angel and cesspools of corruption.

Hammerhead let me in. His face was the color of milk.

I saw Captain Newman head for Room E, where Laibowitz was pounding on the door. When I got to them, Laibowitz was saying, "He's got the goddam bed jammed against the door or something!"

Captain Newman motioned him aside and tried the door. It did not budge. "Mr. Future!" He knocked on the door. "It's Captain Newman! Open the door!"

Room E was silent.

Francie Corum came down the aisle. "I found him at my locker this afternoon, trying to jimmy it open."

Captain Newman rattled the door. "I know you can hear me. Listen! I have news! Important! I just heard from Mr. Past!"

A rustle inside the room.

"Mr. Past—is on his way! To join you. He says he'll never leave you again! Do you hear me? *He'll never leave you alone again.*"

We heard the bed being shoved away. The door swung back on its hinges. Francie shuddered.

Against the dim light, Colonel Norval Algate Bliss stood silhouetted. He had shaved off his beard and mustache. He was clad in a feathery kimono, stolen from one of the nurses' lockers. There was rouge on his cheeks.

"Come in, dearie," he smiled.

The Last Christmas

Fourteen sun-blackened, woebegone Italian prisoners of war, guarded by five MPs in helmets, shuffled down the ramp to Ward 7. Their boots were caked with alkali, their uniforms shapeless from innumerable rubbings on desert rock. Some had sun-bleached knapsacks slung across their shoulders; some clutched bundles, ponchos, greasy canvas tied with rope. At the head of the column was an officer in the once-dashing garb of Mussolini's legions.

You may ask what fourteen Italian prisoners of war were doing five thousand miles from a European theater of war, and why, in particular, they awaited admittance to an N.P. ward? The answer is simple, though you may have trouble believing it.

In November, 1942, our expeditionary forces, under a General named Dwight D. Eisenhower, landed on the northwest coast of Africa and overran Oran, Algiers, Casablanca. Between the valiant British and ferocious Aussies to the east and the clamoring Americans to the west, between the planes that hammered them from the sky and the tanks that chewed them up on the sand, the enemy took a terrible clobbering. At Kasserine Gap, so did we. By May, the "master races" lost almost one million men, eight thousand aircraft, uncounted thousands of tanks and cannon. General Rommel's *Afrika Korps* alone surrendered a quarter of a million prisoners.

As for the Italians—ah, the Italians! They simply were not cut out to be the empire-builders their strutting Duce yearned for. Italian troops began surrendering whenever they could get close enough to the Americans to hold their hands up. They were anxious to surrender only to Americans because they felt inferior to the British, were terrified of the Aussies, and had so many relatives in America that they had confidence in our ingenuous and benevolent nature. They also believed our radio, our leaflets and our mobile loudspeakers, which promised all who laid down their arms instant forgiveness, excellent provender, and boundless understanding. What our propaganda did not achieve, our P-38s did: the Italians went green with panic at the sight of one of our "twin-forked devils," which made a hair-curling whine when they dived and a blood-chilling scream when they strafed. The Italians surrendered in droves.

All this is simple. What borders on fantasy is how 270 of the vanquished Latins got all the way from North Africa to Camp Colfax. It was because of the way some idiot in high station interpreted the Geneva Convention of July 27, 1929, which is entitled "Convention Relative to the Treatment of Prisoners of War." Section II, Article 9, paragraph 2 of that historic covenant, in case you want to look it up yourself, reads as follows:

Prisoners captured in districts which are unhealthy, or whose climate is dele-terious to persons coming from temperate climates, shall be removed as soon as possible to a more favorable climate.

Anyone who thinks about it must be impressed by the wisdom, to say nothing of the humanity, which inspired that provision. It would, after all, be barbarous to send Hottentots to a prison camp in Alaska, or Eskimos, say, to a stockade in Yucatán. Among civilized nations, prisoners of war are surely entitled to a climate as much like their native habitat as their captors can provide.

Since the Italians had been captured on a desert, the idiot mentioned above thought it necessary to incarcerate them in a similar climate. So boys raised in the verdant Dolomites or the fertile valley of the Po, lads from the vineyards of Tuscany or the heavenly lake of Maggiore, soon found themselves on the Atlantic—bound for shuttered trains which were bound for the broiling sands of the Southwest. Our quota, at Colfax, was 270.

They were put to work, with meticulous respect for the rules of war, as labor crews on the miniature base (where everyone slept in a tent) some twenty miles from our post, which General Armstrong had set up for special training in desert maneuvers. Our GIs called it "Death Valley," which was, in fact, a good two hundred miles away. The Italians referred to it with phrases from Dante.

It has often been alleged that Italians, a self-dramatizing people, are matchless hypochondriacs, and that even the hardiest among them express heart-rending anguish over the most minor aches, pains, and twinges. I do not know whether this applies to all the sons of Romulus and Remus, but I can vouch for the fact that *our* Italians were practitioners of suffering without peer.

Some PWs, of course, suffered real injury in the line of their bondage—

hernias, fractures, blows on the head. But a whacking proportion of the rest swiftly acquired ailments that were distinguished by two salient traits: they were pitiful to observe and impossible to disprove. Our first-aid unit in Death Valley was soon deluged by epidemics of aching backs and athlete's foot; putative nausea, heat rash, and ringing ears; disturbances of skin, liver, heart, or stomach that were as subtle as they were exotic. The complaints of our prisoners were of a range and a complexity before which medicine could only stand dumfounded. Even Corporal Laibowitz, no tyro in convenient *krankheit*, was astounded by the Latins' symptomatic genius.

Some of the doctors in Main insisted that the Italians were strong as horses and had simply discovered that they could lighten their servitude by rolling their eyes and moaning "*Mamma mia.*" This did not alter our solemn obligations: No civilized power denies medical care to the ailing. And under military regulations, even a sick PW must be confined in a well-guarded area. The only guarded area in our hospital was Ward 7. That is why fourteen hot, dirty, more-or-less sick sons of Rome were dispatched to us. . . .

Captain Newman was flabbergasted. Our facilities were overtaxed enough without taking on fourteen ambulatory aliens whose symptoms, save for one bandaged and one lame, he regarded more with admiration than alarm. Before Captain Newman would sign any document, he telephoned a protest to Lieutenant Colonel Larrabee.

In five minutes, Colonel Pyser called Captain Newman and told him to get the hell on with his duties. "There's no other place in the hospital I can put those Dagos," was the way Colonel Pyser phrased it. "Examine them, dose them with castor oil for all I care, and get them the hell back to Death Valley! And Newman . . ."

"Yes, sir?"

"The United States is at *war* with Italy, goddamit!"

"Thank you, Colonel."

"Don't give me any of your sarcasm, Newman. You know damn well what I mean: I don't want you to mollycoddle these jokers just because they fake a toothache and sing *Pagliacci.*"

"I will not permit vocalizing in the ward, sir."

"That's not what I'm driving at! Just don't start psy-cho-ther-a-py on those baboons, for God's sake. They are enemy, not house guests. Treat them as if you were in a battle zone, not a goddam health resort, and get them back to their picks and shovels!"

The fourteen PWs were assimilated in Ward 7 with no difficulty. They were not all malingerers. One ran a fever of 103; another had a vicious infection, from some rusty barbed wire, that threatened to require a leg amputation. The youngest, a sixteen-year-old whom the others called "Bambino," cried for his mother, hour after hour. The other PWs made a great fuss over him,

sharing their mail and their Red Cross packages and trying to entertain him
with foolish clownings. They even improvised a Punch-and-Judy show out of
old socks stuffed with paper. But Bambino's anguish did not abate until one
of the Italians got a rubber glove from Francie Corum, filled it with milk,
punctured one of the fingers, and put it in the boy's mouth. Bambino sucked
on it greedily and fell asleep. The comments some of the Americans made on
this infantile regression were brutal; but Bambino's terrible weeping stopped,
and for that everyone in the ward was grateful.

In due course, twelve of the PWs returned to Death Valley. Their places
were promptly taken by others. How could it be otherwise? Ward 7's mirific
attractions—sheets, soft beds, revolving fans, good food, devoted orderlies,
pleasing nurses, a radio, ping-pong—were glowingly extolled by the twelve
who returned from the hospital to the 258 who still labored out in the
desert. Ailments promptly broke out among those 258 with a speed not seen
since the Black Plague. The first-aid unit in Death Valley threw up its hands
and called for the delivery truck. In two days we had nineteen more Italians
in Ward 7. And when *they* were discharged—well, it soon got so that a regular
shuttle ran between Death Valley and our hospital. Every armed truck that
conveyed PWs out of Colfax transported PWs back. On any given day, we had
anywhere from ten to twenty-five Italians in the ward—wheezing with
"asthma" or groaning of constipation, fluttering their eyelids over "heart
murmurs" or thrashing about in the throes of "bladder trouble." "This place is
like Bellevue on New Year's Day," said Francie.

Yet the Italians turned out to be a blessed addition to our lives. Lovable
by nature, they were so glad to be in the cool, clean ward that they knocked
themselves out trying to please us. They laughed readily, leaped to offer everyone help, and seized on any excuse to burst into song. They made beds,
washed dishes, scrubbed floors. Several even began to sew curtains. They would
do anything to avoid being discharged.

They also left no doubt in anyone's mind as to what side they were on.
They prayed aloud for the death of Hitler, whom they loathed, and the disgrace of Mussolini, whom they despised. For good measure, they threw in
disgust with the Japanese, about whom they knew nothing. They realized
that the sooner their country was defeated, the sooner would they be reunited
with their loved ones. Nothing was more precious, more dreamed of, more
beseeched of the Almighty.

Few of the Italians spoke English, but that presented no problem in communication: there was always one or another patient in the ward who spoke
Italian. (Pepi Gavoni did not, to Laibowitz's astonishment.) Besides, the
gestures of our PWs were so eloquent, their pantomime so descriptive, their
speech so melodious, that few of us had difficulty in understanding what they
were trying to express.

It was two weeks before Christmas, 1944 (the last Christmas most of us would ever spend at Colfax, though we did not know it), when an Italian major named Marcello Fortuno and sixteen of his talented countrymen were vacationing in our ward, that Corporal Laibowitz asked Captain Newman for an audience "with me and a committee of the boys," at his captain's earliest convenience.

"I'm up to my ears today," said Captain Newman.

Laibowitz looked at the ears unsympathetically.

Captain Newman consulted his calendar. "Oh, hell, come in at four-fifteen."

At exactly 4:14, Laibowitz entered Captain Newman's office with Gavoni and Lawrence. The three lined up before the desk. They even saluted.

"At ease," said Captain Newman, surprised that they had not already taken seats. "Now, what's this all about?"

"It's about Christmas," said Laibowitz. "There's a beaut of a tree in the Rec Hall, from General Armstrong in person, but regulations don't allow our patients out of the ward."

"We feel our boys ought to have their *own* tree," blinked Gavoni. "Agreed, Doc?"

Captain Newman said, "I see no reason why we shouldn't have our own tree. What else?"

"Santa Claus," announced Hammerhead. "Why can't our boys have a Santa Claus of their own, too?"

"I see no objection to having our own Santa Claus, too."

"That brings us to a serious problem." Laibowitz pursed his lips profoundly. "Right?"

"I don't understand," said Captain Newman.

"That's why I raise the point. Doc, what about the PWs?"

"I don't see what problem they can present."

"That's because you're not a PW. The Italians feel they should be allowed in the Rec Hall on Christmas Eve for the big show, with the whole hospital. They want to be treated like friends, not neurotics."

"That's interesting."

"The Italians can put plenty of life in the celebration, Doc! They sing like maniacs. And they can sing an American song in the C.O.'s honor. Tell him that and we're in!"

"Jackson, I've got to hand it to you. Your recommendation has merit."

"That's because it makes sense," beamed Gavoni.

"That," said Captain Newman, stealing a page from Laibowitz's book, "is why it has merit."

Laibowitz looked startled; he was accustomed to laying, not exploding, dialectical booby traps.

"Is that all?" smiled Captain Newman.

"Yeah—"

"Dismissed."

"—except for the collection."

"What collection?"

"The collection for buying the *tree*, for the ward," said Hammerhead.

"A buck a head from the nurses and orderlies, and two from each doctor," said Gavoni.

Captain Newman reached into his pocket.

"Three bucks from you, Doc," said Laibowitz. "On account you're chief of the ward."

"Get a nice big tree," sighed Captain Newman.

The tree he saw in the sun lounge several days later was not very big and even less impressive. It was, indeed, a rather puzzling tree—at least it puzzled Captain Newman. It puzzled him more and more the more he studied it, and he found himself studying it more and more as the day wore on.

The tree was, for one thing, only five feet high; for another, it looked undernourished. The more Captain Newman thought about that tree, the more he tried not to think about it; and the more he tried not to think about it, the more he did. When he found himself thinking of the tree instead of the patient in Bed 5, who was suffering from hyperacusis, he decided to go to the sun lounge.

The tree was in the far corner. The Italians, Francie Corum, and the Three Wise Men were bustling around it, festooning it with tinsel and trinkets under the direction of Major Fortuno, who was supervising their efforts with narrowed eyes and the hand signals of an orchestra conductor. "No-no-no-*no!* A *sinistra! Bene! Un altro poco. Si! Bravo! Perfettamente!*"

Captain Newman called, "Laibowitz . . ."

Something in Captain Newman's tone warned Laibowitz that no good was being boded. "He is busy with the tree," observed Laibowitz.

"He is also wanted by Captain Newman," said Newman.

"He is coming," said Laibowitz.

Captain Newman stepped into the orderlies' bull pen, which Laibowitz entered with an aggrieved expression.

"Jackson," said Captain Newman carefully, "couldn't you find a—uh—bigger tree than that?"

"If a man could get a giant would he settle for a midget?"

"Don't play volley ball with my questions! Where did you buy that tree?"

Laibowitz studied the ceiling. "Who said I bought it?"

Captain Newman felt a prickle of apprehension. "You went into town three days in a row—I okayed the passes myself—for the express purpose of buying a tree—"

"A man can start for paradise and end up in Flushing," cried Laibowitz. "The trees in town are a disgrace—crummy and all picked over; only anemics left."

"Then where did you get—"

"Doc, some things a man is better off not knowing."

"I'll be the judge of that," said Captain Newman sternly.

"To be judge and jury at the same time is a mistake."

"*Where did you get that tree?*"

"From another tree," said Laibowitz dourly.

"From 'another'—! What tree? Where?" An awful possibility loomed in Captain Newman's mind. "Jackson, is there any connection between the tree in the Rec Hall and the tree on our porch?"

"Not now . . . Doc, you are turning pale. I'll get you an aspirin."

"I don't need an aspirin. I need a gun!"

"Can I put on a blindfold?"

"Answer my question!" snapped Newman.

"You should of been a district attorney."

"Did you get the tree which is on the sun porch—"

"Doc—"

"*Yes or no?*"

"Yes."

Captain Newman sank into a chair. He was wrestling with all sorts of emotions. "How did you do it?"

"With a saw."

"A *saw?* What kind of saw?"

"How many types of saw *are* there?" cried Laibowitz. "A saw. For sawing."

"Where did you get it?"

"From surgery."

"From *surgery?*" Newman exploded.

"You sound like an echo."

"You *stole* a surgical saw—"

"Such an accusation is not fair! The saw was borrowed."

"You *borrowed* a delicate, expensive instrument—"

Laibowitz raised a hand. "Doc, do me a favor. Bust me, to civilian. I prefer it to this chewing out."

"You'll get both! I want the details."

"The details will make you madder."

"That's not possible. You 'borrowed' a surgical saw—"

"It's already returned!"

"Dull as a board, no doubt—"

"No!" protested Laibowitz. "Just bent."

" 'Bent.' That's nice. Nothing could be better for a surgeon, of course, than a bent saw. For crooked patients. It will cut around corners."

"Doc, I can see you are getting upset."

"Upset? I?" Newman laughed hollowly. "Simply because my orderly broke into surgery—"

"I didn't. Don't be hard on Pepi, Doc! He was doing it for the ward. I tell him to get a saw, thinking he'll go to the tool shed, but the poor four-eyed slob sneaks upstairs—"

Captain Newman rose. "Let's quit all this stalling. Tell me the whole story."

"You better sit down."

"I stay mad better when I'm standing." Captain Newman put his hands behind his back.

"You look like Captain Bligh."

"That will be enough, Laibowitz!"

"That tree in the Rec Hall was a good twenty-five feet high!" cried Laibowitz. "The top didn't even clear the overhang from the balcony. They had to ease it down, under and up, to get it in. And then the top couldn't even be seen, unless a guy laid flat on his back! Doc, is that a way to enjoy a Christmas tree?"

Captain Newman wrapped himself in ice.

"The rest," muttered Laibowitz, "is obvious."

"*Be* obvious."

"So I took the saw and climbed the ladder and cut the goddam top off!" cried Laibowitz. "Doc, I made that tree look ten times better! It was a cockamamy tree. Ask anyone. The top *leaned*." Laibowitz illustrated the deplorable deformity of the tree quite vividly.

"And are you so damn stupid," Captain Newman fumed, "as to think that General Armstrong won't see that his tree has had its top chopped off?"

"How will he see?"

"With his eyes!"

"Doc, do I look like a meathead? Would I leave a tree with a flat top? A Christmas tree comes to a point, right? Well, it still comes to a point, because that's the way I trimmed it, after I cut the top off. Doc, so help me, the only difference in the General's tree now is I improved it!"

"It's merely five feet shorter," glared Newman.

"Looks are more important than height," observed Laibowitz.

"Be sure to remind General Armstrong of that when he throws you into the guardhouse. How did you get it out of the Rec Hall?"

"Out a window, through the sheep pen, up the back stairs. No one even got a peep what was going on!"

"Not one of the five thousand blind men on this installation saw you carrying a five-foot tree—"

"We didn't carry it."

Captain Newman closed his eyes. "What did you do?"

"We used an ambulance."

"An *ambulance?* Where the hell did you get an ambulance?"

"Near Emergency."

"Where was the driver?"

"Shooting craps, with Pepi."

"Did *you* tell Pepi to—"

"Certainly. How else could I get the ambulance? . . . This driver is a nut for galloping dominoes."

"Then who drove?"

"Cooshy."

"Cooshy? Cooshy *Finn?*"

"He is a very careful driver, Doc."

"Cooshy Finn is a patient!" exclaimed Newman.

"That's why I chose him!" said Laibowitz. "We can always claim he stole the ambulance when he was off his rocker. Hammerhead told me—"

"Hammerhead?"

"He was in charge of the stretcher."

"The *what?*"

"The stretcher we put the tree on. You would never know it was a tree!"

"Why not?" asked Captain Newman bitterly. "Did you dress it in a uniform?"

"No, I covered it with a blanket. Doc, you would be the first to swear it looked like a corpse!"

Captain Newman put his head between his hands. His groans were many and heartfelt, but they did not make him feel better. They did not seem to affect Laibowitz either. After some piteous sounds, Newman muttered, "You may go—no, wait." He raised his head. "Excuse my asking so hostile a question, Corporal Finaglowitz, but just for the hell of it, and because you didn't spend one red cent for that wonderful, perfectly pointed tree you wrapped in a blanket and conveyed in an ambulance: What did you do with the money you collected?"

Laibowitz drew himself up with dignity. "What we *saved* in not buying a crummy tree went for presents—for my patients."

As I walked around the installation those days, I could hear the new spinet in the Rec Hall banging away in relentless rehearsals: choral run-throughs, close-harmony WACs—and carols, carols, carols. From every radio on the post came glutinous renditions of "Silent Night." Day and night, "I'm Dreaming of a White Christmas" drifted, most incongruously, across the desert air.

In our ward, song after song ascended from the Italians, who exercised their happy voices on the sun lounge. There was a certain mystery about some of the songs they were rehearsing, for they always stopped when an officer was around. Gavoni or Lawrence patrolled the entrance to the ward and signaled back to the sun porch when enemies were approaching. When Francie asked Laibowitz, who seemed to spend every moment he could whispering to Major Fortuno, what all the secrecy was about, the lugubrious Corporal studied a nonexistent spot on her uniform and replied, "The PWs are preparing a surprise."

"I'll bet it will be a good one," she smiled.

He favored her with one of his most enigmatic moues—inscrutable, yet patronizing: "You said a mouthful, Lieutenant."

How can I describe, to those who have not themselves experienced it, what Christmas is like away from home? At no other time does memory serve men so cruelly.

On the battlefields around the world, Christmas partook of paradox to confuse the heart. On military posts in the States, depopulated by fortunates with home leave, it was bittersweet, at best. And in the Army hospitals, where men lay locked in pain, torn by wounds, contending with the accursed heralds of death . . . Many of us offered silent thanks that Christmas "comes but once a year."

The Eve was officially inaugurated in Ward 7 after an early dinner, when Clarence ("Armpit") Garopy, dressed in a preposterous Santa Claus suit, crawled in through a window, unlocked by Lieutenant Grace Blodgett on this special occasion, bellowing "Ho, ho, ho!" through a false beard and hauling three duffel bags, bulging with presents, over his shoulders. Garopy, a scullery helot, was the biggest, fattest soldier Arkie Kopp could recruit for the role. He had a little trouble getting through the window, partly because the duffel bags kept banging against each other like unanchored buoys in a storm-tossed sea, and partly because while Pepi and Hammerhead kept trying to yank him in, two hypomanic patients kept trying to push him out. But Armpit kept bellowing those "Ho-ho-ho"s and charged down the center aisle, snapping a paper whip and shouting, "Hi, Dumbell! Hey, Blitzen!"

Armpit emptied the bags under the tree and the Italian PWs scrambled around, yelling "Ecco! Ecco!" arranging the packages, each of which had a patient's name on it.

The Rec Hall was so decorated and pretty that I hardly recognized it. A huge "MERRY CHRISTMAS—HAPPY NEW YEAR" was strung across the entire width of the auditorium, beneath a canopy of interlaced red and green streamers. Silver stars and balls and twinkling lights gleamed everywhere.

Every door and window was framed with greenery, in which poinsettias nestled.

The auditorium was jammed. Men in wheel chairs lined both sides of the hall, right up to the stage. Only the first row of folding chairs, reserved for the C.O. and his party, was empty.

Down the corridor a clarion "Ten*shun!*" echoed. We stood up as one. Came the rustle of commotion antecedent to order, the pregnant bustle that precedes, and the awesome silence that succeeds, the entrance of Command, mighty and incarnate. Entered General Armstrong, smiling, laden with decorations, his wife on his arm. None but a C.O. could nod with such practiced grace. Immediately behind: Colonel Pyser, two lieutenant colonels with wives, four majors without. What a fine sight our H.Q. staff made as they filed into the front row!

As the ladies seated themselves, with girlish sounds and gestures, I saw General Armstrong nudge his wife. "Honey," he said proudly, "did you ever see such a magnificent tree?"

"Oh-oh," whispered Francie, beside me.

"Mason," replied Mrs. Armstrong, "that *is* a beautiful tree."

"Great tree, General!" said Lieutenant Colonel Liston.

"Perfectly *lovely*," chirped Mrs. Glock.

"Best tree we ever had, sir," grinned Major Frisby.

Fondly, General Armstrong's eyes took in every branch, every string of snow and silver until—he frowned, turning to Major Hornaday. "Say, does that tree look right to you?"

I heard Newman moan.

" 'Right,' sir?" asked Hornaday.

"I could swear—"

"Gentlemen, our national anthem!" proclaimed Captain Frolich (Special Services) from the stage.

A ruffle of drums: we snapped to attention, Newman with particular alacrity, and the hospital orchestra played "My Country, 'Tis of Thee," which is not our national anthem.

General Armstrong was staring at the Christmas tree intently. "Hornaday," he whispered, "I could swear that tree was bigger!"

"Bigger, sir?" Hornaday echoed.

"*Taller.*"

"Perhaps it was the angle from which you originally viewed it, sir."

"Don't be a jackass, Hornaday."

"Sorry, sir."

All during the singing of the carols, General Armstrong kept eyeing that tree, interspersing his singing with side-of-the-mouth comments. His rendition of "Adeste Fideles" went like a descant:

Oh, come all ye faith-ful
>   (They said that tree measured twenty-five feet.)
Joyful and tri-umphant
>   (That tree's no twenty-five feet!)
Oh, come ye, oh, co-ome ye
>   (Think it could've shrunk indoors?)
To Be-eth-le-hem;
Come and adore Him,
>   (How high d'you figure that tree to be?)
Born the king of a-angels
>   (I make it nineteen—twenty, tops!)
O come let us adore Him
>   (Next year, Hornaday—)
O come let us adore Him
>   (—send one of our trucks—)
O come let us adore Him,
>   (—pick up the tree instead of accepting delivery from—)
Chri-ist, our Lord.
>   (—those goddam scoundrels in town.)

"On with the show!" the M.C. cried, and the auditorium rocked with applause.

The Singing Secretaries got a riotous hand, Hoodunit was extravagantly acclaimed, and Amy Beauregard created near-pandemonium, of course, when she sashayed down the aisle in her sequin *décolletage*, blue-lighted by a baby spot, pressing kisses on foreheads as she extolled Mother in sentimental song.

"And now, a surprise!" announced the M.C. "Our Italian PWs!"

The orchestra struck up "Funiculi, Funicula." Down the aisle, up the stairs, onto the stage, flanked by MPs, marched Major Fortuno and sixteen compatriots. Never had the Major looked so elegant: his hair shone, his goatee gleamed, his teeth sparkled.

"Prison-errs, HALT!" Thus Lieutenant Farkus.

"*Molte grazie*," bowed Major Fortuno.

The Italians arranged themselves in a semicircle. Major Fortuno stepped forward, clicked heels, and, reinforced by a slip of paper, orated: "Generale Arma-strong, officers, *medici*, beautiful *signore*: Ina my country is saying: 'Molte grazie!' It mean: 'Thanka you varry moch.' Alla my man say *molte grazie* you! We prisoner—buta no slafe! We lose—buta no punish! We Italian —buta horray America!" The applause was so deafening that Major Fortuno had to bow three times.

"America! What it mean? It's come from Amerigo Vespucci! America! Who discovered? Cristoforo Colombo! New York! Who boss? Fiorello La Guardia!" After naming other great Italians linked to our glory, from Arturo Toscanini to "ballplaying Tony Lazzeri," Major Fortuno concluded: "So ina you honor, Generale Arma-strong, we singa special song!" He raised his hands; sixteen pairs of lips were wetted; sixteen pairs of lungs inhaled; sixteen pairs of eyes burned at their *maréchal*. And when his hands pumped downward, out of sixteen grateful throats poured: *"Oh, di, puoi vedere alla prima luce dell'alba . . ."* They were singing "The Star-Spangled Banner" in Italian.

How can I hope to convey the effect this had on us? We were on our feet at once. We had never heard our great hymn sung in another tongue; nor have I, for one, ever heard it sung with such feeling. After the final, stirring strophe, *"sulla ter-ra dei liberi-i-i, E sulla casa dei coraggiosi!"* our prisoners could do no wrong.

And perhaps that was just as well. . . . Major Fortuno announced their next selection as "olda American Indian song." Again he raised both hands; again they dropped; and this time from the sixteen fervent throats ascended a melody that puzzled me, in accents certainly not Comanche. Nor were they English, Italian, French. They contained a good many gutturals. . . .

Newman's eyes got wider and wider, his cheeks paling, and when Francie turned to him for enlightenment, from one side, as did I from the other, I heard Newman curse under his breath. "Laibowitz!"

Then I knew. Major Fortuno's proud choir was singing a song Laibowitz had taught them in those secret sessions—a Jewish song, a Chanukah song, every sound and syllable of it!

If the Italians thought they were singing an Indian lyric, the Americans had no reason to doubt that, like "The Star-Spangled Banner," the words had been translated into Italian, too. (I leave out some lads from Brooklyn, whose expression suggested that the world was coming to an end.)

Captain Newman turned, surveying the rows of GIs behind us with an expression such as I never expected to see on a psychoanalyst. Corporal Laibowitz was nowhere to be seen among the seated. That was because he was not seated. He was standing—leaning against the wall under the overhang, one hand fondling a branch of the Christmas tree he had made foal another, the other keeping time to the song his innocent agents were singing. His face was a study in rapture.

General Armstrong whispered over his shoulder: "Newman!" Francie winced.

My chief leaned forward. "Yes, sir."

"Got to hand it to those Italians, Newman."

"Yes, sir."

"Damn beautiful language!"

"It—certainly is."

"You understand it?"

"I—don't speak Italian."

"No lingo like it, Newman."

I learned that it is the weak who are cruel, and that gentleness is to be expected only from the strong.

I came to believe it not true that "the coward dies a thousand deaths, the brave man only one." I think it is the other way around: it is the brave who die a thousand deaths. For it is imagination, and not just conscience, that doth make cowards of us all. Those who do not know fear are not really brave. Courage, I think, is the capacity to confront what can be imagined.

I learned that life—so precious, so variable, so honeycombed with richness and delight—is held cheap and trivial in the scheme of impersonal events. When a human life is snuffed out in an instant, without reason, without justice, as so many were in Colfax, how can one deny that all our lives hang by threads of nothing more than luck? A vagrant microbe or an oil slick on the road, an open door, the leak in a gas line, a madman encountered by chance—against these what matters all our painful accumulations of virtue, knowledge, nobility, sacrifice? There is no answer to death, nor to many of the problems which perplex us; there are only rueful accommodations to reality. And what is reality but a fortuitous play of circumstance, indifferent to our hopes or our unutterable aspirations? And what is wisdom but the capacity to confront intolerable ideas with equanimity?

I came to see that every man is subject to fantasies so obscene, yearnings so mendacious, drives so destructive, that even to mention them shakes the gates which we have erected against the barbarian within. Nothing in nature, not the wonders of the firmament nor the enigmas of the atom, is half so strange as man's unconscious—that hidden, heaving sea of primordial impulse in which the most confounding contradictions live side by side: the insatiable hunger for love, the boundless rage to kill; the clamorous Now, preserved from the most distant Then, in scornful obliteration of time; the yearning to be known, the conspiracy to remain unrevealed; the male, the female, their tragic amalgams. . . . Not Xanthus nor Xanadu, for all its measureless caverns, provides so stupefying a landscape. I sometimes think there is a dimension beyond the four of experience and Einstein: insight, that fifth dimension which promises to liberate us from bondage to the long, imperfect past.

In Ward 7, I learned that no despotism is more terrible than the tyranny of neurosis. No punishment is more pitiless, more harsh and cunning and malevolent, than that which we inflict on ourselves. And in later years, I came to see that no oppression is more vicious than that of the more neurotic among us over the less. "For some not to be martyrs is martyrdom indeed." There is an imperialism in virtue, which compels us to acquiesce to those who exploit it. For each of us is a slave to guilt, and acts out lifelong expiation—however disguised, however symbolic.

It is many years now since the war ended. Colfax is a deserted place on a desert few would even want to visit. But what happened there lifted ordinary men into a kind of grandeur, because they were dedicated to a purpose larger than themselves. Most men debase "the pursuit of happiness" by transforming it into a narcotic pursuit of "fun." But there are those sublimely cursed by discontent, and to them happiness comes only when they push their brains and hearts to the farthest reaches of which they are capable. Nothing is more rewarding than the effort a man makes to *matter*—to count, to stand for something, to have it make some difference that he lived at all.

I often remember a Sunday picnic, one rare spring day on the dunes many miles from Colfax. Newman and I were stretched out, our shirts and shoes off, soaking up the sun, watching a continent of clouds drift toward the crimsoning horizon. Francie was sitting beside us, in the partial shade of a saguaro, her honey hair flecked with light, picking up handfuls of sand with that amused composure which rarely failed her, watching the golden grains trickle through her fingers. We had taken a solemn oath, as we drove away from the post, that we would not for so much as a moment think about the war or the ward. From Francie's portable radio, we heard the joyous arpeggios of a Mozart concerto.

We reveled in the beauty of that day. The war, we knew, could not go on much longer. Hodges' troops had punched through to take the Roer dams. Further north, Montgomery's British and Canadians were slashing their way up to the Rhine. Patton's magnificent wildmen had their armor cocked at Trier. Our entire front was alive, rolling for the great river.

The strains of Mozart cut off abruptly. "We interrupt this program to bring you a special news bulletin. . . ."

On an island called Iwo Jima, after seventy-two successive days of un-paralleled "softening up" by aerial bombardment, our Marines, pinned down in treacherous volcanic ash, were being massacred. The Japanese had concealed their cannon in a thousand ridges and terraces and underground pill-boxes, connected by subterranean tunnels, covered with eight, ten, twelve solid feet of cement. Another disaster, more slaughter, men bleeding, cursing, weeping, dying, in mud, sea slime, filth.

"Oh, God," cried Francie. "Will it never end?"

Newman reached over and snapped off the radio. "Sure; everything ends," he said and put his hand out, pulling her down beside him. She buried her face in his shoulder. For a moment the unearthly stillness of the desert enveloped us.

Then Newman said, "My father once told me a story I always think of, when the going gets rough and things look hopeless. It's about Destiny. . . . Destiny came down to an island, centuries ago, and summoned three of the

ABOUT THE AUTHOR

Leo Rosten has combined the best of many worlds in a brilliant career: as a social scientist whose studies of the Washington correspondents and of Hollywood are considered classics; as the creator of H*Y*M*A*N K*A*P*L*A*N, one of the most endearing and enduring characters in American humor; as a writer of movies; as author of *The Story Behind the Painting* and the unforgettable *Captain Newman, M.D.*

Born in Poland, Mr. Rosten was brought to the United States at the age of two, was educated in the public schools of Chicago, studied at the London School of Economics, traveled widely in Europe, and received a Ph.D. from the University of Chicago. He was a senior staff member of the RAND Corporation, has taught at Yale University, and served as Ford Visiting Professor of Political Science at the University of California, at Berkeley.

Mr. Rosten's versatility embraces a distinguished career in government: special consultant to the Secretaries of War and of Air, chief of the Motion Picture Division of the National Defense Advisory Commission, deputy director of the Office of War Information, consultant to the Commission on National Goals.

He serves on the executive board of the Authors League of America and the National Book Committee. He has won the George Polk Memorial Award, the Freedoms Foundation Medal, and citations from the Commonwealth Club and the National Conference of Christians and Jews.

Mr. Rosten is Special Editorial Adviser to *Look* magazine, where he is writing the widely acclaimed series, "They Made Our World," portions of which appear in this book—a series called, by the Great Books division of the Encyclopaedia Britannica, "surely one of the most distinguished series ever to be published in a popular magazine. The rare combination of scholarship and creative insight has made Leo Rosten one of America's foremost practitioners of the art of writing . . . about serious subjects."